Capacity Building Series: Volume III

Accelerating Juvenile Reentry

*A Practical Capacity Building Model
for Sustaining Aftercare*

Books in Capacity Building Series

Volume I. *Building Capacity from the Bottom Up:*
The Key to Sustaining Local Services (2024)

Volume II, Second Edition: *Decriminalizing Mental Illness: A Practical Model*
for Building Sustainable Crisis Intervention Teams (2024)

Volume III. *Accelerating Juvenile Reentry: A Practical Capacity*
Building Model for Sustaining Aftercare (2024)

Volume IV. *Accelerating Adult Reentry: A Practical Capacity*
Building Model for Sustaining Post-Release Transitional Services (2024)

Capacity Building Series: Volume III

Accelerating Juvenile Reentry

A Practical Capacity Building Model for Sustaining Aftercare

James Klopovic

with

Nicole Klopovic

AFFINITAS PUBLISHING

Capacity Building Series: Volume III
Accelerating Juvenile Reentry: A Practical Capacity Building Model for Sustaining Aftercare
Copyright © 2025 by James Klopovic, DPP and Nicole Klopovic, PA-C

Published in the United States by

AFFINITAS PUBLISHING

Cover and interior design: Nick Zelinger, NZ Graphics
Virtual Assistance: Kelly Johnson, Cornerstone Virtual Assistance, LLC
Editing: Peggy Henrikson, Heart and Soul Editing

Publisher's Cataloging-in-Publication
(Provided by Cassidy Cataloguing Services, Inc.)

Names: Klopovic, James, author. | Klopovic, Nicole, author.

Title: Accelerating juvenile reentry : a practical capacity building model for sustaining aftercare / James Klopovic, with Nicole Klopovic.

Description: First edition. | [Morrisville, North Carolina] : Affinitas Publishing, [2025] | Series: Capacity building series ; volume 3 | Includes bibliographical references.

Identifiers: ISBN: 978-0-9982372-9-9 (paperback) | 979-8-9850119-9-9 (hardcover) | LCCN: 2024925837

Subjects: LCSH: Juvenile delinquents--Deinstitutionalization. | Juvenile delinquents--Services for. | Juvenile delinquents--Rehabilitation. | Community organization. | Organizational effectiveness.

Classification: LCC: HV9069 .K56 2025 | DDC: 364.36--dc23

10 9 8 7 6 5 4 3 2 1

First Edition

Printed in the United States of America.

To my mother, Audrey Tucker Klopovic, whose courage, determination, kindness, and support of her five children made her all that a mom should be and more. She was a true blessing with a charming, disarming Australian accent. Her influence helped shape my character, and she encouraged me in all my endeavors.

Kids in trouble with the law have deep capacity to learn and change.
– Benjamin Chambers, Communications Director,
National Juvenile Justice Network

Acknowledgments

This project began with a discussion about how to construct grants that make a difference at the North Carolina Governors Crime Commission in the latter 1990s. Doug Yearwood, my colleague and friend, sparked the conversation and helped me define Capacity Building for the thousands of grants we were involved in for years. Then he encouraged me nearly daily through seven years of research for and then writing of the Capacity Building Series.

Many, many more people were involved to bring about this book and its three companions. I interviewed dozens of people, and others commented on and critiqued the many new concepts. They were a test of fire for these pages. It would be impossible to name them all, but I still stand on those shoulders!

In addition, I must mention the remarkable publishing crew of Team Affinitas. They take this muddy clay of a writer and carefully mold him into an author. Peggy Henrikson is truly an editor extraordinaire. We've spent untold hours deciding the best way to explain, describe, and promote these ideas. Nick Zelinger is my great graphic designer—tops, really. He takes a plain manuscript and creates something beautiful, a treat to read. And my faithful virtual assistant Kelly Johnson is ever helpful with publishing details, and I am thoroughly amazed at what she can do with internet technology.

Finally, acknowledgments can't be made without mentioning my daughters, Cindy and Nicole, who are in my heart every day, even when we are far apart. Nicole is the cofounder and CEO of The Nicole and James Klopovic Family Charitable Foundation, which we formed to support public programs that do good in the world. This Capacity Building Series will be its operating manuals. The Foundation and Nicole are the reasons I write.

Specifically for *Accelerating Juvenile Reentry,* the third volume in the Capacity Building Series, I owe a debt of gratitude to the following, who were leaders in this field when I conducted my research:

LaMar Davis, Executive Director of **Choice,** Baltimore, Maryland, enthused about his life's work making throwaway children respected and building the next generation of change agents. Kate Carver, the Choice Director of Community Partnerships and Rae Gallagher, the Choice Director of Operations are true "Movement Builders."

Tim Decker, Director, Missouri Division of Youth Services with the **Missouri Model,** is changing how state government should function in the 21st century. Phyllis Becker, Deputy Director of Youth Services, defines the movement of this therapeutic approach to guiding youth and families to productivity in the community. Gail Mumford, Senior Associate with the Annie E. Casey Foundation, which has the Missouri Model as a focal program, brings a true appreciation for the youth served by the Missouri Model. Pili Robinson, Director of Consulting Services for the Missouri Model, is replicating this remarkably successful model.

Don Devore, Director of Operations for **VQ** (formerly VisionQuest) for Delaware, is leading the research that will determine how to match assessed individual youth needs to specific evidence-based practices. Rich Berry, VQ Chief Operating Officer for Evidence-Based Services, is discovering the complicated process for how to make a defined service work at various sites; it's the work of years.

Christa Myers, Project Director for **Reclaiming Futures** at the Logan County, Ohio site and Michelle White at the Montgomery County site are changing how troubled teens, boys and girls, are treated by reforming the juvenile court system toward brokering services.

Chris Ellison, Director of Student Services for **Rite of Passage**, Silver State, Nevada, is artfully blending current criminal justice systems with evidence-based programming to produce evidence-based results in a new wave of therapeutic residential settings.

Kim Castano, Executive Director of **Aspire,** Joe Hodgson, Director of Quality Management, and Logan Walters, Chairman of the Board, demonstrate that "throw-away kids" can and do succeed.

Rich Steele, the Director of Policy and Program Development for **Models for Change** in Pennsylvania, led this organization from five pilot sites to all 67 counties in little over five years.

Thank you all. James Klopovic

There is no knowable limit to change or growth; and perhaps
there is nothing impossible but thinking makes it so.
– Will Durant

A Note About Artificial Intelligence

We encourage you to use this remarkable tool to enhance your idea as you build your program's capacity. However, it must augment planning, operation, and sustainability. This book on Capacity Building represents years of work studying and documenting how outstanding people have made adult reentry and aftercare *work well in practice.*

Therefore, yes, take advantage of AI, but keep in mind the following: AI *does not and cannot* substitute for the extensive "street view"—even "worm's-eye" view—research covering what works in building this practical, proven model. AI cannot assess the local politics, personalities, processes, and procedures you will use to turn your good idea into a working, sustained program.

Secondly, and most importantly, AI can give you the sense of moving forward while hindering your progress. As a planner, you can get *stuck in analysis* with the *feeling* of moving forward. In the end, you must *act* to see what works for you, in *your* community, with *your* idea.

We wish you the best.

James Klopovic and Nicole Klopovic

Contents

LIST OF FIGURES

PREFACE:
THE BIRTH OF CAPACITY BUILDING

I began thinking about Capacity Building in the early 1990s. After retiring from the U.S. Air Force in 1987, I joined the North Carolina Governor's Crime Commission (GCC) for a second career. Somehow, I was assigned to the Analysis Section that evaluated grants. It was light-years away from what shaped me growing up on a farm and two decades with the military. The GCC is the pass-through agency for federal grant funds, which are filtered through the governor to North Carolina's 100 counties and more. Every state has such an entity. Over time, billions are distributed throughout the country, a collective, massive, continuous stream of tax dollars. There is much room for improvement; a great deal is at stake.

Throughout my 25 years at the Commission, I observed and participated in the granting of millions of dollars in thousands of grants *just* for North Carolina. We managed well over 400-500 grants each year. The GCC processes more now, I'm sure. One year, one major committee of four received just over $70,000,000. All that money could have been spent much more effectively. . . . But how?

I noticed that some grantees "got it." They significantly changed their communities for the better and continued to do so. Others, not so much. I began to study what does and especially what doesn't work. Thank goodness enough goes right to be instructive, even illuminating. Their lessons learned had to be organized, told, and retold. I began to see that nearly *all* grantees never critically looked at the potential they'd have if they concentrated on building their idea to *last* from conception. They needed to evolve past the chaos and rapidity of continually implementing and not achieving permanency. Out of this musing, Capacity Building was born. Old ideas demanded novel rethinking, top to bottom and back again.

As I began my research on the topic, I visited the site of a highly successful juvenile aftercare, where I announced my intention to organize and explain how to do aftercare. The executive director, with the steely-eyed sternness and resigned but resolute voice of years of experience declaimed, "You can't understand, let alone organize, this thing we do. It's all chaos." Thus, he threw the gauntlet.

It wasn't far from the truth to say folks came to work, waited for the first thing to go wrong, then hustled to plug the dike with a longing eye to five o'clock. It was crisis management in action. So much time and potential wasted. Still, many local service projects made their ideas work out of sheer passion, brains, and intestinal fortitude. But largely, grant-funded projects lived for the next grant—*if* it came. It was a plan to fade away or fail outright. Success was achieved mostly by chance, a lot of work, and a little magic. Staff didn't know how to remove themselves from the chaotic crisis cycle of immediacy, which came at the expense of looking beyond it to permanency. More importantly, it prevented them from creating a success template for the next project—paying it forward.

Figuratively, I picked up the gauntlet. What now, thought I!? Capacity Building demanded an overhaul of the current approach, which began as a list of good things to do to deliver local public services—77 of them to be exact. However, all of these "good things" were an incomprehensible jumble that defied systematic organization and thus meaningful implementation. The order had no rhyme or reason.

Then it dawned on me that everything has a beginning, middle, and end—a Life Cycle. With this concept, chaos becomes a linear process. It bows to true planning, priorities, evidence, and *order,* increasing the effectiveness of collective talent and will. People could understand a Life Cycle. Better yet, they could apply a calculated sequence of proven practices with an eye to building an idea that lasts as long as the problem it addresses endures—finally to stable permanency. Moreover, stakeholders could muster a matrix of other essential talents and services to the cause of the idea. True synergy is possible where the whole becomes greater than the parts.

By then, I was focused on federal policy analysis and saw the need to do better granting—in fact, *much* better granting. Fortuitously, I pursued a doctorate in Public Policy. The topic was to define an evidence-based process to build *Permanent Solutions to Permanent Problems* at the local level. I demanded of myself to design a dissertation that was practical and would make a material difference in people's well-being, neighborhood by neighborhood. This was where problems and their solutions mingled, waiting for inspiration, sweat, and a *plan.*

Now great rigor came to play in studying how to accomplish govern*ance* (the how) not govern*ment* (the what)—through granting in this case. My goal was to help programs realize better results by doing more effective, sustainable program development. I spent seven years earning a degree devoted to Capacity Building, which took on new meaning and practicality with rigorous investigation.

I saw the sensible wisdom of this new approach called Capacity Building. Although a few programs are currently using it with great success, it's slow to catch on because it challenges the system of top-down government with bottom-up-and-back-again governance. It's a new way of building lasting public programs that improve our neighborhoods with collaboration between all three levels of government (federal, state, and local), as well as the private and private nonprofit sectors. Capacity Building from the bottom up presents ways to build permanency using selected local services and talent to solve local problems. This collaborative matrix becomes focused and more—much more—than the sum of its parts.

To begin, I needed to define a universal, pervasive, and persistent problem to analyze and for which to suggest solutions. This problem had to be reentry, which is a concern, I can safely say, of *every* community in the country. Tackling it had to involve a community-wide strategy, and it had to start with prevention of the problem in the first place. Thus, it needed to include:

- Keeping our *children* in school and helping them be successful—by far the most successful crime prevention action we can take.

- Helping our *mental health consumers* to stay out of the criminal justice system and remain at home or in the workforce as productive members of their communities.

- Supporting our *troubled youngsters* to get back on the path to self-sufficiency and good citizenship.

- Helping *those who run afoul of the criminal justice system* to return to respectability and productivity as a part of community.

These steps represent a comprehensive strategy for reentry, township by township. Furthermore, a municipality can begin with only one element of the strategy, depending on their resources and especially their determination to succeed. This model for public services is based on prevention, intervention, and resolution of a universal, intergenerational problem. After all, having *no* reentry strategy is extravagantly expensive in public dollars and individual suffering, which these capacity-built programs could help alleviate. For those willing to address these issues, Capacity Building is the way.

Remember that discussion with the program director who said taming the chaos of services can't be documented? Well, this book is part of a four-volume set documenting just that—taming chaos, bringing order, and permanently solving a universal problem, one project, one community at a time.

This is a major life work for me—and its own reward. As Henry David Thoreau wrote in Walden, "If one advances confidently in the direction of his dreams, and endeavors to live the life which he has imagined, he will meet with a success unexpected in common hours." Who knows where these volumes will go and what effect they will have. I do know that whatever happens, it will be good. At least, these volumes in the Capacity Building Series can guide the generations that follow me in building local service ideas that are *Permanent Solutions to Permanent Problems.* If even one effective, lasting program results, it's been worth everything it's taken to realize these volumes and this dream of a lifetime.

– James Klopovic

Don't judge each day by the harvest you reap but by the seeds that you plant.
– Robert Louis Stevenson

How to Get the Most Out of This Book – A Checklist

The following Figure 1-A, Capacity Building Checklist for Juvenile Aftercare – PHASES I-III, with Key Action Items and Effective Practices presents a "snapshot" of 21st-century Capacity Building. It's a good place to start because it offers an overview of the sequential process of developing your idea proven by the model programs discussed herein.

The checklist is just a few pages by design—simple but not simplistic. It works.

- Review this action-oriented checklist—and think about it.
- Read the book, take notes—and think about it.
- Refer to sections in the book as you develop your program—and act accordingly.

The rest of the book delves into details. Figure 1-B on pages 236-239 repeats this checklist as a review.

Figure 1-A. Capacity Building Checklist for Juvenile Aftercare – PHASES I-III, with Key Action Items and Effective Practices
Phase I: Plan and Implement
1. **Structure leadership to build and preserve core values.**
Effective Practice: Publish and distribute a signed state-level joint policy statement that commits agencies to the new vision of aftercare.
Effective Practice: Organize senior core stakeholder groups according to bottom-up, community-based aftercare critical functions.
Effective Practice: Organize your overall operations staff as Task Teams responsible for specific program core values.
Effective Practice: Organize site-level leadership around a strong judge.
Effective Practice: Organize services delivery stakeholders according to their expertise with and influence on building and using evidence throughout your program.
2. **Assess capacity to deliver services by understanding your client.**
Effective Practice: Assess organizational capacity to deliver services as preparation for implementation.

	Effective Practice: Define your transitional services in terms of your target populations.
3.	**Narrow your scope to include what can be done.**
	Effective Practice: State a vision with a purpose that is motivating by its challenge and tempered by scope that considers what can and can't be done.
	Effective Practice: Define the project scope in terms of your target populations' needed competencies for productive independence in the community.
4.	**Design analysis and evaluation to preserve core programming components.**
	Effective Practice: Design a logic model for the chain of outcomes to define project results and means to get there.
	Effective Practice: Operationalize impact analysis and process evaluation according to core components to ensure evidence-based practice fidelity.
5.	**Plan for stable resources.**
	Effective Practice: Conduct annual strategic planning devoted to sustaining resources, which include personnel, equipment and material, and funding streams with multiple goal-oriented purposes.
6.	**Build evidence-based services on an evidence-based program and processes.**
	Effective Practice: Build an evidence-based program and processes to support your evidence-based practices.
	Effective Practice: Build a single plan for individualized, comprehensive treatment that focuses on post-program aftercare.
	Effective Practice: Collect data that support the evidence-based practices adopted.
7.	**Build key staff to support and deliver strengths-based services.**
	Effective Practice: Select staff with a multi-step vetting process.
	Effective Practice: Create an organizational structure that's lean and flat, in which everyone must be qualified and ready to deliver line services.

Phase II: Operate and Stabilize
8. Operationalize the plan.
Effective Practice: Practice hands-on developmental leadership and train to sustain.
Effective Practice: Continuously engage the citizens.
Effective Practice: Engage collaborative leadership skills, especially with external change agents.
Effective Practice: Understand programming readiness to help determine capacity to deliver defined services.
Effective Practice: Extend capacity assessment into a statement of cost effectiveness.
Effective Practice: Carefully limit project scope to keep from overextending service delivery capacity.
Effective Practice: Become data driven by putting the components of evidence gathering in place.
Effective Practice: Develop a dashboard of results-based accountability.
Effective Practice: Maintain resources by keeping stakeholders informed.
Effective Practice: Have the money follow youth targeted by aftercare.
Effective Practice: Have the aftercare services continuum emphasize capability for independent living.
Effective Practice: Create a workplace to tap intrinsic motivation.
Effective Practice: Tame turnover by managing employee and leadership succession.
Phase III: Sustain and Expand
9. Sustain operations via brokered services and mapped service systems.
Effective Practice: Sustain the brokerage of services.
Effective Practice: Map the terrain of service partners to identify barriers to client service access.

10. **Expand incrementally and locally.**
Effective Practice: Designate a single body to guide strategic planning for expansion.
Effective Practice: Design a strategic planning process for modest expansion.

Now you have an overview of how the elements of Capacity Building fit together. The bugs have been worked out. This checklist is your personal consultant, continuously at your side. The rest of the book explains each step in detail to answer your questions or lead you to the appropriate answer.

Herein is *wisdom* attained from experience. Visualize the **Life Cycle** of your idea. This makes your vision real.

Herein is *logic*. Build your idea with **Key Actions**—what you need to do when you need to do them. See your project taking shape.

Herein is *purpose*. **Effective Practices** are just that—*effective*. You must act, but not haphazardly without a mission.

Process matters. Moving relentlessly, productively, with this proven process is the antidote for confusion and failure. Again, the process is *simple* but not simplistic; it's *suitable* for any good local service program.

One of the best aspects of Capacity Building is that you will mold your program to your local circumstances, politics, and people—and especially to your mix of staff and partners. It will be *yours*.

As you progress, add, edit, and refine your path. That way, you're building your implementation plan of action for your *next* idea—or to help *others* make a permanent difference as well.

The aim is to help create communities where people can live, work, play, be content, and *thrive*.

Capacity Building is 21st-century governance. *Lead it.*

CHAPTER PREVIEWS

Chapter 1: Introducing Juvenile Reentry Aftercare
The introduction in Chapter 1 gives you a good idea of the Why and What of Juvenile Aftercare capacity building. It also introduces you to the seven Reform Model programs that freely shared their expertise. The Why and the What are important analyses to begin to form what you will do in your community for your unique circumstances. This book then takes you into realistic all-important action. It also explains the Life Cycle for these programs and how that concept is helpful in developing your program. Finally, you receive a comprehensive checklist of action items and effective practices for bringing your idea to fruition. Chapters 2 through 4 discuss the three main phases of a program's Life Cycle.

Chapter 2: Life Cycle Phase I – Plan and Implement
In this chapter, topics under consideration include: leadership, assessing services for your clients, determining the scope for your program, analyzing and evaluating to preserve program fidelity, determining and attaining sustainable resources, building on evidence-based services, and key staff for strengths-based services. The chapter wraps up with practical, inspirational points staff of the Model programs offered.

Chapter 3: Life Cycle Phase II – Operate and Stabilize
You've planned and implemented services; now this chapter focuses on continuing effective, efficient operations. It discusses: developing leadership, assessing capacity and cost effectiveness, limiting scope creep, establishing means of evaluation and analysis, building resource streams, designing services for life skills, motivating staff, and planning for succession.

Chapter 4: Life Cycle Phase III – Sustain and Expand
This chapter explains how to stabilize your operations with brokered services and mapped service systems. It also discusses how to safely expand your program incrementally so it doesn't fail but can begin to realize transformation.

Chapter 5: Thoughts on Reentry and the Aftercare Reform Movement
Chapter 5 provides a final overview of the innovative concepts involved in Capacity Building, such as: bottom-up organization and communication, local ownership and commitment, matrices of evidence-based, strengths-based services, brokers for services,

effective practices, assessment of risk and resiliency, and further suggestions for collaboration with public agencies.

Chapter 6: A Look Over the Horizon – The Reform Public Servant-Scientist.
The final chapter offers suggestions from successful practitioners for the future of aftercare. Implementing their ideas would help expand and strengthen these aftercare programs and capacity-building concepts.

INTRODUCING JUVENILE REENTRY AFTERCARE

Chapter 1

INTRODUCING JUVENILE REENTRY AFTERCARE

The most important thing we can do with the people we are working
with is to get them to believe in themselves—that they can do it.
[The essential task is] . . . building the capacity of people to act on their own.
– Luz Vega-Marquis, Annie E. Casey Foundation (2012)

The Why and What of It

Juvenile reentry is the story of a movement to reform our juvenile justice system from the bottom up. It takes a new perspective that includes intensive, essential community-based aftercare, which completes initial reentry efforts begun by the juvenile justice system. Its foundation is about building capacity to address problems and community engagement.

The best approach to ameliorating involvement in the criminal justice system is to provide services as early as possible, both for prevention and for individuals who have already become involved. We can't fully address aftercare/reentry for juveniles unless we make a good effort to get children, especially those with troubled beginnings, ready for success in primary and secondary school. That's why any municipality is best served by building a continuum of services—first to *prevent* failure in life then to address involvement or dependency on public services. It's also why we detail programming for building permanent solutions to permanent problems in the four-book series on Capacity Building. These books present how to develop successful programs to help children, the mental health consumer, juveniles, and adults. Thus, this volume on juvenile aftercare is part of a continuum of some of the best programming a municipality can adopt and how to do it effectively.

Basically, this Capacity Building approach is based on two major philosophies: building programs for permanency and bringing many talents together such that the whole is much greater than the sum of its parts.

Taming the "Chaos"

As explained in the Preface, this book began at the site of a highly successful juvenile aftercare, where I announced my intention to organize and explain how to do aftercare. The highly experienced executive director responded sternly: "You can't understand, let alone organize, this thing we do. It's all chaos." Thus, she threw the gauntlet.

Her statement did hold a lot of truth. Just a casual observation of local service programs throughout the state bore witness to management by crisis. Many staffers, especially those at the helm, poured the first cup of coffee then waited for something or things to go wrong so they could tackle the day. They never had enough time or opportunity to think about how things were done and how they could be done much better. So how to begin?

After many discussions at many sites and attending conferences and classes on community building, an idea emerged to begin organizing the chaos. The Life Cycle. Everything—everyone, every animal, every plant, every car, well you get it—has a life cycle, and so does an idea for a local public service. Everyone understands a life cycle. We now had a mechanism to talk about and explain how this great idea of aftercare should be framed and built. The concept communicates critical functions and sequences that can be fashioned, implemented, and permanently built.

For simplicity's sake, services must be:

- *Planned and implemented* – Of all functions, planning is the most important overall task. Yet it's where most public projects fail.

- *Operated and stabilized* – This is where staff figure out how aftercare works in *their* municipality. *All* are starkly different—from the people to the politics to the way things get done. But when a core of motivated people with a good idea focuses on a good idea, it does happen.

- *Sustained and expanded* – This stage is the goal. It's when your idea becomes permanent and can begin to close the services-to-needs gap. In the case of juvenile aftercare, this gap is wide and persistent.

Chaos is now more than tamed; it is dominated. The sites we investigated improved by thinking about their Life Cycle. Now staff had a structure for taming the chaos and delivering even more successful aftercare.

> **Each phase of the life cycle illuminated key features and their subsequent best effective practices and how to properly conduct each one.**

They could explain what they did, when they did it, with whom they did it, where they did it, and the ultimate criticality—*how* they did it. The Life Cycle also formed the template for investigating and supporting dozens of local programs (some in different services) and scores of staffers over several year. Each phase of the life cycle illuminated key features and their subsequent best effective practices and how to properly conduct each one. The building blocks of an idea became practical, proven, and doable by any municipality by any group of likeminded local citizens.

Juvenile aftercare can be done, should be done, in any municipality willing to commit to and accomplish the proven sequence of work. Much more than that, success with aftercare establishes a proven path for any subsequent service idea.

Building Permanent Solutions to Permanent Problems

Building lasting juvenile reentry programming is an excellent example of building permanent solutions to permanent problems—the essence of capacity building. Why? Setting the youngest among us on the path to being productive good citizens and neighbors is the best of our occupations—because whatever we do is generational.

Thus, it's vital to be holistic and collaborative in whatever you do. Holistic means to work effectively with local public and private organizations, government agencies, and community leaders to identify the most pressing juvenile issues. Then design effective, sustained solutions. Focus on the best services and involve people who specialize in juvenile programming. Build what's best according to those services and providers, led by your program vision and purposes. Make friends, compatriots, and champions along the way.

Collaboratively realize collective intelligence, another expression of the whole being greater than the parts. Evaluate the impact of your efforts continuously over time, and strategically, practically, and by the data, adjust. Tailor your strategy as needed to ensure that your investments, especially human capital, are creating lasting positive change in the community. Remember that less, well done, is more.

Promoting Community Empowerment with Civic Engagement

Local action is the most potent of state and federal programming. Local citizens define their own problems and their own solutions using their own resources. Empowering residents and promoting civic engagement are crucial for addressing long-term issues at the municipal level, where the heart of the matter lies. Therefore, you need to support actions that enable community members to participate in decision-making processes and take ownership of local solutions. This places transparency and accountability where it should be: on your neighbors, your local service providers, and your local government officials and their governance. (I note a vital distinction again: Governance is *how* you do the work of government, which is what you do, thus the correct, better focus.) When people are actively engaged in shaping their communities, they are more likely to advocate for and sustain permanent solutions to their problems. The heart of this new way of building communities is threefold:

1. *Building capacity and collaboration* – Building the capacity of local service providers and fostering collaboration between organizations bound together by a single vision can lead to more sustainable, then sustained, solutions. Positive change doesn't last unless the program does. Strengthening communal effort helps create long-term success.

2. *Intelligent systems design and advocacy* – Some problems persist due to systemic issues. Programming that focuses on effective process, dynamic policy improvement, and systemic reform can create lasting solutions by addressing root causes of problems.

3. *Community-led initiatives* – Empowering communities to identify and address their own challenges can lead to sustainable solutions by emphasizing enthused community engagement and communal ownership.

These strategies are widely recognized as effective ways to address persistent problems at the local municipal level where it matters.

When realized, and it will happen, success builds on success. It promotes individual and collective enthusiasm, creativity, and energy. Much good is felt and realized. Collective Intelligence blossoms. You're not building a program so much as a way of life and providing an example for doing smart public services, project building, and communal advancement. One success breeds two more, and so on.

> **This Reform Movement, a new way of thinking, is based on local buy-in, faith in youth, capacity building, and evidence-based action.**

Top-down public service agencies cannot successfully accomplish the reentry process, which is best served by the community, with the ultimate responsibility for its citizens. Keeping a youngster from failing at life requires a transition away from crime to the community and success as a productive citizen. This usually means earning an honest living to support a family, which requires a new perspective.

This Reform Movement, a new way of thinking, is based on local buy-in, faith in youth, capacity building, and evidence-based action. The consequences of successes over time are enormous. It requires our public institutions to take the lead from the community to fund and assist with assembling the matrix of public, nonprofit, and private resources necessary to complete aftercare.

Basic is the belief that all children can succeed at being independent and productive. A child ushered to good citizenship and productivity brings a generation of returns. This view requires rethinking the punitive/control-based philosophy of dealing with juveniles. Service delivery must take the view that juveniles are capable and can respond to strength-based modalities.

Because each community is different, the focus here is on capacity building's universal yet critical features of leadership, capacity assessment, scope, analysis and evaluation, resources, services, and key staff. These features are all explained herein from the perspective of successful aftercare practitioners as those features matured with the growth and stabilization of their projects. Their overarching goal from the outset was to build *permanent solutions to permanent problems.*

The wisdom of these practitioners is captured in suggestions and the most effective practices for each critical feature. Productive process reigns, chaos is tamed, participants can see a bright future. The ideas that follow are based on data and actions proven by repeated practical application and observable progress. The community is the focus. Top-down agency public services simply cannot deliver services effectively without a true collaboration of shared ideas with and resources from the community. This aftercare reform envisions a day when the public sector functions as a broker of all available services.

The culture of top-down control must evolve to bottom-up collaboration. It's a movement of humble people with bottomless, boundless belief that children *and* their families can conduct their own fulfilling lives with targeted, intensive guidance. Insights from decades of experience gleaned from successful practitioners running important aftercare programs have resulted in a major realization: Teaching the individual and the family unit to correct their own shortcomings, seek their *own* services, and contribute in their own way is the best means to achieve fulfillment in the community. This Capacity Building Movement recognizes that reentry, done properly, only begins the process of ensuring success for children. Capacity-building aftercare is about guiding children to develop competencies that last a lifetime. We can then only imagine the effect of a good citizen "paying forward" their good fortune.

The programs and people described and referred to in these pages are reforming how government can work to support our youngest citizens. Moreover, they demonstrate how philanthropy can be done, how communities can nurture better residents, and how people—especially high-needs youth and their families—can stand on their own, quite capable of contributing. The study sites demonstrate client by client, family by family, that the top-down agency control model is not the entire answer; it is only part, just the start, of the solution to the problems of juvenile delinquency.

Slowly and surely, our public systems are moving from "silo" agency services characterized by compliance and control to communal efforts based on disciplined care and strengths. They are demonstrating how the inherent strength of a wayward young person can be directed positively by truly collaborative systems beyond just a single agency. Then stakeholders can focus on the goal of helping communities become more wholesome. And finally, the belief that those served can emerge from difficult circumstances increases. All progresses from the bottom up and back again in an ever-informed cycle in which people and institutions become more aware of how to better serve with each iteration. Communities build where citizens can live, strive, and *thrive*.

The exemplary programs that are the basis of this examination are positive proof that minds, cultures, and inertia can be changed. These "overnight" successes are anything but; their entrepreneurial founders have been struggling, failing, and getting up to do this work again and again for decades. For example:

- *Rite of Passage,* which began years ago in a teepee with 12 "discarded" children was approaching 1,000 employees nationwide at the time of this writing and will inexorably expand.

- *The Missouri Model* began decades ago with the brave move to close the state's central correctional facilities for youth and redirect those resources to small community-based day and residential facilities with remarkable results.

- *Models for Change* in Pennsylvania, begun by the Annie E. Casey Foundation, went from five pilot sites to commitment from the entire state, all 67 counties, to do community-based reentry-aftercare in just over *three years*. The initial data, which told the story of real progress and measurable impact in the community, was so irrefutable and compelling that each county wanted in.

These agencies prove that working with high-risk, high-needs youth and their families can be done. Their wisdom, experiences, processes, procedures, philosophies, and even checklists are there for us all, just for the asking. These pages describe the new way of leading with this Movement to Capacity Building from the bottom-up to build permanency with ideas that are made to work.

The programs profiled in these pages model effective movements—in their communities, done their way. Movements, especially in the public sector, are usually centrally controlled lists of recommended actions that try to make systems more efficient and effective but, unfortunately, do not. They usually represent the result of the convenient reshuffling of complex and multilayered bureaucracy. The result simply becomes more cumbersome, especially when federal, state, and local policies are stacked one upon another. Each level adds more complexity, confusion, and chaos. Real, long-term improvements are glacial and minimal compared to their potential and need. Realize also that the implementation and effectiveness of any policy directive is determined at the local level. Local bureaucrats choose what they implement and how they do it. It could, no, *has* to be better.

In the end, what these large public systems propose to do is still top-down, too broad, or too narrowly defined, insulated silos, so reform ends where the limits of agency responsibilities end. Working reform must be felt by individuals in the community. Thus, we chose the model programs herein to demonstrate that community implementation of a good idea works. What better idea than one that focuses on our youth.

These models provide the basis for many field-verified effective practices. They prove that real reform can be designed, implemented, and sustained. They can be bottom-up, inclusive, intensive, data driven, and long term. Plus, they can be based on the innate strengths of those (youth) served rather than just addressing "risk factors." These models, constructed with existing local capacity, deliver an array of necessary services defined by the target populations. Although this is remarkable, it's intuitive that services should be defined by the people served, not by a distant policy statement.

> **Through these long-standing and well-working programs, this necessary, intuitive approach to improve social dysfunction *with the help of target populations* has been defined.**

When a program is not built right, it fades away or dies from the assaults and pains of implementation. While the program dies, the memory of a failure never does, making it difficult to proffer another good idea. However, through these long-standing and well-working programs, this necessary, intuitive approach to improve social dysfunction *with the help of target populations* has been defined. How sensible. The many people who contributed to these pages suggest the character of their peers and their programs. They suggest reform away from an agency attitude of cooperating on terminal programs to municipal collaboration on permanent solutions to realize a vision. People are energized by their work. Following are insights, characteristics, and strengths of those working collaborations.

- *They build problem-solving capacity.* – Successful model stakeholders know intuitively from the first days their ideas crystallize that services must be supported by a good business structure. This is the exact opposite of the current control model, which tends to leap to a service that floats on air, largely oblivious to a foundation that will sustain it. When capacity is the focus, leadership grooms the next generation of model builders, line staff, supervisors, middle management, and their replacements. They rarely take on more than can be done well; they know their capacity and the community's capacity to deliver permanent resources. Choice, for example, is based on a continuous flow of volunteers who are supported by AmeriCorps. Staff get intensive training and mentoring that never ends. The close and continuous attention blooms in intrinsic motivation. Services are based on data and any action's contribution to goals. Added responsibilities are assumed only after support, especially funding, is secured. Aftercare practitioners understand the life cycle of realizing their idea.

- *They reform systems for efficiency and effectiveness from the bottom up.* – These juvenile services practitioners understand they're conduits. They channel troubled youth from local agencies such as the courts to the community, where transition away from bad decisions to productivity happens. Kids and their families become part of the solution, not the problem. And they respond in kind by the thousands. This is a systems way of thinking, which includes the target populations, community resources, and public and private partners. These practitioners continue the work of transition begun by social agencies, and, for example, the courts and corrections.

- *Actions are based on data, data, and more data, but only what is useful, understood, and easily gathered.* –These successful programs embrace technology. Gathering data is a way of life. Data is the essential element of an evidence-based practice and its foundation, the evidence-based process. An evidence-based therapy, for example, is devilishly difficult to do right, as the players, place, and conditions differ with each application. Delivering a service or evidence-based practice as it was intended means tracking training, videotaping group therapy and dissecting it, and measuring and analyzing client progress. Minute details are vital. This mentality of continuous data collection carries through to daily operations. Staff track processes for efficiencies. Measures are realistic and progressive, where a young person moves from small gains in a group to eventual program graduation with the skills to continue to self-improve. No trivialities are collected simply to fill a quota or an artificial outcome. Data must be useful. The mantra becomes less is more, a constant theme of capacity building. One chart telling the story of cost effectiveness carries the day at a budget meeting.

- *Staff plans sustainability.* – Models are built to last. They must be, as reentry is continuous and costly. Procedures are documented. The programs open new sites only if the will and the means of support at the new locations are established. Staff develop data as flows of information, not occasional sterile reports of numbers. They immediately record interaction with a client and usually dissect it the same day! Realistic goals produce real results that are used to justify programming and resources. Fidelity of evidence-based services is paramount. Staff who can't adapt to the tenets of the model leave of their own volition or are asked to leave, but only after rigorous training and mentoring to see if the staffer can fit, that is, contribute to team cohesion, vision, mission, and success. Program leaders and staff continually look for ways to weave their model into other locations, agencies, and systems. They always ask, "What's next?"

- *Progress is incremental.* – Growth is not haphazard. While every stakeholder is looking for the next opportunity, a new site must be able to support the model and the processes. Practitioners interviewed from each site remarked about not expanding because other sites were simply not meeting the criteria for expansion, even after pleading to give them a try. These practitioners are in the risk business, and they do take risks; however, too much is at stake to assume unacceptable risks to what has been proven to work. They do it right—over time—or not at all.

- *Rebuilding lives begins in the community.* – The community holds the keys to resocialization. Public agency services and controls reach their limits and can end. At that point, the community is strongly advised to seamlessly continue dedicated support for families. These youth can take years to rebuild their lives, long after they gain independence from the courts and most public assistance. In other words, formal control of agencies must yield to community involvement and pro-social strengthening.[1] They emphasize interconnected active engagement, collaboration, and continually strengthened constructive social values. Communities become more and more resilient, more capable, and more cohesive by building people and neighborhoods that thrive in a virtuous cycle. It's synergy, pure, simple, and elegant.

> **Communities become more and more resilient, more capable, and more cohesive by building people and neighborhoods that thrive in a virtuous cycle.**

- *Expectations are realistic and necessarily challenging.* – Getting through these programs is tough. Critics may call these models "hug-a-thug" until they experience and understand the necessary rigor of what happens for an at-risk or troubled youngster. The realism comes not in the absurd top-down agency demand that the result of a sponsored program must be 90 percent employment. The realistic expectation for improvement may rather be that clients straighten up their rooms and attend group. They first need to get to group and be willing to participate for any hope of improvement. Small steps are realistic steps; behavioral modification and skill building take a lot of time. Yes, there is nurturing, which capitalizes on strengths. However, youngsters and families are accountable for achieving goals, responsible for resolving their difficulties, and in charge of how and how well they resocialize within their community. This completely reverses the control model of transitioning wayward youth, which "provides" services and assumes responsibility for the youth. Assuming another's responsibilities just does not work. The art of it all is to illuminate the path to self-determination.

- *People are the focus.* – One of the goals is to establish genuinely caring relationships between everyone involved in a child's life. This begins with the youngster and the family recognizing and building strengths to counter risks all of them have. Then, every level of staff is continuously prepared to deliver a pro-strengths model of skills building and, of course, believe in what they are doing. These programs hire and build determination. Even though this is some of the hardest and most frustrating work imaginable, inspired people emerge, and thus all obstacles must fade away. Only the objective of an able young adult matters. And relationships, friendships, are built with stakeholders and partners from the community to the governor's mansion as these programs deliver on promises. Such programs are the epitome of credibility because they succeed where other programs fail.

- *These programs exhibit a real will to win.* – It sounds trite, but failure really is not an option. If it were, none of these programs would exist. Those that don't get these fundamental laws have "failed"—and some spectacularly. The difference in these highlighted programs is that those involved learn. Standards are extremely high. Environments are built in which, yes, process and delivery failures are expected—but no blame is cast, corrections are made, and all move on to the next "opportunity" to fail and improve. Again, it's about process, not personalities and turf. Integrity, truth, grit, passion, and creativity matter. Good people are shaped by being asked to tackle opportunities, not just avoid problems. Everything is for the long term. The vision is dynamic and motivating as it's just a touch out of reach, but worthy. There's a sense that we are building something truly great.

- *The mission is cultural change.* – Part of the accomplishments now enjoyed by these successful programs is that they have figured out working collaborations with key agencies, decision/policy makers, and providers. This collaboration, not just cooperation to the end of the day, means fitting into existing systems and being connected to community resources. Minds are being changed by the example set by model program staff; people in the collaborative mindset see the physical evidence of high expectations and intensive evidence-based aftercare. One by one they evolve from enforcing rules and regulations to being brokers of services, as in the case of probation officers in these cameoed programs. Their enthusiasm for this real cultural change sometimes only grows when they see their caseloads reduced with each successful outcome. Seeing is believing.

- *Evidenced is the multiplier effect of the whole being greater than the sum of its parts.* – Inclusion is vital. But only with those who contribute materially to the success, preservation, and institutionalization of the model. Program founders and managers realize that the propensity to include everyone is counterproductive and the enemy of progress. These practitioners are masters of bringing together a critical mass of talent and energy—not too big, not too small.

- *Models are based on a philosophy that kids and families can change.* – The basic theory of change, now proven, is that strengths-based nurturing focused on kids *and* their families in the community *works*. It works when evidence-based practices and processes are applied and maintained. Fidelity is sacrosanct.

- *These programs build believers.* – They attract, train, nurture, and promote people who are not just passionate about the work, they believe high-needs youth and their families can be responsible, accountable, and then capable, contributing, and productive citizens. They are there when this happens every day.

Let's pause for an observation that only comes from the field over time, with the people doing the "impossible" and with investigative rigor. It is

> The basic theory of change, now proven, is that strengths-based nurturing focused on kids *and* their families in the community *works*.

this: Most children who may be a bit undisciplined or flirt with risky or bad behavior only need a gentle nudge to keep them on track to reaching their potential. The effect is staggering over time. This is justification enough to sustain a proven idea. And these programs do that, by the thousands of youngsters. Think about it.

One of the engines of change is the Annie E. Casey Foundation. The impetus for this model of capacity building is captured in the Foundation's seminal essay, "A Road Map for Juvenile Justice Reform," which begins by stating:

Our nation's juvenile justice systems are poised for a fundamental, urgently needed transformation—and not a moment too soon.[2]

The problem is stated plainly—that ". . . juvenile justice has probably suffered the most glaring gaps between best practice, what we know, and what we most often do."[3] What we need are effective practices. The essay says what should have been said much sooner:

- *Children are not adults.* – Trends in juvenile justice practice blur or ignore the established differences between youth and adults.[4] The fact is that youngsters make mistakes. Some are regrettable, but most children grow out of making bad choices. This is the concept of desistance. All but a few who misstep or worse, respond well to mature, structured guidance at the right time in the right way.

- *Wholesale incarceration is not the answer.* – Indiscriminate and wholesale incarceration of juveniles is proving expensive, abusive, and bad for public safety.[5] All youth need the same things to assume a productive place in society. They need social skills, and an education that leads to a career, whether technical or professional, that supports a household. They also need the discipline to be responsible and accountable, and especially the ability to persist. Every step further into the criminal justice system is proving to be increasingly criminogenic, while building great impediments to the strengths and social supports that lead to success. Once wayward youth suffer the drumbeat that they are "losers," they begin to believe it and act accordingly.

- *Families are critical.* – Juvenile justice systems too often ignore the critical role of families in resolving delinquency.[6] The hallmark of these successful evidence-based programs and fundamental to their success is that families are involved in the child's therapy and may very well be directed to therapy on their own. Families must be capable of continuing to guide their offspring long after they graduate from a program. They are the true aftercare a young adult needs.

- *Prosecuting minor offenses disrupts normal development.* – The increasing propensity to prosecute minor cases in the juvenile justice system harms youth with arguably no benefit to the public.[7] Getting tough on crime has swept up many low-level offenders and completely disrupted or stopped their normal development away from crime and to formal education in a regular school. While under court supervision, many begin or continue the path to long-term dependency on public services—or worse, recycle in and out of the criminal justice systems. Recidivism rates in correctional facilities are abysmally high when compared to treating those who cycle through with proven strengths-based models in their own communities.

- *Resources are apportioned better.* – Juvenile justice has too often become a dumping ground for youth who should be served by other public systems.[8] Many of the youth served by these model programs have multiple problems. They may have problems such as substance abuse, learning disabilities, physical disabilities, very poor social connections, mental illnesses, criminal and gang involvement, and a family with a generational history of difficulties. These issues can be successfully treated with community-level services at dramatically lower costs than the juvenile justice system. This is especially true with a strengths-based, nurturing approach inclusive of the family. Note also that the participants in these Movement programs are not "creamed" for successful program participation. All but the most incorrigible, habitually violent offenders or sex offenders are taken. The majority simply need that nudge to the more rewarding path.

- *Unequal justice persists* – System policies and practices have allowed unequal justice to persist.[9] The Casey essay points out that minority youth who are arrested are "more likely to be detained; more likely to be formally charged in juvenile court; more likely to be placed into a locked correctional facility … ; once adjudicated more likely to be waived to adult court; and more likely to be incarcerated in an adult prison." The system actually proves to be criminogenic. This deeper and deeper penetration into the criminal justice system is where very expensive, increasing levels of punishment are the first alternative in cases where it does *not* have to be. These programs are proving that more productive alternatives exist.

The story of local capacity-built juvenile reentry programming is based on believers. These passionate people know they can do more together. They know others can change when they're given compassion with high expectations, and that the best place for this change is in the community. Program officials interviewed believe that cultures can evolve if that evolution is incremental, sustainable, and mutual. They do it with an indomitable spirit of dreaming beyond what seems possible while building sustainable capacity from the bottom-up if the evidence supports their actions. What this evolution of local services must do is help as many people as possible realize that troubled youth can succeed; that these programs *work;* and that public will to invest in their communities is *essential* to changing minds to the reform way of thinking.

This is the story of how these remarkable people with extraordinary ideas and spirit represented by the models cited in these pages are revolutionizing how we usher our children to adulthood. Youngsters act the part they're allotted—bad or good. If detention or prison is their lot, then they work hard at being "cons." That is who they are. Likewise, if troubled youngsters are put in a home setting and expected to contribute, then they do. In this environment, based on their inner strengths, they are skilled, smart, and determined. Like just about everyone else, they want to succeed. It's notable that so many just need a nudge to stay the course.

> **A critical task of the Movement is to ensure communities continue this work.**

Accelerating Juvenile Reentry is the retelling of successful lessons for how to implement high performing, sustainable governmental services. Simply put by a key Missouri Model founder, "Invest a little—get a lot." This is a message of hope. These believers prove it can be done.

The Capacity Building Movement, as we call it, is the approach these programs take. Program staff from the buck-stops-here department head to the lowest vision-motivated line staffer have a bone-deep belief in positive youth development which is pro-youth, pro-treatment, and pro-strengths. However, it may be all for naught if the community is complacent. Communities need to give youth and family the skills and ability to cope. They need to nurture the innate qualities it takes these youngsters to become productive, and even fulfilled, to the best of their abilities. In addition, this public support should be at the right time for the right reasons and preferably terminal, without resulting in dependency. A critical task of the Movement is to ensure communities continue this work.

The challenge is to keep the Movement going. Don't assume it will not wane despite its decades-long experience of working out what is most effective to build program permanency. Public services tend to cycle in and out of favor. Remember "Three Strikes"?

This sensible movement for juvenile aftercare will be sustained when people continue to learn and apply what works. Following are smart things to keep in mind when contemplating what to do with youth transitioning from a brush with the system on their way to productivity.

To Consider Before You Start

When you begin building permanent solutions to permanent problems, it's important to get in the right frame of mind. According to several senior juvenile aftercare program officials, the goal of beginning is to do just that. Action, deliberate action, matters. Commit to the work by getting a nucleus of people together to devise an implementation plan according to the life cycle of your project. No need to rehash the volumes of justification to work with high-needs youth.

When done properly, and by the example of the proven models herein, change agents will come to *you* for your services as they have done for these programs. This was especially true with Models for Change, which has proliferated throughout Pennsylvania. The *means* for reform in Pennsylvania were not obstacles, because the idea was well thought through, laid out, realistic, and ready to go. "The real challenge in juvenile justice budgeting is not the size of the investments, but rather the quality," according to the Annie E. Casey Foundation.[10]

Quite important are three initial and critical elements,[11] according to the Foundation, which resulted in the seed money for the Choice program:

1. *A champion* – Initially, choose a champion with the fire to lead, who will be your executive director.

2. *Board of directors* – Next, assemble your board of directors, who are crucial stakeholders chosen for their expertise specific to your idea and the fire to work.

3. *Reform model* – Then, choose a communally identified and agreed upon reform model.

When these elements are established, focus on your objective. That objective, to be clear, is:

To help struggling youth reduce their involvement in the criminal justice system and dependence on public services while they become mature, independent, and capable.

From that, the vision materializes then the mission and goals take shape. According to the director of consulting services with the Missouri Model, this mission is:

To change cultures from control to strengths-based interaction with clients.

This mission can be achieved, according to this director, when agency staff believe that all but a few youngsters are not incorrigible. It is not enough to get them through your program; they must thrive long after they graduate. Notice this word—*thrive*. The overall goal here must be thriving citizens. Thriving means one has the dignity of a good career as the individual's talents and desire dictate, and one can earn and keep respect. It's a situation in which the individual can contribute to the common good. As difficult as that goal may seem, it's being achieved every day for thousands of formerly troubled youths and their families. Potential is becoming reality.

When preparing, focus on the youngster's path to finally arriving successfully in the community. Build permanent business and services capacity to weather the vicissitudes of public programming and the vagaries of funding. One of the program directors in Missouri advises to translate as much as you can into policies and written directives without hamstringing creativity and flexibility. Build a community services delivery infrastructure as conservatively and frugally as possible. Adopt a policy of less, but doable, is more. If what you're doing, whether it's an evidence-based program or an evidence-based process, doesn't work, don't hesitate to cut it, he suggests.

The senior executive for Choice summarized years of successful work with Ameri-Corps at the University of Maryland, Baltimore County with the following advice:

- *Be clear about the population you are serving and the partners who will help you.* – This is way beyond the youngster who comes to you from the courts or is referred by a clinic. Define the players, partners, and patrons according to a strict definition of success and the contribution of each to it. Yes, clients are also essential partners.

- *Celebrate champions.* – Follow your star performers and continuously tell their success stories. Be clear that every entity in these model programs has an opportunity to become exceptional. Yes, this includes but is certainly not limited to staff, board members, supporters, donors, volunteers, and especially your young clients. They are your best argument for your program—and don't forget their parents who need to be active participants and believers.

- *Build your program's reputation.* – All is for naught if *everyone* in your program is not credible. This is another bottom-up phenomenon. The credibility of your line staff conducting groups, visiting a family, or searching the streets for a client who "forgot" an appointment is vital. Credibility is a matter of simply delivering on promises and understanding your role within the community.

Small things matter and speak volumes about you and your sincerity in this enterprise. Say what you will do and do it. Be on time and prepared for a meeting. All participants must be congruent in word and deed.

- *Blend cooperation* – Successful programs are the constellation of senior leadership, management, supervision, and line staff, who all work as one. Easily said, tough to do unless it's part of planning. When staff coalesce, you can see it in the confident, competent smiles of all—especially the executive director. You can feel it in an enthusiastic, organized, forward-leaning board. You can observe the pride in place with artwork by young students and be swept up in the joy of young children who clamor for the attention of their teachers. See how they train, problem solve, and serve—together—even to being in a classroom learning together, each learning how to critique the other.

- *Be aware of limitations and define outcomes.* – Set realistic expectations. Know what can and especially cannot be delivered well. Be prepared to say no to a bad idea no matter how tempting or how timely an unexpected but encumbering grant, for example, may be. Yes, and particularly difficult is saying no to a good idea if its time has not come.

- *Build on existing organizations.* – Why reinvent services delivery infrastructure! Thriving practitioners are masters of demonstrating to agencies public and private how their proven models and way of doing business *multiplies* agency resources and significantly advances common goals. Whole physical plants such as detention and central residential centers and their associated funding streams are turned over to these programs since they are much more cost effective. It's not easy; the officials interviewed mutually telegraph the struggle.

- *Focus on process.* – Make sure the processes of getting things done are efficient and effective by doing the right thing the right way. Outcomes are fractured, poorly realized, or not realized when the operations under them are ineffective, inefficient, or focused on the wrong thing and doing it poorly. Understand that the project has a life cycle, which must be taken in sequence.[12]

> **Make sure the processes of getting things done are efficient and effective by doing the right thing the right way.**

- *Build a plan then act on it.* – Planning pays exponentially, the Choice executive director emphasized. Negotiate the process and make space, physical and timewise, to do planning, he says. Note a particular mindset of the successful: These practitioners are in a constant state of discontent. They feel more can always be done, refined, even perfected. Of course, we are talking about the inspirational leading the inspired. More basic than the effect of good leadership is that bottom-up leadership, informed from the line and the field, is self-fulfilling.

- *Be ready to implement.* – *Before* you agree to start, gather key partners in the community and ensure their commitment in terms of financial and political aid and participation. This wraps up initial planning, which must end for anything to happen. It is safe, even fun, to plan the days away, but only action proves the plan. Planning is a continuous process, however, because these programs iterate toward better ways of doing this work.

- *Train, train, then train some more.* – Preparing staff is just a mention here. Stay tuned for much more. Training is comprehensive and intense. These model programs get the criticality of training, which is continuous. Even group sessions are almost immediately critiqued for nuances of therapeutic technique from which every participant learns. People are trained in their jobs and cross-trained in other essential skills. No duties go wanting when people need time off or even resign.

- *Be aware of problems.* – But not to the point of paralysis. Programs become successful because staff remain ready to confront obstructions or glitches. They actually see them as opportunities to be better. Problems in these programs are part of the day and taken as a matter of course. Difficulties, if anticipated and resolved before they become serious, strengthen systems and the people running them. Chaos happens and can be tamed. This says a lot about the attitude observed in the field. There's a problem-solving atmosphere of not casting blame and encouraging calculated risk. Staff sincerely thrive while grappling with challenge.

- *Build on model fidelity.* – Every practitioner interviewed for this meta-model passionately discussed how reliability is maintained at all costs and with all effort. These pages contain a theme of evidence-based programming, processes, practices, and services production. If any one of these strays from what is proven to work, the indicators of progress and measured effect begin to fall off. In fact, this dispels one of the myths of evidence-based practices that they can be picked up part and parcel and plunked down in another location. They cannot. To successfully transfer from one location to the next, an evidence-based practice must be in an environment of total data-based activity. Then it can be molded to the new circumstances instead of the other way around, while maintaining fidelity. If not, your evidence-based service fails to produce the numbers, falters, then crumbles. This is way beyond hijacking a crafty idea that may have worked elsewhere.

The concept of having an evidence basis for an entire program returns us to the seminal work of the Annie E. Casey Foundation.[13] The core strategies for the Juvenile Detention Alternatives Initiatives are based on good numbers. Thus, they include smart things to do when contemplating a juvenile reentry program. In fact, using accurate data in providing local public services is a reform in itself. Note how this is stated. Data as a detached entity *distracts* from mission accomplishment; it must be *built into the process* of delivering aftercare services even as the idea to do so forms. The irony is that good data analysis is one of the first things given short shrift, left unattended, or abandoned all together. This neglect is also a first step to failure.

The evidence of progress must be accurate, which means it must be correct and timely, and it *must be put to use,* the sooner the better. According to the Pennsylvania Commission on Crime and Delinquency, decision making must be data driven.[14] Data must be used to dissect problems and their nature, understand alternative actions based on it, point to the best of those, and rule out the fog of unsubstantiated opinion. Furthermore, data set the stage for agreement.

This approach implies a good strategy exists to create a true continuum of services. Success is rightly defined as involving one child, one family at a time. Client services are individualized, uniquely planned, and intensely shepherded through program completion and projection into the community. This means staff assume the responsibility and vision of continuing aftercare from the beginning.

Juvenile aftercare is much more than a program; it's a way of life. Children are best served by preparing them for meaningful independence. Evaluation of evidence-based programs, staff, processes, and clients is continuously supported by the technology to do it.[15] The Aspire executive director is immersed in how her program is running and should run. She's so engaged she visualizes who should be at the table, when and where they should be working on what, and especially how things should run. These people think (and dream) not in terms of their agency or program; they "see" how systems will work together. This is the epitome of a thought experiment that becomes bricks, mortar, and thriving youngsters. It's leadership at its finest.

With this introduction of aftercare in general, let's move into a discussion of the individual model programs that provided the wisdom presented here.

The Model Programs and How They Were Chosen

This type of study is one of the most gratifying because it's about our youngest citizens and how to guide them into successful adulthood. The gifts extended to society are incalculable, plus it's immensely satisfying to observe youth learning, growing, and being happy at what they're doing.

Selection of these programs was necessarily stringent as numerous programs address juvenile reentry. We have systemic ideas emanating from the criminal justice system, especially via correctional facilities, for example. These are concerned with aftercare but usually only with services emanating from the agency. The support is terminal, provided just at the beginning of personal transition to the world of adulthood. The goal of aftercare is completed in the community, the neighborhood, and the family, and thus we focused on community aftercare.

Community-based ideas for aftercare are realized by private and nonprofit entities. These programs continue and complete the aftercare work started by government services, which are large umbrella companies, and the justice system of courts, corrections, and law enforcement. Drilling down into the community, municipalities build resource centers to tackle the job of transitioning youth. Within a city are entities that combine and focus federal, state, and local providers on this task. Selection is further complicated by the fact that many, many programs say they are doing juvenile reentry, but few get it right—or so say practitioners involved in the work.

Thus, the selection process of model programs to study had to winnow a host of juvenile reentry programs. We culled out a few that were in fact changing current institutional culture and reforming systems. In the process, we determined how juvenile reentry should be done, now and especially in the future.

> **The goal of aftercare is completed in the community, the neighborhood, and the family, and thus we focused on community aftercare.**

Recommendations for possible study sites were taken from criminal justice professionals, private providers, decision-makers, and program practitioners. Their referrals were based on programs they observed most improved youths' lives and con-tributed to community well-being—the ultimate goal of public services delivery.[16] What were the few programs that had worked out the best way to go about aftercare? We looked for survivors.

Site selection was particularly vital because we were to publish and disseminate the lessons these program officials and practitioners had learned, in some cases over decades. The programs we finally chose had survived nearly every mistake imaginable and had successfully solved endless problems. They had trampled over project-ending barricades and had gotten more from stakeholders than was previously possible. They became a permanent solution to a permanent problem.

The winnowing process was necessarily multi-pronged. First, juvenile reentry projects were generally grouped into three categories: residential, day care, and after-care. Rather than investigate a single approach to reentry, these categories added to the richness and depth of the data collected. Each model approached skills building for troubled youth from different angles. Together, they represent a comprehensive continuum of services. They suggest what services and methods of delivery they found best and importantly, how a community might approach combining the matrix of services unique to their aftercare effort. Along with this winnowing and targeting, we searched the internet for promising programs and consulted academic experts who conducted research into juvenile reentry.

This input was triangulated to arrive at 18 possible candidate sites for investiga-tion. A preliminary interview to screen sites for more in-depth interviews was conducted to get firsthand knowledge of the suitability of the potential study site for this method of action-oriented investigation. We reviewed the literature, perused documents, and conducted on-site observations and ultimately very productive personal interviews. Phone calls also helped with the selection process by allowing impressions of intangibles. We were able to ferret out stakeholder willingness to par-ticipate and project sophistication, which could be evidenced by at least a formalized organizational structure, written procedures, and a system of resources development.

Talking to program stakeholders and practitioners provided insight into the maturity of the projects. Maturity was discerned by the program having passed through the stages of the program's life cycle: 1) plan and implement, 2) operate and stabilize, and 3) sustain and expand. Enthusiasm for what they were doing was indi-cated by their willingness to participate in interviews and share what they had learned and were doing for subsequent aftercare efforts. Their sophistication of operations as evidenced by their formal organization and written procedures and policies demonstrated stability and an ability to expand or have their model replicated by other aftercare practitioners.

The phone screening resulted in seven sites that represented the phases of program evolution, various methods of service provision, varied demographics, and various geographic locations from rural to large metropolitan areas. Much of the data were then gathered telephonically while repeated visits to select sites provided the necessary hands-on perspective vital to this type of inquiry.

Everyone contacted was not only willing to participate; they could not wait to tell their story. These champions collectively made the point that system-wide reforms must be made, demonstrated it can be done, and explained how to do it.

Next, let's look at the remarkable study sites represented.

The Choice Program

The Choice Program is a community-based, family-centered case management approach to delinquency prevention and youth development.[17] It began in 1987 in the city of Baltimore and has since expanded, at the time of this writing, to Baltimore County in its entirety. It has a dual mission to assist at-risk youth and prepare the next generation of college AmeriCorps volunteers to become civic-minded change agents for reform by serving in other communities and positions of influence. Many go on to stellar professional public and private careers.

The program provides intensive advocacy for high-needs, court-involved youth and their families by applying a strengths-based model to monitor, mentor, and link youth to resources for success, education, a job, and services. The model also promotes protective factors such as better peer groups, success in school, and better life choices. These factors mitigate the risks of circumstances such as gang involvement, anger issues, and criminal involvement while empowering participants to become productive, successful people. High expectations and a rigorous schedule instill responsibility and accountability. They also experience the best of teamwork.

Staff are mainly volunteers from AmeriCorps who are highly trained in Choice methods of intensive, face-to-face aftercare and serve a demanding year in service as Community Service Learning Fellows.

The program has been successfully replicated in other states. It's extremely cost effective and is measurably successful by enhancing academic success and reducing arrest rates, for example. A Maryland Juvenile Justice official noted that Choice is successful because it does what the criminal justice system as a stovepipe service cannot do.

The Missouri Model

Correctional officials in Missouri realized there had to be an alternative to the top-down institutional model, so this model is "reinventing the practice of rehabilitating youthful offenders."[18] Officials closed all statewide, centralized youth correctional facilities in the early 1980s and channeled those resources to small, local facilities. Most notable are the smaller community group homes and a continuum of residential and non-residential program options located nearer to participants' homes. Participants respond remarkably well to therapies that focus on strengths rather than compliance and punishm

The mission of The Missouri Model is based on the notion that "Every young person served by the Missouri Division of Youth Services will become a productive citizen."[19] This model offers an alternative to traditional incarceration via intensive youth development group therapy, education, and family and community engagement. They consistently have better outcomes, such as decreased recidivism and improved public safety, academic performance, and employment rates compared to institutionally incurred expenses that attempt to do the same thing. And all at dramatically reduced costs.

The Missouri Model is a state sponsored, child friendly residential approach that does not coddle. This is important, as children respond to caring discipline, order, and guidance. It's the difference between beginning the morning with a sincere "good morning" versus the lights being turned on and the order to "Get up!" With this humanized yet tough approach with high

> **Participants respond remarkably well to therapies that focus on strengths rather than compliance and punishment.**

expectations, all-important small successes such as keeping a room in order gradually lead to growth. These programs prove demographics are not destiny. Select youth are nurtured as family, not as criminals, and the youth respond in-kind. The model has a deceptively simple structure and philosophical basis:

- *Size* – Small and non-prison-like facilities, close to home
- *Focus* – Individual care within a group treatment model
- *Safe* – Safety through relationships and supervision, not correctional coercion
- *Skills* – Building of competence for success
- *Family* – Inclusion of families as partners
- *Community* – Focus on community transitions and aftercare

Thus, this initiative reduces reliance on expensive secure incarceration, improves public safety, reduces racial disparities and bias, saves money, and promotes juvenile justice and services delivery reforms. It epitomizes better allocation of resources with better effect than the centralized model of control and coercion. The ultimate evidence of success with this model is that it's being replicated nationally.

Models for Change

Models for Change[20] is a systems reform idea begun by the John D. and Catherine T. MacArthur foundation. The guiding principle is that children deserve an opportunity for education, a job, and productive participation in their communities. The Foundation further believes that these ends are best served by reforming the culture of compliance. These models incorporate:

- *Intensive aftercare* – Aftercare is intensive, strengths-based, and meant to enhance capabilities for success and productivity after program services stop.

- *A community base* – Alternatives to juvenile justice responses recognize that real aftercare happens at home.

- *Right sizing* – Smaller local facilities enhance services delivery and effectiveness.

- *An evidence base* – Selected services must be evidence based, i.e., demonstrate good results.

- *Comprehensive case management* – Mental health is part of case supervision.

- *Targeting of needs* – Juvenile indigent defense recognizes the needs of the target population.

- *Equality* – A sense of racial and ethnic fairness/disproportionate minority contact seeks realistic equality of opportunity.

The four pilot states of Pennsylvania, Illinois, Louisiana, and Washington at the time of this writing were working on how to better serve youth after a brush with the criminal justice system. More states are working within this model on mental health services, indigent defense, and disparities.

Models for Change works with stakeholders who represent the continuum of resources, facilities, and services a youngster needs to transition to better choices and productivity in society and away from the progression of bad choices that lead to delinquency and crime. Working on preventing bad choices is much simpler, more effective, more rewarding, and less expensive than any criminal justice system involvement. Models for Change is intuitively a good approach as it's preventive in philosophy, approach, and practice.

This community-based approach demands accountability while participants are treated fairly by the juvenile justice system. Practitioners at each pilot state and site are free to structure how they go about reforming their systems. That is, provided the systems are reasonable, effective, and developmentally appropriate, while ultimately holding participants and their families responsible for results.

Pennsylvania was the first state selected by the MacArthur Foundation to conduct Models for Change. It was chosen for this study because of its history of juvenile justice reforms and pioneering work in the implementation of Balanced & Restorative Justice. The goals that continue to guide this effort include the following:[21]

- *Align* with the philosophies of Pennsylvania's juvenile justice system and the state's family advocacy network.

- *Integrate* with ongoing system reform emerging from Models for Change, Pennsylvania.

- *Design and implement* a strategic model that authentically includes the voices of all stakeholders, advances evidence-based approaches, and produces measurable and sustainable productive change.

Pennsylvania is quite advanced in this work facilitated by reform-minded leadership. Leaders have built forward-thinking consensus with stakeholders who understand the work. They know how to succeed with this strengths-based nurturing, not coddling, model of treating juveniles. Pennsylvania exemplifies for all these models how to do the work of cultural change. They are moving from extant justice system models seeking to control youth to combining resources and programming to prepare youth for adulthood.

VQ – formerly VisionQuest

VQ is a comprehensive youth services entity that's being replicated nationally in Arizona, Pennsylvania, Delaware, Texas, and Florida.[22] This alternative to corrections has been evolving and making a difference since 1973. It combines nurturing residential aftercare that borrows from Native American traditions marking the transition from

childhood to adulthood with experience-based learning, and evidence-based practices.

Note entities included in VQ's mission and the program's priorities for them:

- *Children* are safe, valued, and honored.
- *Families* are respected and supported.
- *Staff* are trained, supported, and appreciated.
- *Communities* are protected, impacted, and involved.

VQ, with its roots in Native American culture, is reforming programming to
address the unacceptably high rates of recidivism associated with the one-way-in and
one-way-out corrections model. Staff recognize that families must be involved in the
work of reentering society and a child needs stability directly after discharge. They
know they must continue support well after the child and family are on their own
again. To do this, VQ practitioners restated their core values in a 2012 Annual
Report:

- *North – We value our circle.* North promotes mentorship, unity, integrity,
  a balanced team, accountability, and our unique legacy of ceremony
  and innovation.

- *East – We value a safe environment.* East creates an opportunity for youth,
  staff, and families to heal, openly communicate, and reach their highest
  potential.

- *South – We value our youth and staff: Past, present, and future.* South means
  we are committed to high-quality services, fidelity, and fairness. Staff are
  our most valuable resource.

- *West – We value growth and change.* West positively impacts staff, youth,
  families, and community while promoting spiritual maturity.

VQ synchronizes juvenile reentry with collaboration, accountability, community,
family involvement, and a coordinated continuum of individual care until the
transitional process of success in the community
is complete. In other words, VQ is reforming
corrections by reinventing juvenile reentry and
aftercare.

> **Staff recognize that families must be
> involved in the work of reentering
> society and a child needs stability
> directly after discharge.**

Reclaiming Futures

Reclaiming Futures[23] began because the community had little in the way of neighborhood-level drug treatment services for high-needs youth. This model of juvenile reentry is reforming how a state juvenile justice agency can be integrated into the community to complete the process of reintegration. It's system-wide change that promotes collaboration. The model seamlessly connects courts, probation, and evidence-based treatment with community service providers for court-involved youth. Juvenile justice system staff collaborate with public and private service providers to deliver positive, pro-social activities and drug and alcohol treatment. They include character-building activities and involve adults as mentors and examples of good citizenship. The model takes a strengths-based approach to youth development that guides youth through treatment and beyond the juvenile justice system into the community. Services are tailored to each youth with a six-step process that's continuously assessed for impact and progress while clients are in residence and reconnecting to family and community.

Reclaiming Futures youth have complex needs, especially after release from court supervision. At that time, they and their families can be disconnected from services and under influences that could return them to the courts and correction. This model, supported by the Robert Wood Johnson Foundation and proliferating throughout the country, efficiently links leadership across agencies and across sectors from public to private to nonprofit entities. This is another model program reforming the systemic, departmental response to juvenile delinquency by focusing on community as ultimately responsible for whether its young citizens fail or succeed.

Aspire Youth and Family

Aspire[24] is a private alternative day and after-school program that delivers case managed behavior plans to youth ages 10-17 who have a history of difficulty with school and life. This high-needs population with substance abuse and behavioral/emotional difficulties is assisted in year-round small classroom settings. It uses a successful empowerment model with evidence-based practices such as The Seven Challenges faced while overcoming substance abuse. Their Kids at Work program, which is in most cases free, teaches life lessons via culinary arts. Simply, this model conveys the message that *you can do it*. As Aspire is evidence-based, it gets results.

Most notably, the study site in Clyde, North Carolina, has a 13 percent recidivism rate at the time of this study versus a 40 percent recidivism rate documented with similar local North Carolina youth not in Aspire. The cost of program attendance is on a sliding scale or at no expense to clients and their families for those who can get Medicaid or insurance reimbursement. Similar to the new breed of models reforming juvenile reentry, Aspire focuses on strengths, with high expectations and individual responsibility and accountability. Aspire staff and providers surround their clients and their families with support, individual and group counseling, outpatient services, and a regimen for success in school, at home, and in the community.

Rite of Passage

Rite of Passage (ROP) began in 1984 in a tee pee with 12 troubled youth and at the time of this study has more than 40 programs in 15 states.[25] Its original purpose was to fill the large gap in aftercare. ROP serves high-needs youth that come to its programs from institutional settings or are sent directly from the courts. Basically, this multimodal approach offers clients opportunities to succeed within their communities and with their families. Through accredited junior high and high schools at each ROP site, their students receive special education services, career education, and opportunities to participate in organized team sports, all in a therapeutic environment. The regular school experience is complemented by comprehensive community services, residential treatment programs, behavioral health services, and gender-specific programs. Services are again strengths-based, emphasizing skills development with individually tailored and managed services. Experience with various therapies and methods of service delivery over the years has led ROP to use specific evidence-based and practical approaches that include the following:

- Social learning theory to enhance education
- Risk/needs assessments using a validated risk assessment tool
- Understanding unique youth characteristics (responsivity related to culture, trauma, gender, etc.)
- Individualized treatment plans
- An effective behavioral management system
- Effective program implementation
- Understanding staff characteristics and roles
- Quality assurance/fidelity of practice
- Effective practices in community supervision

The program's core strengths result from years of reflection, action, and evolution.

- *Knowledge and skills* – Decades of experience have produced staff who are highly effective in working with youth and their families.

- *Corporate assets and human resources* – Their skilled workforce does it all—from operations to conducting therapies to running the schools.

- *Culture of innovation* – ROP staff continuously develop and integrate effective practices that are reforming how aftercare is delivered.

- *Value to families and communities* – Services are delivered at a fraction of the cost of institutionally supported services and, with remarkable results, are returning youth to productivity in the community.

How to Use This Life-Cycle Action Process

First a disclaimer: The meta-model presented here is an amalgam of superior programs that transition troubled youth back to their communities from troubled circumstances, usually after being involved with the criminal justice system. It is *not* an exhaustively comprehensive how-to manual for your reentry programming effort. It is, however, a beginning—a general guide filled with the wisdom of your fellow practitioners. It's the first-of-its-kind *progressive checklist of proven action items* that take an idea for local services from inception to permanency. Its strength and uniqueness lie in recognizing that success results from defining a problem locally and using local resources and people devoted to succeeding to solve it.

The suggestions have arisen from experience over time, from making mistakes—and learning! You'll find rigorous, sound evidence throughout. From this written mentorship, you can establish your own process and determine your own path to improving your community.

I have come to know program officials well who would say, "*Plan* like there is a tomorrow; *work* because you have a purpose; and *persist* because you are making a difference." Plan intensively and inclusively, they say. You must become quite competent at planning because it never ends. The paradox is that the plan must result in action. Good planning will result in an awareness that the time is right to begin. Secure a few rooms, hire a few good people and train them well, and get the referrals going. Run your operations to build permanency from which you can increase the numbers of troubled youth and families served enough to document real results.

Dream the dream that's just out of reach, a little uncomfortable yet worthy. Such dreams tend to happen as these programs prove themselves.

You *can* build a potent, sustained program built on capacity, supported by evidence, and surrounded by incremental but continuing successes. Thank goodness these programs have made sacrifices over the decades to prove exactly what does make a difference and how to do it. It just takes time and faith that strengths-based intensive personalized therapies, bottom-up collaboration of resources, and post-discharge long-term community services are the way to go.

> **From this written mentorship, you can establish your own process and determine your own path to improving your community.**

LIFE CYCLE PHASE I – PLAN AND IMPLEMENT

Chapter 2

LIFE CYCLE PHASE I – PLAN AND IMPLEMENT

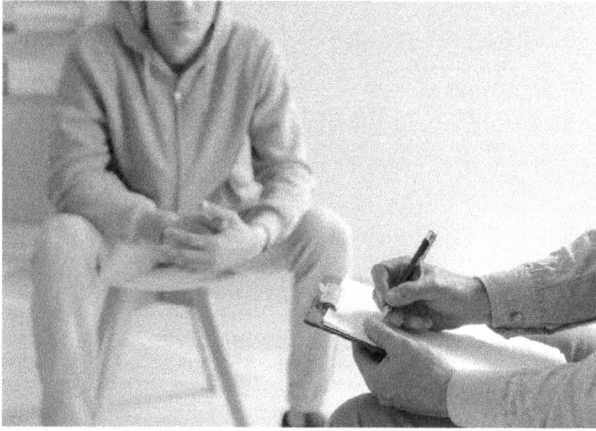

There is no easy way from the earth to the stars.
– Seneca

The Model for Juvenile Aftercare Services

Make no mistake; we are peeking into the daily operations of sincerely good programs and the thoughts and actions of truly accomplished people who do great things because they are compelled to do so. They are driven to succeed, though intelligently. The drivers of change who have created these programs do the myriad things that make the difference between a failure, a so-so program, and one that leads the nation in innovation and relevance. They are paving the road of the Movement to justice system reform and, by extension, the reform of how public services can be delivered.

Every one of these program professionals put the lion's share of their time into gathering the right people, whom they guided and inspired until they epitomized the mantra *Failure is not an option.*

Interviewees reflected on the qualities of those who are attracted to be part of these programs. At every level, passion and a real hunger for this work was evident. Everyone knows where they fit and are unblinkingly certain they have a vital role to play. For example, everyone at every level can talk to one another about the work at hand. They might discuss a nuance in a therapeutic session just completed or converse about generating support. People are hands on, creative, and quite comfortable tactfully challenging the status quo by asking *why not?* They don't simply accept the way things are.

Fundamental to this process is making friends. The people working these programs are masters at building relationships—and not shallow or temporary ones, but relationships that are long lasting and heartfelt. Relationship building begins with the first days of planning and never stops. It's a force multiplier with real consequences and great potential.

The executive director of Choice, the model intensive aftercare program in Baltimore County, Maryland, commented that it's not enough to know and maintain relationships only with people at various levels of decision making. He makes it a point to truly know his whole staff and spend time with them.

Staff are persistent, dedicated, and especially groomed enough to be more productive than they thought possible. Thoroughness in whatever they do is expected, tactfully demanded, and willingly given. These practitioners, who come from years of field experience, gather like minds and are okay with productive confrontation. They find themselves efficiently doing the work of the day and calmly handling the snafus. They are problem solvers and enjoy a challenge, especially when it comes to working with their counterparts in the system. They aren't deterred by barriers and bureaucracy, and certainly don't waste time unproductively. They understand that efficient processes are the key to effective service delivery. They are anything but desk-bound, hidebound clock watchers. As a researcher, I found them to also be fun people.

Slowly, agency staff learn how processes are supposed to work on *their* terms in *their* language. They're encouraged to become part of the Reform Movement, away from the control model exemplified by hierarchical public service agencies. They move to the strengths-based model of capitalizing on positive skills and behaviors demonstrated in forward thinking transitional intensive aftercare youth programming. Court officials soon see that youngsters taken into one of these programs spend a lot less time under court supervision and are much less likely to reappear in court. This saves agency staff money and time they don't have to squander. Judges, for example, most times do not have a community program that focuses on strengths-based programming and are forced to use the criminal justice system. When one of these community programs does take root, judges are usually its champions. Communal leadership is integrated into every site launch.

The change in culture moves from reluctantly accepting what comes from public service agencies to collaborating with them in a bottom-up virtuous cycle. It is so counterintuitive because relevant action happens at the point of contact. Children and their families are then seen as community resources rather than problems to control. An official with a state-level division of youth services observed that Choice is vital because "It does what we can't do." How can a parole officer, for example, have daily contact with clients and their families and have at least five face-to-face contacts per week plus phone calls? Choice does this with teams of AmeriCorps volunteers well trained in reaching this difficult population of formerly delinquent youth. This type of concentrated service is not uncommon in these model programs. They are proving that street-level—not agency-level—contact is the way to greatly improve the juvenile transition rate.

This is the epitome of a matrix of willing partners targeted and specifically selected for their contribution to the vision. Reflection travels back up the chain of services to inform all about how things are working, in a never-ending cycle of application, feedback, improvement, and back again. This new (old) way of doing things works and provides an example and inspiration for other communities.

This evolution in culture is strictly orchestrated, with bold commitment from program top leadership. It filters down to that staff visit to pull a young client out of bed to join the day's group session.

Plan and Implement Delivery Systems

We now enter the discussion of the critical features of building juvenile transitional services delivery systems. Yes, *systems*. This is not about the services you plan to deliver; they are inconsequential if you don't build the *business underneath the business* of those services. We repeat, the failure of a public service is incalculably harmful. Not only does the target group, in this case our youngsters, our most promising group, suffer—perhaps for a lifetime—but any great idea thereafter will meet with cynicism and obstruction. This must not happen.

Planning is where your efforts will rise or fall. It's the most vital phase and the one most neglected. Planning is tough, because there seems to be nothing material for the effort except maybe a few sheets of paper. Yet those papers are platinum. So, the person with the initial idea must be inspirational enough, talented enough, and determined enough to compel the few believers to plan well to the day the idea is sustained.

Planning is tough for many reasons. Staff can't see the plan as bricks being laid on a wall. They would much rather jump right in and start counseling or doing what they're good at and what's comfortable to do. Then the money runs out. Now what!? To have a good chance at building the legacy of changed lives, you must plan as if your professional life depends on it—because it does. Then, with confidence, implement for stability and build program capacity for permanency. This is how remarkable ideas become remarkable programs that make a difference that matters.

> **Planning is where your efforts will rise or fall. It's the most vital phase and the one most neglected.**

Thus, this study focuses on what happens at active sites, where staff are face-to-face with troubled youth and their families and the work of preparing them for successful independence. That's where reform takes root. It bears repeating that you will define features critical to your situation. However, this universal sequence of action items must be followed because any omission can risk weakening or even ruining your work. The model of critical features and effective practices is not a hierarchy of things to do, but it's a rational sequence. Planning should touch on each critical developmental feature, its action items, then the grail—effective practices. You need an overall focus, the sum of the vital parts. If anything, stakeholders emphasize staffing is the overarching concern, even though it's mentioned last as it threads throughout all three phases of the project life cycle. So do all the critical features, action items, and effective practices. Their commonality is people. It's through intense and lasting relationships that this work is completed and sustained. Because a project idea usually takes shape with a nucleus of community advocates, we begin with what to do about leadership.

1. Structure Leadership to Build and Preserve Core Values.

While the people shaping an idea may not initially see the light of bottom-up strategies, they can feel the heat of systemic weaknesses, even failures, and subsequently act to construct a program that capitalizes on the strengths of all stakeholders. But where should one begin? Almost everyone going about the business of starting a new idea has been through the visioning process and has been left somewhat lacking in direction afterward. Where did the promises of good ideas go? These change agents who make ideas work realized they were a part of the problem of top-down thinking and acting so they set out to change how they viewed and conducted aftercare. To paraphrase the very observant founding mother of one of these model programs, they set about understanding their dreams and hopes and agreed on them. Then they committed to them with the attitude that failure was not an option and obstacles were but opportunities to strengthen the process.

The leadership structure that emerged from onsite discussions with program staff and stakeholders elaborated four focal points for aftercare. They described how a very large statewide strategy such as Models for Change may be structured around and by the juvenile from commitment to aftercare to capable independence. The structure included overarching *policy,* state-level *directorships,* mid-level *operations officers,* and finally the *teams* in the matrix that delivers services. It's advisable to start small and doable with a single site, just as Aspire in North Carolina has done.

Variations include local efforts such as Choice in Baltimore, which is now penetrating other locales as sites take root and flourish. Or perhaps Rite of Passage, which began with a few high-needs youth decades ago and now is spreading nationally. Lessons can be learned from each program. The main lesson of capacity-built local aftercare is that bottom-up, community-based, and strictly applied strengths-based therapies *work,* no matter the scope of application. But when the programs began, creators had a grasp of the work at hand—not too much to be overwhelmed, not too little to be ineffectual.

The Center for Delinquency and Crime Policy studies outlined principles for this Movement of youth reintegration into the community as productive citizens:[26]

1. *Responsibility and freedom* – Prepare youth for progressively increased responsibility and freedom in the community.

2. *Interaction and involvement* – Facilitate youth/community interaction and involvement.

3. *Community support systems* – Work with the offender and community support systems on qualities needed for constructive interaction and the successful return of capable youth to the community.

4. *New resources and supports* – Develop new resources and supports as needed and defined by the focal group of youth and established with the service delivery infrastructure.

5. *Monitoring and testing* – Monitor and test the youth's and community's ability to work productively together.

In a Joint Policy Statement on Aftercare, 2004, the Commonwealth of Pennsylvania secretarial-level stakeholders stated their commitment to community-based aftercare, Models for Change, with the governor and people of Pennsylvania. This 17-point position paper left no doubt as to what would happen when the model took root. First, it defined aftercare:

Aftercare is the combination of services, planning, support, and supervision that begins at disposition, continues while a youth is in placement, anticipates the youth's release from placement, continues until the youth is discharged from juvenile court supervision, and extends thereafter through connection to other opportunities, supports or services, such as those provided to dependent children.

Services would be justified by need and be timely. Agency services would be coordinated and integrated; they would work toward common goals and share resources. The expectations were that a youth would be prepared for school or a job, have services continued after agency involvement, and have supports required for any youngster preparing for adult responsibilities. They put this commitment and earnest intent into *writing*. The basis and intelligence of this approach is recognizing that *all* children are at risk.

Effective Practice

Publish and distribute a signed state-level joint policy statement that commits agencies to the new vision of aftercare.

Eventually, with a tremendous amount of work, this document changed Pennsylvania youth services in profound ways. This insightful approach greatly reduced the number of court-involved youths, improved the efficiency of resources, and bettered communities. Further, community safety and security improved, court dockets and caseloads saw a bit of relief, youngsters stayed out of trouble and jail, and resources were more efficiently allocated at great savings. Within three years, every county was committed, which proved that strengths-based environments and communities are the keys to successful transitional services. The program provided proof that public agencies can collaborate on an evidence-based vision to reform aftercare and its agencies. The new system included 17 major policy statements (italics this author's to emphasize key terms):

- *Tailored action* – Aftercare begins at disposition and is tailored to the individual needs and capacities of each youth.

- *Focused planning* – Juvenile probation officers and residential treatment staff collaborate on a *single plan,* developed within 30 days of placement. The plan integrates treatment and aftercare services, including appropriate education placements and goals developed in consultation with the appropriate school district.

- *Dynamic planning* – Juvenile probation officers, in cooperation with residential treatment staff, host school district representatives. As those served move closer to leaving the facility, these representatives *refine the plan.* Refinements include post-release provisions that establish the provided services and planned conditions of supervision.

- Community-based comprehensive oversight – Systemic oversight ensures that placement facilities link their "supervision, care, and rehabilitation" within the facility to the plan for treatment and supervision *in the community.*

- *Goal of competency* – "*Competency development"* is a key, well-defined part of residential treatment and of post-placement expectations.

- *Judicial involvement* – Juvenile court judges at disposition review hearings routinely inquire about a youth's aftercare plan. They enter court orders, anticipating discharge, that are sufficiently detailed to *give direction to probation officers or treatment staff.*

- *Guiding principles* – Juvenile court judges and juvenile probation officers *further the principles* set forth in the Juvenile Court Judges' Commission Standards Governing Aftercare Services.

- *Targeted involvement* – Juvenile defenders and prosecutors *attend all disposition review hearings.*

- *Systemic involvement* – Juvenile defenders *visit their clients in placement.*

- *Victims' involvement* – Upon their request, the *views of crime victims* are invited and considered in aftercare planning and at dispositional review hearings.

- *Accountable aftercare* – The aftercare plan addresses the youth's activities related to *accountability* to the victim and community.

- *Continuum of care* – All probation officers have the skills to fulfill their obligations as *monitors* as well as *planners* for re-entry and *supporters* of youth who have *left residential care.*

- *Proportionate aftercare* – Intensity of supervision is *proportionate to the risks and needs* of delinquent youth. Proportionate also applies to targeting resources to proven services.

- *Services that follow the child* – County children and youth agencies *keep their doors and cases open* to youths who entered the delinquency system from the child welfare system and who should be receiving foster care and other services as "dependent children" upon release from a residential facility.

- *Appropriate adjudication* – In appropriate cases, county children and youth agencies support the petitions of delinquent youth to be decreed dependent children *prior to their 18th birthdays.*

- *Transition to the mainstream* – Resident school districts *promptly enroll* all youth who wish to return to public school. They work with the host school district and juvenile probation to ensure a *seamless transition* to an appropriate setting.

- *Evidence-based decisions* – *Evidence-based prevention programs* such as the Blueprints for Violence Prevention are considered for post-discharge services.

Review the above closely, as it's a matrix solution to a thorny problem from the bottom up and back again. Rather than the usual top-down, remote policy declaration, this document began at the bottom by describing the desired measurable result for aftercare for all participants and the wider citizenry. It described what capacities public agencies would have to build. Most important, the document outlined the need to build self-sustaining bottom-up services for "life after MacArthur," the day when that foundation's seed money ceased.[27]

Model programs focus on four distinct groups of change agents: those at the head of the program, those with cross-organizational responsibilities, those leading the site, and the direct service providers.

Effective Practice

*Organize your overall operations staff as Task Teams responsible
for specific program core values.*

So, we now turn to how to organize senior stakeholders or core partners.

Key to designing the most suitable organization for this new take on juvenile justice services is to recognize the unique functions of aftercare and how each level is responsible for keeping core values. Original program leaders are practical, process-and-action oriented, and technically proficient, according to a Missouri Model founding official. In other words, they are working leaders who not only set and carry out policy but also have the training and experience to comfortably jump into a group therapy session, for example—and many times they do.

Leaders of these programs are also aware of their place in and effect on the movement to reform justice systems. They are redesigning how services are delivered in the public sector. They recognize that changing monolithic systems rests on a foundation of immutable beliefs in an alternative way to go about juvenile justice.

The Missouri Model, an exemplary and forward-thinking model, recognizes that implementation requires changing the top-down, control-oriented system. Then values can pave the way for modifications that recognize the primacy of the community and how to combine resources from the bottom up.[28] The program vows to adhere to the following:

> **Key to designing the most suitable organization for this new take on juvenile justice services is to recognize the unique functions of aftercare and how each level is responsible for keeping core values.**

- *Embrace core values.* – Everyone involved in the Missouri Model, internal and external, must believe in strengths- and community-based aftercare.

- *Operationalize core values.* – The mechanics of change, facilities, staffing, and approach all must be put in place as the manifestation of core beliefs.

- *Protect against internal drift.* – To preserve fidelity of the Model, the program hires and trains good people. Transparency is the hallmark of arresting drift away from the processes and tenets that demonstrated success in the first place.

- *Sustain external support.* – Relationships, again, are everything to a movement. This Model cultivates them.

Missouri Model founders have a creative take on assembling overarching leadership. They have an appointed liaison board, and half of the six appointees are Democrats and half are Republicans. This structure serves to make the body reasonably immune to changes in the governor's mansion. Capacity Building at its finest. Note, too, that this concept can and should be implemented at any level of government as people build the infrastructure of governance. They enjoy remarkable continuity in political support, policies, and practices. If possible, those appointees are required to commit to a long-term tenure.

The next level of leadership, program directorships, is exemplified by Choice, which is run remarkably lean, another marker of these model programs. The director has two chief deputies. The one for Community Partnerships oversees staff for Human Resources, IT, Quality Assurance, and Research. The one for Operations oversees two assistant directors, one for Recruiting and the other for Education. They also receive splendid administrative support from The Shriver Center at University of Maryland Baltimore County. This co-locates them with shared office space in proximity to their source of AmeriCorps volunteers, who come from the University student body and become Community Service Learning Fellows. These Fellows are the line-level service delivery agents who do the bulk of the work with program youth. Yes, this exemplifies a matrix of relevant services versus stovepipe insulated services.

To demonstrate the leanness of the Choice organization, the three lead executives directly supervise their deputies and eight service coordinators. Those eight each work with three community-based Fellows, who cycle annually. This arrangement provides manning of their successful brand of intensive aftercare at all their active sites, which are organized by program tasks.

Effective Practice

Organize your overall operations staff as Task Teams responsible for specific program core values.

Task Teams are how Choice leadership integrates operational functions to launch new sites and maintain model integrity. These values-oriented teams define Choice culture based on the belief that "Thoughts become words, words become actions,

actions become habits, and habits become our character." They have three Task Teams: one for Quality, also responsible for research and data, one for Training, and lastly, one for Recruiting and Retention. While this may not seem too remarkable on its surface, the inspired part is that each functional team is responsible for, essentially the keeper of, assigned core values. Brilliant. The Training Team is accountable for the *learning environment,* and the Recruitment and Retention Team is responsible for *inclusion,* for example. The director of program operations shares: "When programming is launched, managers and staff keep and model core values and basic techniques." The team concept makes that happen. The director of operations enthuses that buy-in is intense, and creative energies are released by "maximizing talent." Imagine a work environment in the public sector in which your talent flourishes and "work" is no longer work.

The Quality Team is responsible for the quality assurance process as the name implies. Notice they do not say quality *control.* Quality cannot be controlled but it can be assured; it must be teased from reasonable standards, goal-oriented policy, and dedicated, well-trained staff. Further, this team ensures that services are delivered with integrity, one of Choice's core values. They always seek to answer key questions, according to one of Choice's key executives. For example: "How do we ensure we do what we say we will do?" and "What does success look like?" Thus, they analyze the theoretical, qualitative, quantitative, and practical aspects of major recommendations. They align all actions with core values and contribution to programmatic goal accomplishment with an eye to the evolving stability of the program.

These leaders and practitioners continually work to understand exactly who is served, what providers do, and how they do it. They detail the duration and intensity of a service. They gather a stream of good ideas. But before an idea, large or small, is adopted, they will have interviewed a full 80 percent of Choice staff and stakeholders for their view of it and insights into it. If expanding to a new site is a consideration and that site doesn't understand or support the Choice model of strengths-based transitional programming, Choice staff move on. They know what they are doing.

Choice is a learning culture for practical reasons. The program has a 100 percent annual turnover of AmeriCorps Fellows, so training of new Fellows is continuous. The atmosphere is one in which people have permission to make mistakes. Those mistakes become grist for discussion and critique

> Imagine a work environment in the public sector in which your talent flourishes and "work" is no longer work.

with an eye to personal and programmatic improvement and progress. No detail is too small as they know that the correct minutia represent a miracle in the making.

The Community Service Fellows have regular check-ins with the human resources staff to give them an opportunity to discuss how it's going, notes the director of community partnerships. Everyone gets regular input on the overall health of Choice and the efficiency of processes. Staff are encouraged to participate in learning and implementing change based on their own research. This creates an atmosphere of sharing and idea prioritization regarding their goal-oriented work. When they meet, they have *no* Robert's Rules, according to the Choice senior director. There is "one voice—one vote."

Their next step is to imbue this successful business model with youth and families. This philosophy and manner of going through the day naturally passes on to key external helpers. For example, a casual request for data from a parole officer is quickly evaluated for feasibility then delivered. A few more of these "favors," and they have converted that parole officer to intensive, strengths-based aftercare and the bottom-up Movement. The point of contact can be anyone from Choice. All are concerned with improving the organization and services delivery.

Organizing by task teams goes iterations beyond training. Choice also has a mission to qualify emissaries and change agents for community work in general and for transitional work specifically. The Training Team works hand in glove with the Recruitment and Retention Team to publicize the Choice alternative for community service. They develop a pool of the best young civic-minded college students via the AmeriCorps program, bring them on board, and mentor them by building a lifetime relationship. They train them and guide their enthusiasm as they connect the work of transitioning youth to community services. Nothing is left to chance as each recruit gets training, supervisory support, tutoring, and coaching. They are made to understand success from the perspective of youth and their families on their caseloads. Many students remain in this type of work. Others progress to jobs that influence what they learned to do with Choice, such as becoming program executives, service providers, and lawyers. It's a picture of credibility, fidelity, and performance. Obstacles just fall away.

A note of caution and realism: Don't underestimate how difficult this level of work is, mainly because of differing opinions about how to handle troubled youth. For example, some school officials hold the opinion that wayward youth are discipline problems to be shunted aside, usually to the courts or suspension from regular school.

However, Choice officials are gradually demonstrating that most troubled youth have strengths that become the basis for success in school and beyond.

Now we work our way down the leadership chain to how these sites organize location-level leadership. This is to be distinguished from the last level of organization, involving line-level service delivery staff and specialists.

Effective Practice
Organize site-level leadership around a strong judge.

At the site level, in the Reclaiming Futures model, site teams comprised of "Fellows" come from the courts, juvenile justice, treatment specialists, project directors, and the community. The judges are the absolute key, as they are for all these programs, because in the case of Choice, they set the direction of the Fellows' tasking and provide motivation to juvenile offenders that only a judge can. "When I call for a meeting," observes one highly experienced juvenile judge, "people come."

Community Fellows, which may include local agencies, service providers, and parents, are the most difficult to keep enthused, according to a Reclaiming Futures site director, who has been with the program since its inception.

> The Fellows, who represent critical services along the path to success in the community, are charged not with services delivery but *systems change.*

Therefore, project staff make a point to train and include Community Fellows in program decision making at every opportunity.

Each locality chooses their Fellows slightly differently, according to the locally defined need and purpose. The Hocking County Reclaiming Futures site staff selects members from the pool of youth advocates and services organizations, law enforcement, residential centers, the school district, the juvenile detention center, and mental health organizations. The Fellows, who represent critical services along the path to success in the community, are charged not with services delivery but *systems change.* This is a bit of brilliance. Notice how function changes from business as usual to cultural change, in which individuals then communities progress and transform. In handling everyday business, these programs are teaching stakeholders in our public agencies that punishment for juvenile delinquency is not the answer for most youth. This has the added benefit of helping sustain interest in the experiment to treat wayward youth differently. Including as many stakeholders as possible in deciding how a program is to be run is very much "shared leadership" according to the site director of Logan County Ohio Reclaiming Futures.

Fellows are intensely involved in the work of implementing the program and operating their sites by networking with other sites and working closely together. They're in constant communication, formally and informally, with regularly scheduled meetings weekly, monthly, and quarterly as needed. These meetings exemplify organization based on purpose, efficiency, effectiveness, and collegiality. Some of the duties of the Fellows involve working through the issues related to client assessment, treatment planning, and connections to needed services. A large matter is ensuring the fidelity of evidence-based services. For example, Reclaiming Futures stakeholders consider or employ Seven Challenges, Motivational Enhancement Therapy, and Cognitive Behavior Therapy, of the many modalities employed by transitional services.

From the outset, an inordinate amount of time is spent on what to do to be evidence-based. Practitioners ruminate about it—what it is and how they know it when they see it. Especially, they discuss how to manage and implement anything that's evidence based. They want to know how it equates to savings and goals, and the extent to which it's effective, according to the Models for Change director for policy and program development. A brief mention of evidence-based practices is enough for the moment, as much more on this topic follows.

Nothing is taken for granted. Stakeholders, especially program officials, are constantly working through issues, never satisfied, always reaching for a little more, according to the Logan County, Ohio, Reclaiming Futures director.

Effective Practice

Organize services delivery stakeholders according to their expertise with and influence on building and using evidence throughout your program.

Surprisingly, leaders are less interested in *why* we need evidence-based practices than they are in the *how* of it all. Notice they are geared to action. Staff, from top to bottom and bottom to top need to understand, support, and promote the concept of proving the effectiveness of the program in its entirety. This supports the adoption of a proffered practice that has its roots in valid research. This investigatory vetting process maintains fidelity, which will ensure overall effectiveness across different settings, from session to session, from therapist to therapist.

Yes, searching for and using services with an evidence basis is preferable, but most services employed at the local level are not evidence based. The reason is simply because so few have been investigated and profiled to show given results over time. It's just too expensive, technical, and time consuming. And even if a practice is evidence based, fidelity is wickedly difficult to maintain. So, what's a practitioner to do?

The answer is to err on the side of practicality. Choose services because they change lives and contribute to the program's goals. Continue to assess them in house to realistically ensure results that are meaningful to target populations and local stakeholders in that order. If those you serve are progressing, that justifies, if not compels, continued support from such local stakeholders as county commissioners or town council members. Have as a condition of services selection, a goal to collect the practical data and do the analysis that builds the evidential argument for the service in question. This, again, assumes that the overall program and processes are evidence based. Experience demonstrates that any effort at analyzing a practice produces some of the highest payback by enhancing program justification.

Now, just how should your service delivery teams be organized? VQ services-oriented teams are mainly comprised of a chief judge or judges, parole officers, line staff, and youth "decision makers." Of this group, line staff are most critical, according to the VQ executive in charge of evidence-based practices. They're the "four-star influencers" in a department or in a therapeutic setting. Due to their years of experience, "they know what works." These people are the change agents for the program and the service brokers for future services that may be acquired. They are living proof that the therapies they practice work. And they are opinion leaders who can look at a recidivism statistic, see the financial argument in favor of or opposing the program, and then communicate that argument. This vital talent is essential come budget planning time.

So how does program leadership influence these influencers? They will ask, why do a suggested practice at all? Point out to them what is in it (this program) for them. A parole officer or a court counselor will see their caseloads reduced; a judge may have a few more options for strengths-based sentencing; an elected official may see the economic sense of funding—most important for a politician. Demonstrate the effect on program clients. Then make the economic case that evidence-based practices save time and resources and make money. The return on investment of working with our youngest citizens is demonstrable. Great savings of time result from stopping the endless loop of recidivism with each successful formerly delinquent youngster. They make money because youth who stay out of the criminal justice system are productive neighbors contributing to the common good.

Put these structures for leadership in place as quickly as possible. Good people properly placed, trained, and motivated will be the engines of development and progress as you implement the plan by stages.

The next criticality we consider is capacity assessment, determining just how many of your services you can deliver effectively. Again, the overarching philosophy is "less is more."

2. Assess Capacity to Deliver Services by Understanding Your Client.

Capacity assessment is all about understanding your client and your organizational capacity to deliver justified, specified services that work and are efficiently, effectively, and frugally done. All services must be cost-effective. Your program must compete with hardcore fixed expenses and thus must "save" money and show a "profit."

While you're assessing your capacity to deliver services, build your readiness to implement the services. An in-depth knowledge of the clients you serve determines how they need to be served. This, in turn, determines what to do and to what degree you can deliver the services. Understanding your organization is vital if only to gain the buy-in the process demands, as key program staff council. Each of these model sites has spent and continues to spend an inordinate amount of time doing capacity assessment because they know by sometimes brutal experience it is productive and vital. Don't assume, for example, that the plight of the young male approximately 13-18 years old is completely understood and thus the response to their needs is well known and all you need to do is set up shop and begin attending to their needs.

Analysis of capacity can be as simple as understanding how to use a waiting list to determine ongoing demand as the Aspire program of intensive aftercare does, which helps them adjust staffing. Conversely, capacity assessment can be quite lengthy and complex if a statewide effort is anticipated. In fact, the Models for Change implementation team conducted assessments that determined state, site, and client readiness *before* they began delivering the first proven therapy session. In keeping with the bottom-up nature of reform, line staff are instrumental in planning, which is unheard of in top-down systems. Line staff are especially helpful in program-wide understanding of the limits of capacity. Plenty of proven help from which to learn and profit is available just about wherever you may look. The trick, again, is to see its opportunity and know how to use it.

> Do capacity building well the first time, as it will become the template for the continuous process it must become.

Consultants and implementation tools such as checklists are ready to be of service. Staff suggest it's helpful to use a little of both to get started. Done properly, capacity building is continuous. You can't deliver what you can't justify and support. This detailed capacity preparation prevents program staff from "over-promising and under-delivering," according to the Choice executive director. Do capacity building well the first time, as it will become the template for the continuous process it must become. Preserve the basics, develop a learning environment, and be consistent, staff at these model sites admonish. Each new program idea and each new site make unique demands for services.

References in the literature and experts can become a crutch, so beware. References to what should be done make capacity assessment sound simple, but the experts only have time to impart one aspect of the entire process. Plus, they're in and out of a consulting arrangement with no buy-in to program results. Work with experts, staff say, but recognize their limits.

Effective Practice

Assess organizational capacity to deliver services as preparation for implementation.

Marguerite Casey Foundation Assessment Tool

One of the best resources you can use is the Marguerite Casey Foundation Assessment Tool.[29] It's a diagnostic instrument best used by staff because it teaches the process of planning and managing a transitional services enterprise. Its originators recognize that, of all the facets of a successful program, building capacity from the bottom up is *the* primary purpose of any activity. Luckily, all the groundwork has been done in the form of this tool.

Open the Marguerite Casey Foundation website and download the Foundation Assessment Tool (in Excel).[30] (See endnote for the link.) In the Introduction, you'll see that the tool helps you rate the following four capacity elements:

- *Leadership Capacity* – The ability of organizational leaders to inspire, prioritize, make decisions, provide direction, and innovate.

- Adaptive Capacity – The ability of a nonprofit organization to monitor, assess, and respond to internal and external changes.

- *Management Capacity* – The ability of a nonprofit organization to ensure the effective and efficient use of organizational resources.

- *Operational Capacity* – The ability of a nonprofit organization to implement key organizational and programmatic functions.[31]

A capacity assessment or readiness tool should provide a quantitative overall score for your capacity to serve or readiness to begin services, and you will know the areas in which you need to focus. Notice you can—and need to—*act* on each one of these statements. Don't let yourself be "hypnotized" into "analysis paralysis." Always ask, how do we implement these results and *act*.

You'll also gain a baseline understanding to monitor growth, capitalize on strengths, and correct weaknesses. In general, you'll be able to make better decisions. The Assessment Tool supports making decisions objectively, more thoroughly, and quite important, sequentially. Action then is more analytical, rational, and mission focused. Otherwise, capacity building might tend to be haphazard. This tool warrants consideration as it addresses the weaknesses of building the service delivery systems and thus where and how the matrix can be strengthened. It also addresses the essentials of internal programmatic capacity, which will focus your analysis of readiness. It establishes a baseline understanding of program health from which you can monitor progress and identify weaknesses ("opportunities," staff would say). The Casey capacity assessment tool can help you earn essential commitment from stakeholders while limiting participation to those few who are essential and committed by word, deed, and work.

As the program stabilizes, this tool becomes an implementation checklist for expansion, the function of which is essential to closing the services-to-needs gap at your site. The assessment summary is part of an expansion checklist, should you wish to increase your effort elsewhere. Expansion must be analytical, gradual, and data based, not a grand emotional gesture.

Also note that although this example readiness scale is quite comprehensive, it does not consider that you must thoroughly understand your clientele, a topic we'll address after we consider capacity.

Practitioners at most sites also use consultants, who come freely from the foundations that back these reform ideas. Foundation trained and based consultants have decades of experience and bring effective ideas from other sites, especially technical assistance about how to implement evidence-based practices. The Models for Change consultants from The MacArthur Foundation, for example, worked full time. Their mission, besides technical assistance, was to help with cultural change and teach why and *how* to do a better job of overall implementation. They focus on practices, policies, and problems while generating "face-to-face buzz," according to the director for policy and programming at Models for Change.

Quantifying the unquantifiable is a bit of magic, but this assessment summary does it. It has four levels of preparedness for each capacity element in each of the four dimensions. Under Leadership, for example, CEO/ED Analytical and Strategic Thinking has four levels:[32]

- *Level One* – Somewhat uncomfortable with complexity and ambiguity; some ability to analyze strategies

- *Level Two* – Able to cope with some complexity and ambiguity; about to analyze and periodically generate strategies

- *Level Three* – Quickly assimilates complex information and able to distill to core issues; welcomes ambiguity and comfortable dealing with the unknown; develops robust strategies

- *Level Four* – Possesses keen and exceptional ability to synthesize complexity; makes informed decisions in ambiguous, uncertain situations; develops strategic alternatives and identifies associated rewards, risks, and actions

Key staff and stakeholders have averages for each dimension and an overall score that's graphically represented. And, as the assessment requests, staff can focus on four of 59 capacity elements to strengthen that are "most interesting." This then becomes a plan for strengthening an existing program or implementing a new one.

The initial purpose of capacity assessment is to determine organizational readiness to implement. It can also deter the impulse to begin or expand too soon. This impulse is particularly evident in the public sector as starting an idea or expanding one can serve as a personal expedient, usually political. Starting "by the numbers" compels prudence and enhances the chance of success for those served.

Once a program is in the operational phase, the same assessment tool should be used to continually evaluate the program capacity to deliver selected services and adopt new ones. Certain questions are helpful to answer during this process:[33]

- *Timing* – What are you committing to? Is the timing right for a new way of thinking and doing?

- *Practicalities* – How much time and what resources will be entailed in the endeavor?

- *Sustainability* – Can we sustain the effort to endure the changes in philosophy of treatment and culture?

- *People* – Do we have the right people in the right places, equipped and trained to do the right things? Do they know their roles and how they fit in the organization, i.e., how they contribute to accomplishing organizational goals?

- *Commitment* – How can we get buy-in and commitment from key people and agencies, public and private?

- *Data* – Do we have the information systems and qualified staff to develop relevant data and information?

- *Success?* – How will we know if the program is succeeding or, if failing, how to correct deficiencies?

- *Payoffs* – What is the payoff of success to key stakeholders? In other words, what is the cost-effectiveness of the program and how can it be used to justify furthering the program?

- *Relationships* – How do we maintain critical relationships?

Model programs answer these questions through research, analysis, and regularly scheduled, productive (vision/mission goal-oriented) meetings of selected staff, advisors, and perhaps consultants. In other words, they put in place structures such as well-run, regular meetings, necessary to work out essential planning issues. They address each question until a satisfactory resolution emerges then move on to the next question. They never go for "perfect" information; they continue until it "feels right" then get to work.

The plan to act must always be detailed enough to ensure workflow but flexible enough for contingencies—because things will not go as planned. Diversion from the plan is a law; embrace it as proof you are doing the right thing or know how to do it the right way. Growing pains are a good thing.

Now add to operational assessment the client risk assessment to understand the strengths and risk factors of your target population. Risk assessment must be done in conjunction with understanding the details of operations and services delivery beyond risk and resiliency factors of those

Understanding your youngsters is basic to building capacity and operational readiness.

you will serve. To be clear, you are serving both high-needs youth *and* their families. The profile of this population varies by location, according to practitioners interviewed for this model program for juvenile aftercare. This is another way of saying your program is yours because your target population is yours.

Understanding your youngsters is basic to building capacity and operational readiness. Initially, understanding is achieved through profiling your clients during program planning, then during operations, when you consider referrals for your program. Profiling continues individual by individual, so you are continually in touch with your clients' needs and how best to address them. Profiling those you serve should become part of readiness and part of ongoing data development. Model programs gain much needed insight into service delivery by constantly assessing clients. Your clients determine the services you must provide or contract, which in turn relates to how you support those services with personnel, facilities, administration, and funds.

Probably the best resource for doing this is the Models for Change source document from the MacArthur Foundation: *Risk Assessment in Juvenile Justice: A Guidebook for Implementation.*[34] It approaches this essential task in terms of systems, discussing the effect of aftercare systems on one another and how they should work together while building permanency. This is the definition of vital continuity and the way organizational development in the public sector should and can be done.

Effective Practice

Define your transitional services in terms of your target populations.

By knowing those you serve, you can then design your matrix of local services. For example, your charges may be largely defined as being in poverty and perhaps affected by community violence and/or an inordinate frequency of domestic violence. Conversely, youngsters may have good teachers, a mentor, and a supportive home life. With these supports, your youngsters can overcome difficult circumstances, especially if your program is a permanent, functional matrix of tailored services.

By being disciplined in comprehensively and honestly defining risks and strengths of those you serve, managers and staff can make better programmatic decisions. This is especially critical in planning for the day when the responsibility for the youngster is transferred from the public systems, mainly the criminal justice system, back to the community. All with an eye to transitioning them fully to the family, where the real responsibility for transition lies. A successful child is a successful adult, with great intergenerational implications.

An alternative school principal commented that his students "can go on to more schooling, get a job, or be lost to the streets." The community and the family oversee the result for each youngster. As the report states, in collecting essential data to continue to improve programming and accomplish stated goals, you will better understand the risks of youth reoffending and match interventions accordingly. If anything, the guidebook resulting from the capacity assessment tool is appropriately thorough, and it's practical and proven by effective application over a range of circumstances, time, and sites.[35] It ensures that implementation will succeed as much as possible because it's based on the newest and continually evolving theories of how to foster youth development. Those theories recognize that aftercare is about youth progress toward usefulness as a citizen, where desistance (avoiding crime) is part of the natural development for most adolescents.

The capacity assessment tool report also recognizes that public systems are not the answer but part of the answer for youth returning to school, home, and the community—that risk is not destiny. The executive director for Choice had an interesting insight: "Understand your client so you understand what you *cannot* do." Capacity assessment is the process of "understanding what is possible." Most youth need surprisingly little skillful and well-timed prodding for them to do the right thing. After all, most of the youth in these programs really do want to succeed at life.

Another great idea comes from the bottom-up Movement leaders at Choice. While each of these sites displays a high-end facility with technology, Choice takes it a step further. It has a dynamic GPS map of possible clients according to their offenses. First, they ask, "Who is eligible?" Then they ask if there's a staff-to-client fit to the in-home, face-to-face nature of their model. At this point, these potential referrals are matched to available resources, not the other way around. Staff and decision makers at these model sites also have the courage to walk away from a "deal" if it doesn't fit. GPS is ready made for capacity assessment and using it is rather brilliant. With mapping, leaders can physically see where need lies—its shape, density, and implications. All these ideas serve to build permanency.

The Cary Group correctly concludes that to conduct evidence-based practices, the organization itself must be evidenced based.[36] You'll find a more detailed discussion further along, but a brief mention of this theme is relevant to the work of capacity assessment and thus to capacity building. The Cary Group checklist[37] suggests the following components of sustaining evidence-based change, which is a variation on the theme of capacity assessment (italics are the author's):

- *Cultural alignment with readiness* – Becoming evidence-based is a cultural change; it's not business as usual. Minds will have to internalize the differences and compel action accordingly.

- *Proper use of assessments* – Assessments of organizational processes and service delivery systems are well advised to constantly analyze, both quantitatively with assessment instruments and qualitatively by peer critique. Perhaps even videotape an EBP therapist in group, for example.

- *Effective staff-offender interactions* – The Missouri Model, for example, bravely closed all centrally located youth prison-style facilities in favor of small, disbursed, community home-style residencies. These welcoming facilities changed the culture from punitive, control-oriented responses to aberrant behavior into laboratories for continuous positive behavioral change.

- *Continuum of programming* – Stability includes stabilizing processes along the path of services delivered by each service provider along the way. This is born of a conviction that a youngster must be equipped to go home—to stay.

- *Quality assurance (QA)/performance data* – When done properly, QA ensures process efficiency and effectiveness, while performance data gives regular, near-daily numbers on program goal accomplishment. Make the distinction that this is not quality control. Quality can't be controlled, but it can be assured.

- *Organizational supports* –Your program cannot exist in a vacuum. Remember the strength of what you do is based on relationships between your partners, collaborators, and clients.

This is a relatively simple checklist to run and can be a good introduction to the design of your evidence gathering, analysis, and use. Contact these program officials, who are a quick internet search away, as they are remarkably willing to share lessons learned. Why reinvent the tried and true? Evolve together. Another take on the whole being greater than the sum of its parts.

When capacity is built systemically,[38] many virtuous unintended consequences arise that are more consequential than the usual cost-benefit estimate. Leadership, for example, is rightly bottom up. This system provides numerous opportunities for communication, which continuously builds relationships and buy-in, according to the chief operations officer for VQ. Previously, remote providers and consultants, who are usually on a fee-for-service basis, were compelled to be active stakeholders, especially when they saw VQ invest its own money in a new site. All stakeholders are vested in, if not compelled to support, program fidelity and success.

With buy-in, according to Missouri Model executives, action is data driven, which means decisions are real-world, street-level relevant. More important, objections to program change or expansion are more readily answered. Resources are economized, apportioned, and more effectively used. Better choices are made at various decision points as youngsters are steered through the criminal justice system—starting with intake and progressing to the court hearing, then to program placement, and finally, to release to aftercare.

Along the way, many opportunities arise for diversion and avoiding the spiral into further penetration of the expensive public systems, where formal public systems involvement may not even be needed. Proba-

> The bottom line is that this approach gets to the root causes of misbehaving, bad choices, and school failure and addresses those causes.

tion actions are better for example, as this service evolves as a channel to services away from unneeded program revocation and return to incarceration. By combining standardized assessment, both programmatic and individualized, and judicial procedure armed with data-based aftercare programming, the system becomes more responsive. All the while, it evolves from the traditional control model to the evidence, strengths-based, and community models. Also, the assessment tools are now validated for a balanced understanding of risks counterposed with strengths, which steers case management away from those default and expensive agency fixes. The bottom line is that this approach gets to the root causes of misbehaving, bad choices, and school failure and addresses those causes.

It's a win-win-win situation, according to a Models for Change senior executive: The system wins, the community wins, and the child wins when their growth potential is revealed. Remarkably and in growing numbers, as the graduates of these programs are uplifted, so are their families. Meanwhile your idea moves inexorably to its potential.

While doing capacity and client assessments, organizational readiness for implementation evolves to an anticipated start date. Then sustainability evolves to support more services and finally to prudent expansion to meet municipal needs. Analysis of capability is an analysis of readiness to proceed.[39] Choice, for example, sets a date to begin and works backwards; of course, it's had more than 25 years of working out the bugs to make this style of implementation work. But Choice does not begin a site until they have solid buy-in from appropriate stakeholders and, if possible, a local program sponsor, a champion. It's another start-date criterion, which is to be ready "when the money hits," according to the Choice executive director.

At the risk of over-simplifying, we'll note a major difference between departmental public services such as the criminal justice system and local, permanent matrices of service programs. The "system" acts on something *after* it has gone wrong, for example, after a youngster becomes a discipline problem flirting with delinquency and criminality. Matrix services, on the other hand, are designed for permanent solutions to permanent problems by capitalizing on youth strengths and potential with highly cost-effective measures.

The project progresses synergistically as critical features are addressed, each pulling the other forward in the planning process. Leadership grows in commitment and cooperation. Capacity assessment helps limit the gaze of what can be done, which fits with the essential task of determining project scope—the next critical feature to discuss.

3. Narrow Your Scope to Include What Can Be Done.

Notice this critical action statement: Good program planning and execution is not about how much you can do; it's how *little* you can do to ensure the idea is foundationally sound . . . by the numbers. Pause and think about this. Trying to do more than is feasible courts chaos and failure.

The process of determining scope, or scoping, is so much more than you might think. It's important to introduce this topic not as the process of visioning, proposing a mission statement, and establishing goals. Rather, it's the intricate task of being practical about what can and especially what cannot be done, according to the executive director of Aspire. The term "scoping" as it's largely done now, deceptively conceals the absolutely necessary work it demands. It's about zeroing in on the essentials and understanding how each is a vital, sequential part of the building process. It's remarkably easy to get distracted.

It's a matter of understanding and living the balance between doing too much or too little, moment to moment, which is a test of leadership and staff focus. That is, can you dream big and be deadly realistic as to what that dream demands? Can you measure the meaningful benchmarks, for example, monitoring grades and attendance before, during, and *after* your intervention? Counting the number of graduates is easy, but it doesn't test behavioral change. When assessment is done correctly, you can see what you're doing well and you aren't doing so well and take the necessary actions to correctly adjust course. This assumes you realize how to correct before a little bother becomes a program threatening crisis. Prevention, action, and timely correction matter. Are you ready for your sponsors and opponents to hear the results? Be vigilant with measures of improvements in your target population.

Do you understand *exactly* what you cannot do so you can recognize "mission drift" or vision drift or goals drift or measurements drift to unrealistic lofty statements? All these questions and more mark the struggle transformational program professionals have when considering scope. Simply, program scope deserves intense initial attention. It needs to be designed into daily processes as a guide for minute-to-minute decisions and operations. It helps to understand what real results are, and you need to revisit that measurement validity regularly, at least annually. Any efforts spent on scoping are some of the most productive investments of time. Scoping is critical to every aspect of program building.

Effective Practice

State a vision with a purpose that is motivating by its challenge and tempered by scope that considers what can and can't be done.

Let's continue the discussion of scoping, which starts with visioning. Ah, visioning. How many of us have been in visioning meetings that are fun, challenging, collegial, lengthy—and misguided. Some general guidelines are appropriate. The statement of scope needs to define what you intend to accomplish and, by extension, what you will *not* do. This is tough as people love to dream and expound on that dream. Scoping is earthbound and frank. From this come goals and their measures of success, quantifiable and qualitative. Quantifiable means the right numbers at the right time. Qualitative means process or that which is descriptive in function. As the vision is shaped and reshaped

> The statement of scope needs to define what you intend to accomplish and, by extension, what you will *not* do.

many times over, understand constraints, stakeholders, resources needed, personnel specifics, support systems, politics, management systems, and the demands of services that must achieve clarity in a few remarkable words. Let us dissect the mission of VQ:

> *VQ is a national comprehensive child, youth and family services organization, committed to providing successful and effective services while adhering to the highest professional standards. With nearly 50 years of experience, VQ provides children, youth and families with a trauma-informed and guided centering practice to promote their highest potential.*[40]

They serve youth and their families—specifically, those who have experienced trauma. This narrows the target population and prevents drifting, oh so subtly, oh so inexorably, into other populations that are a temptation to serve. This business is a calling to help, not a "job." Services, more specifically intervention services, are innovative and delivered with high standards of fidelity. These standards are proven by rigorous investigation, which preserves certain methods, usually by employing evidence-based services that produce desirable results.

The life experiences born of Native American tradition sponsored by VQ entice those of us in the helping careers. Indeed, over the years, its youth-focused programs have taken VQ on character-building experiences over mountaintops, on camel rides, sailing on tall ships, to historic reenactments, on overland cattle trail drives, and on cross-country bicycle rides. Children are restored—to themselves, to their families, and to their communities as productive adults with bright futures.

One VQ site has a shared residence, a small driveway basketball court, and a sense of community. The first of these experiences for many of the youngsters—it's home! Each of these remarkable programs also recognize staff by investing heavily in developing the whole person, whether they're a client or a member of the line team. Team members have the proper training, education, and career development and a working environment that recognizes talent, creativity, and industriousness. Thus, more can be done with the modest means allotted and bequeathed to these programs. Goodness and capability are valued with frugal, targeted, productive investment in time and dollars. Their work is founded on these principles (italics by author):[41]

- Children and youth are safe, respected, and honored.
- Families are protected, strengthened, and educated.
- Our team is developed, supported, and encouraged.
- Communities are engaged, valued, and involved.

Notice the hierarchy of attention: Kids are first. Top-down focus on public agency goals is not mentioned. This is a way of limiting goal creep to assuming more responsibilities without the wherewithal to accomplish them. It states values and it provides an outline for objectives that can be quantified. For example, when focal groups are valued, supported, and run by trained staff, the community can expect to see safety and security enhanced, and its young citizens build themselves to independence from dependence. Take the natural extension of scoping to define what you value.

The Choice program values serve as an example:[42]

- *Bottom-up leadership and practice* – Staff and leadership encourage a bottom-up approach to social change based on sharing the best approaches to transitioning youthful offenders.

- *A learning community* – Everyone teaches and learns in a learning-driven community.

- *Teamwork* – Team members value the dignity of individuals and make a massive collective effort to reform agency-based transitional services.

- *Stewardship* – Sound business practices recognize that making a difference requires sustained effort and an eye to program permanence in the community.

- *Honesty* – Staff and leadership do all this while being open and honest.

Values in these programs are the "thoughts that become words, which form actions that become habits that define character," according to the Choice senior staffer at the University of Maryland Baltimore County campus location.

Next comes defining objectives and concomitant results that follow values-driven goals. This is the foundation of your plan to deliver on promises—your strategic challenge. "If you don't know where you're going, you'll end up someplace else," observes one of our foremost modern philosophers, Yogi Berra.

Results are defined by various limiting factors such as available trained staff, resources, facilities, and support, including transportation and adequate technology. What you want to accomplish implies how to go about it in terms of milestones and tasking, which is daily work and, by exception, to guard against any necessary activities that lie outside the newly formed scope. Treat activities sparsely and only by what they contribute to the whole. When an essential group of people come together to begin a project, the list of issues will be lengthy and at times maddening. Program staff say to simply try to prioritize issues and handle them one at a time. But always be moving forward. A good place to start, according to one senior executive, is to identify issues that will have the most political support and the potential results that are most important to the people served. Then, start collecting data that measures progress, or lack thereof, toward your goals.

A cursory internet search reveals guidelines for designing project scope, although they're somewhat simplistic. They seem to concern agonizing over vision, mission, goals, and measures . . . again. Model programs go further than the internet prescriptions to define core beliefs. The best council comes from the websites for model programs and staff themselves. If it's within budget, perhaps even if it isn't and the promise of the idea warrants it, you're advised to have an outside facilitator help initially to keep the "visionaries" from spinning out of control. Engaging a third party is worth the expense if only to prevent idea and measurement bloat that comes from each stakeholder wanting their measures of performance or goal accomplishment to be the preeminent ones. Seek referrals for consultants to be satisfied that you select one who has a stake in the success of your effort; be wary of the "free" technical advisors that hail from federal sponsors.

> **Identify issues that will have the most political support and the potential results that are most important to the people served.**

When you do start, start with the result of measures of community wellness regarding client and family functionality and work backward to intermediate and immediate stages of progress. Consider process goals to ensure what you're measuring leads to overall project goal accomplishment. Then automate your measures such that line staff can keep data as it happens. Thus, data are live and relevant. The biggest benefit of measure and data that work is staff and partner buy-in. Furthermore, your budget requests will sparkle with hard numbers that justify what you do and more of it.

Yes, you can have measurement creep also. In that case, measures lead to little real consequence but still take as much in time and resources as meaningful measures.

Effective Practice

Define the project scope in terms of your target populations' needed competencies for productive independence in the community.

What does it take to ensure that young clients learn new skills and can apply them when they become independent? Once immediate subsistence needs are considered (housing and regular meals are particularly problematic to procure for justice-involved youth), clients and their families can progress to the next level of support. The first supports they need are practical.[43]

Youth need the skills to earn and keep a job that will give them some potential for a living wage, which means they need vocational skills. Besides a fractured family circumstance, many have some sort of disability or substance abuse problem, so counseling and access to medical help are vital. This is their "continuity of care" prescribed in their case planning. However, this support typically ends when sponsored programs end, which is usually when the terms of a court ruling are satisfied, just when the youngster is beginning to show promise.

There also needs to be continuity with any federal and state benefits they may be due, such as Medicaid or housing assistance. Most of these young offenders will return to the social situation that abetted their troubles in the first place. Ideally, their families should have some guidance from aftercare specialists on how to address their difficulties and counseling for how they can participate in the aftercare process. It's thus necessary that families have continuing contact with program staff, if that can be arranged. Ultimately, your charges must learn to be responsible, so that must be the foremost earned skill of their time with an aftercare program. Consider what you might measure to this end.

Chain of Outcomes

A *chain of outcomes* is a tool that helps differentiate between and visualize the progression of inputs, measures of work, outputs, and true results, or outcomes. The biggest insight of a chain is that you can see the difference between outputs and outcomes, which can be confused and ruin scoping.

Outputs involve numbers without real meaning upon which you can base corrective decisions in operations and programming. A simple example is the number of students you have in an after-school program, which gives no indication of how the youngsters are improving. Numbers must demonstrate how well the target population is doing and thus how you are realizing program goals and vision.

Using children in an after-school program as an example, *outcomes* measured could be improvements in school readiness, such as real progress in basic skills such as math, English, and social studies. The difference, then, between output and outcome is wide and deep. It represents the difference between being stalled and progressing to what matters most to those served and thus eventual improvements in community well-being. Everything needs to be connected and related, one action and measure leading to the next. Thus, the chain analogy.

The chain of outcomes tool is useful because most programs stop data collection and analysis after initial out*puts* are met. These are usually limited to simple measures, such as the number of people attending a class, whereas an out*come* tells the story of desired behavioral change. Outputs are easy to collect but may have little connection to program goals, only the veneer of leading to an evidence base. The youngsters involved continue as before, and to compound the problem, scarce public funds are squandered, and precious time and talent evaporate.

The chain, in terms of transitional services, instructs practitioners to consider outcomes for youthful clients and, by association, the program, agency goals, and lastly, community goals. Again, this is a bottom-up treatment focusing on cost-effective impact rather than the status quo of top-down, cherry-picked measures of loosely shaped agency goals. The former builds program strengths, and the latter justifies agency status quo to minimal effect or declares victory so to move to the next "initiative." Preliminary measures have their place but as *part* of the continuum of the chain of outcomes. Define measures specific to your agency's goals and then plan your analysis and evaluation strategy. Measures must assess the individual where they live. This will be discussed in depth in the following section.

Let's begin with what are termed ultimate measures of results, i.e., those that strengthen community wellness:[44]

- *Ultimate* measures—largely *numbers*—are still a start in defining target population progress. Note the last measure in this category, which hints at the potential that the program may close the services-to-needs gap, slowly, meaningfully.
  - o Employment rates
  - o Post-program high school graduation rates
  - o Continuing education rates
  - o Reductions in criminal justice system involvement, e.g., re-arrest rates
  - o Rates of continued sobriety
  - o Rates of program graduates who remain successful in the community for extended periods

- *Intermediate* measures assess program effectiveness by refining post-program measures. These are usually expressed as *percentage* rates. Note the progression from numbers to more meaningful percentages.

- o Program completion rates
- o Rates of return to regular school
- o Reduction in recidivism rates
- o Reduction in detention rates
- o Rates of continuation in community-based services
- o Improvements in sobriety rates

- *Immediate* measures are an indication that resources are being employed correctly, that is, that effort has a chance of changing behaviors for the better. These are usually expressed as numbers.
  - o Rates of change in referrals
  - o Rates of change of clients in the program
  - o Rates of change of clients in detention
  - o Reduction in the number of school suspensions
  - o Reduction in the number of fights at school

This is a good start. Notice how one leads to the other. Now program staff must assess capabilities for success.

Ask staff and stakeholders over and over, admonishes the Choice national director, if goals and measures are really goals and measures and if they tell the incremental yet progressive story of program effectiveness. Yes, we are still considering program scope.

Know that scoping is a process of questioning how things are done and how well the program is doing. For example, do program skills lead toward employment, or are they merely a goal in themselves? Does a school visit by staff impact recidivism? Ask why and how a measure is important. Key staff at Choice developed their goals with the intent that they would also build relationships as an essential goal— and hold themselves responsible for implementing the work behind lofty statements. Remember, too, that measures of effectiveness and results are rather hollow unless the processes that underlie them are efficient. Thus, your results analysis strategy must also outline a permanent, evolving analysis.

The people working at exemplary juvenile aftercare programs who were interviewed for this descriptive model of how to build and conduct a viable program were exemplary themselves. They were always conscious of the necessity to make the hard connection from vision to mission to beliefs to goals to objectives to processes, then finally to consequential results.

A word of caution here again: Less is more. First and foremost, limit your scoping participants to those who can materially contribute and compro-

Speaking dollars to budgeteers makes your position stronger.

mise; they must believe in the model. A Choice senior staffer concerned with the scope of his program had a further suggestion. He said that program leadership would be well advised to keep the participants informed as to their purpose and regularly validate what staff are doing to contribute to goals. The best indicators will translate into a simple cost effectiveness argument for the program: X money produces Y savings that can be used for Z programming or expansion. Speaking dollars to budgeteers makes your position stronger.

Remember that staff are responsible for *using* data to improve process efficiency and keep *daily* work goal oriented. The more you design measures into your program, the more you must collect, analyze, and use them. Dynamic, meaningful measures are a great way to structure monthly staff meetings, by the way. It takes considerable time, effort, and especially talent to master the work of gathering data, analyzing, and disseminating it, even for a few measures. Monitoring program outcomes is only part of the data story. The nature of measuring performance is that data demands more data in that once one thing is investigated, more areas seem productive to pursue. Scope creep in action. A good program collects outcome data on services and especially on the fidelity of measurable, productive services. It's tough to set up a scoping process so it's practical thus useful; but these model programs suggest how to do it for maximum effect. Scoping naturally leads you toward how you will analyze and evaluate your effort.

4. *Design Analysis and Evaluation to Preserve Core Programming Components.*

Why are results important? The bottom line is that determining credible results usually determines if a program continues or not. The answer, however, is different depending on the context in which it is asked or the person who is asking about it. It's germane when considering juvenile transition and the tussle between agency and measures meaningful to teens, their families, and especially the community. You need to measure performance to make sure your resources are all invested in attaining the results you intend to achieve. There's a difference between attaining a meaningful goal and getting results for numbers' sake. Goals are formed with thought about your intended endpoint and deciding how to get there, continuously correcting your actions if you're off track. Just getting results may have little to do with the purpose of the project. Analyzing your project for a result is itself a process. The way you get to be evidence- thus results-based is as vital as achieving a worthy end.

Again, it is one of the themes of this inquiry that the former of defining measures is the *what;* the latter of the way you go about measuring things is the *how.* You have probably deduced by now that the how of it all is the more important of the two. Yet in actuality, it's the most neglected—*except* in these model programs. They practice this duality to a sharp point and with great appreciation for the realities of measurement in the chaotic setting that is reform minded and about troubled youth. A Reclaiming Futures executive opined that becoming evidence based is a shaky proposition; it is "tough to translate, tougher to implement, and tougher yet to maintain."

The Choice program has one of the best understandings of how to define what must be achieved. They begin with Theories of Change (see Figure 2), which describes the process of achieving long-term goals—one theory for the overall program and those for subprograms, such as jobs and education. One theory is for the overall demonstrable effect, and the other is for a demonstrable effect of a particular service, such as Functional Family Therapy. Choice must have data and evidence that it works for myriad services before they adopt one. And then they want continuous, dynamic proof that the adopted program functions as advertised.

Effective Practice

Design a logic model for the chain of outcomes to define project results and means to get there.

This logic model (on the following page) is deceptive in that it displays the wickedly complex reality of how to connect stakeholders with programming for stated aims. It starts with stakeholders and activities and making sure they improve youth outcomes and strengthen communities—a difficult connection. It's a great statement of a chain of outcomes. Study how each input becomes a functioning, responsible young woman or man.

What is a logic model? The term is quite overused and misunderstood. It is the "mechanism by which an intervention or program works."[45] Despite the seeming agony of creating one of these models, it's the fastest way to physically, tangibly define the purpose of a program and how it can *function.* Let's take a trip across this curious map, otherwise known as a *chain of outcomes,* which term this author prefers.

Figure 2. The Choice Program Theory of Change Logic Model

Community Need: effective, cost-efficient community-based alternative to youth detention
AmeriCorps members delivering Choice Model services reduce recidivism and retention of youth in the community

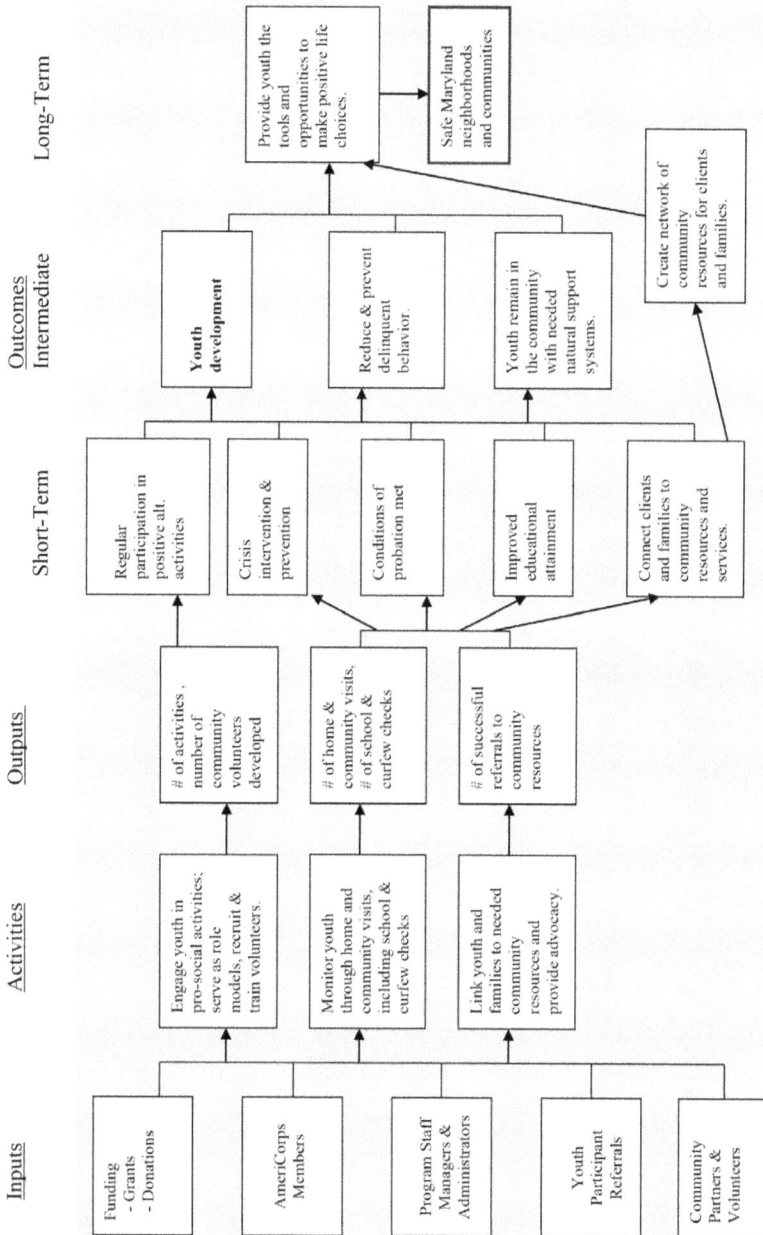

A chain of outcomes depicts how resources and people combine to achieve a common goal. Inputs are the components needed to do work. The chain of outcomes lists people and funding. Consider adding facilities and operational support to the equation. Alone, just about any task can be accomplished with these building blocks, but they need direction. Staff want to help youth make positive life choices that result in safe neighborhoods, so activities should be defined to fulfill that goal.

At this stage, outputs, which are the components of the chain that are measured, need to be connected to a stated end, in this case, safe Maryland neighborhoods and communities. *Numbers* are collected so that agencies may discern that the work is headed in the right direction. The project can still go astray as numbers are relatively meaningless unless connected, unerringly, to what needs to be accomplished long-term, permanently. Numbers are easy to collect, thus most local service projects end data collection by counting things and perhaps computing rates of change. Deeply pursuing how effort improves the community is difficult by magnitudes, and thus the prospect of it is prohibitive; this stage of determining initial outcomes, counting things, is where most projects tragically end their analyses. This model is insightful as it describes activities resulting

> A chain of outcomes depicts how resources and people combine to achieve a common goal.

from first outcome indicators, which are necessary to progress to the next stage of outcomes, intermediate measures. Make sure you include this progression in your model.

Until you convert the logic model into practical work, it's merely a creative exercise. Don't stop with merely computing percentages or rates of change. Look at improvements in behaviors such as reducing fights in school, increasing graduation rates, reducing recidivism. Then *progress to* being a functional service for and in the community. Because your idea, in this case, helps a wayward child to a meaningful place in the neighborhood.

Much more must happen before agencies can demonstrate that their projects are successful. Note how the measures are connected. Again, remember: Less done well is more; this can't be said enough. Determine a few good interim measures connected to one or two long-term measures that are realistic, practical, and easier to assess. A good goal should be to arrive at a one-page briefing of a chart demonstrating a return on investment for local leadership at budget time. It should show a "profit" from funds invested, with a less-than-subtle message that it's a "pay me now or pay much more later" situation. Your program must compete well with fixed line-item expenses and few dollars for new ideas. Only three main points and a chart going in the right direction are dramatic and most important—and compelling because they can be remembered well by leadership.

The first long-term measure the model arrives at is a young adult who can make positive choices and influence improvements in his or her neighborhood. This would be improved if long-term, or ultimate, measures were quantitatively defined in the very beginning of planning. This establishes what the project needs to accomplish and, by extension, suggests a strategy for how to get there. For example, the project can measure the retention of a job for at least a year after graduation. This is a good measure. And better measures usually mean better decision making and programming. Aiming for long-term goals is practically difficult if only for the fact that graduates are difficult to track after they leave the program. It would be illuminating to try to track even a few who may or may not have successfully completed the program. At the very least, just tell them to "Stay in touch." Much can be learned from successes and failures. Don't forget the failures. A troubled teen with a stable job is an indication that the agency's work is producing results. If they continue to struggle, even recidivate, well, what will you do? How will you modify/improve what you are doing?

Patience, discipline, and realism are what make these models work. It took VQ 12 years of utilizing Functional Family Therapy (FFT) before they saw recidivism rates decline. But the established track record of FFT justified continued funding to struggling sites until they began to show progress on stated goals, according to a VQ executive. It takes as long as three years post-implementation of an Evidence-Based practice just to see if it *might* work. Funders may want their money to be spent on EB practices, but the imposition of this requirement may be unrealistic and can be damning. These successful practitioners face a time-consuming and brutal reality. Their work is about cultural change, which many cannot abide because they're comfortable with the way things are. Or equally damning, they want "results now." Program executives realize that after many experiments with services, evidence based or not, any service can fail to live up to its promise and must be exchanged with other core services, read axed.

The progress through this chain of outcomes in programmatic terms would be that your evidence-based practice (input) moves from immediate to intermediate to ultimate outcome. Let's take, for example, the evidence-based practice of Parenting with Love and Limits, which combines instruction on parenting practices with therapy for struggling parents. It's promising as it works on decreasing risk factors and increasing resiliency in the teen (immediate outcome). This, in turn, results in the ability to make better choices (intermediate outcome) seen in the reduction of recidivism and less substance abuse by the teen. The ultimate outcome is independent functionality at home. This is a happy virtuous cycle, not uncoincidentally achieved by Capacity Building, taking a good idea to permanent fruition. Families are noticeably improved in the process because part of the logic, whether written or practiced, is that families must participate with the teen in healing, which strengthens the entire family.

The executive director of Choice suggests the most meaningful measure to pursue is a reduction in delinquency. In a chain of outcomes, this would be an intermediate measure on the path to realizing a functioning individual.

The Aspire North Carolina executive director suggests measuring *school* (academic improvement), *home* (obeying parents), *community* (safety), and *mental health* (reduction of symptoms) improvements, as these are core measures and goals of a successful aftercare program.

The bigger question is: How does this strengths-based, evidence-based theory of behavioral change lead to real improvements in a social condition? Simply put, is the process of converting a plan or a theory into meaningful goal-directed action *doing what it theorizes?* It *can* be done by putting your chain of outcomes into operation.

Effective Practice

Operationalize impact analysis and process evaluation according to core components to ensure evidence-based practice fidelity.

You'll have two levels to put into operation. The first level is for the overall program, which contains a host of service practices. The premise of this model and the wider work is that the most important task is to build capacity support under the evidence-based practice. Not the other way around, in which you implement a practice with no supporting business foundation other than terminal funding, perhaps a lucky grant. Program business strength comes before practice strength can be possible.

Any service practice must have a support system of leadership, administration, and continual operational funding. This support takes time to establish but is necessary to be able to afford the lengthy time it takes for the service to establish itself and flourish.

The VQ executive responsible for evidence-based services sees performance and process measurement as an opportunity to enhance their model. Look to the model developers, internal sub-contractors, and evidence-based advocates for suggestions as to benchmarks and measures. Delivering a service with fidelity is not a discussion of results; it's a lengthy process that can take years to see your new program finally work.

Because it's so important, let's digress a bit and consider how your selected services will be implemented with analysis and evaluation, providing proof of the concept in meaningful results. This determination is essential to your planning phase. Implementation research is codifying how to go about implementing practices that work in your milieux, your unique municipality. It's advised to have core components in place to enhance and strengthen the conduct of every therapeutic encounter.[46] You will need the following:

- *Clear context* – Guiding principles, or core values, must be articulated. This includes a detailed description of clients you intend to serve and *not* serve. Notice here the fundamental theme of success is more of what you don't do than what you do. Simply, don't bite off more than you can support with permanent infrastructure—way beyond funding.

- *Clear core components* – This means to specify exactly, in writing, how your practice will function to achieve stated goals.

- *Clear active ingredients* – These are the subcomponents. They must be defined well enough to allow them to be taught, learned, and performed as specified by their research profile. That profile should specify the conditions under which evidence of results was proven.

- *Clear practical performance assessment* – Ensure the process of delivering the practice fits within the philosophy and core values of your program. This requires that assessment be nearly constant—for example, via a post-therapeutic critique by a mentor therapist. This is practice fidelity. It's ensuring that the same research-proven delivery practices and outcomes happen between therapists time after time and from site to site, whether it's across the street or across the country.

Notice yet another theme: Correct analytical process results in action. You must *do* the right thing the right way. But do the work of answering the who, what, when, and where only if it results in the appropriate how question. How is the only question that results in action. It demands taking the first step and the next. Action alone determines the correct, productive direction—even determining that the idea is a failure and must be stopped is progress. It's good to know what doesn't work as it informs what does work.

Once the core of the service model is understood, then design the process for

> **Welcome data collection, knowing that discipline in data design, investigation, and application become part of the very breath of your program.**

evaluation.[47] You need to accumulate enough data to signify that the service is working as prescribed.

Allow a quick, hopeful digression here. Some in the field tend to shun developing good data, perhaps because it can be technical, time-consuming, and confusing. Don't succumb to the supposed daunting nature of it. Experience has shown that once in place—that is, the policy, hardware, and software of it all—everyone participates. Then all staff can see real progress—the real fruit of their labor. The people running these model programs simply love seeing the numbers go in the right direction, which suggests that the program is strengthening. Welcome data collection, knowing that discipline in data design, investigation, and application become part of the very breath of your program.

First, the processes of evaluation and analysis should consider key relationships. Specify who will do the data collection, data analysis, and reporting and how. Then design program components, develop a logic model on a chain of outcomes, and write evaluation questions and data points that are measurable. While this is difficult to set up and may require expert help, program staff soon learn how to weave this into the fabric of the practice. The process strengthens the whole program's evidence basis.

Little things mean a lot. For example, Aspire evaluators, "*data*tectives," track how long it takes a new referral to get a first appointment. This is a superior initial measure. When done right, as in Reclaiming Futures, you will see service quality develop, partnerships strengthen, and cost effectiveness improve.

Be realistic, model program practitioners urge. You may simply want to maintain functions in the regular school setting. First, a client needs to attend school. Then, they must behave well enough not to get expelled, and eventually attend more regularly. They can then learn it's acceptable to sit at the front of the class and work for extra credit or retake a test. They hopefully won't be labeled as "lazy, stupid, and disruptive" so they remain lost, and the program then is lost. Perhaps then skills learned in a group may begin to work. In other words, comments a VQ executive, task completion is a measure of success.

The Aspire program seeks to see its teens function without harming themselves and their families. What a remarkable statement about the needs of those served and their larger social circles. Of course, behavior such as this must be addressed first before further progress can be made. Then program staff expect their charges to return to and stay in school, make better choices, and function more respectfully with their family members.

Realistic measurements require an artful distinction between having to report what sponsors want and recording the little successes that are collectively significant and may be all that can be expected. Data has a purpose, and it comes with a price of time and resources. Analyze with focus. Intake at these sites is a full diagnostic of the youth. While in school at Aspire, practitioners count errors in reading then track reading level and comprehension to see that those competencies increase as the program progresses. They have check sheets to monitor classroom behavior, how the students are corrected, and the number of times a youngster must be separated from the group for one-on-one attention. Parents provide perceptual ratings used to measure monthly improvement in their child's display of responsibility. GPA is monitored pre- and post-program. Academic and behavioral performance on return to regular school is noted. That's measurement! When these measures are used to strengthen program delivery, the program continually improves, as seen in graduation rates and successes outside of court supervision.

Analysis and evaluation are important beyond the nuts and bolts of the processes. What you are doing is building a permanent program, ready for the day when expansion is right. Then you can begin to penetrate deeper into target populations rather than wider and perhaps carelessly to seemingly needy populations, which may only serve to dilute your efforts. You can qualify a site for expansion by the numbers from your evaluation and analyses.

Again, don't forget to put your budget arguments in terms of dollars. That is: *We saved a certain number of dollars, and with that money, we can offer these services. With continued return on investment, we can do much more of the same.* Of course, all this assumes you have the resources to do so.

5. Plan for Sustainable Resources.

Developing resources is a major theme throughout this book. Every critical feature of the life cycle of a project is somehow materially concerned with sustaining resources, which in turn sustain the endeavor. Sustainability bears mention at this time because planning for permanency cannot be separated from capacity. SAMHSA (Substance Abuse and Mental Health Services Administration) plans for continuing support post grant by keeping stakeholders involved and informed with regular communication.[48]

Include stakeholders in planning for stability, and most important, focusing their resources on services that have impact in improved, even saved, lives.

You are urged to refer to the back matter in this and the other three books in this Capacity Building Series for references and resources. Each volume has various perspectives and numerous ideas on how to sustain operational support, political and practical funding, and tangible goods. Also, a large body of information on this topic is just a few clicks away or with a few phone calls to experienced local aftercare project practitioners. The purpose, therefore, is not to duplicate what is readily accessible but to add some insight to the most effective practices on how to proceed. In this case, it's to have a continuous, high priority resource development process.

Secure resources depend on your funding campaign, funding resources, and the processes by which you procure them. The best of these programs use a multipronged approach aimed at multiple sources to build steady streams of physical goods, volunteers, *and* funding. The idea is to build reliable streams to include in your budget. Yes, even a bake sale can build a history, a stream of funding.

Each model we discuss has a priority for capital and human needs. Aspire, North Carolina, for example, focuses on four essential resources: program personnel, professional services providers, transportation, and in-kind donations of physical goods in lieu of money. In fact, the Aspire program is "on the radar" of a major university for the university's cast-off computer hardware whenever there's an upgrade. Reclaiming Futures in Hocking County, Ohio, has foundation funding as well as federally and locally funded sites, despite being in a somewhat depressed locale in the Appalachians that has little industry.

A senior Choice executive states the campaign to develop resources slightly differently. Start with a sound idea and the dogged desire

> By attaching to a stable entity, a new service model also attaches to the strengths of that organization.

to serve a specific type of client who's not being served, then begin applying for support. Also, attach to a stable organization, as Choice has done with the University of Maryland Baltimore County. Choice benefits from Shriver Center administrative assistance and office space on the University campus and access to volunteer students who become the backbone of the intensive aftercare services it offers.

By attaching to a stable entity, a new service model also attaches to the strengths of that organization. These include a respectable name, connections to influential decision makers and resources, a history of service support, certain established results, and improved or at least established processes of operation. The Pennsylvania Models for Change gets a range of support from county-level governments in every one of their counties.

Be good stewards of your funds, the Choice executive cautions. This means having good fiscal controls and complying with the wishes, rules, and regulations of funding entities, especially grantors. Implied is the deceptively simple advice to be "diligent with recordkeeping." Likewise, be attentive to those things that don't work out, yet suggest answers to make corrections, not excuses. Do what the data indicate, which is a strong case for program integrity, intent, and initiative. Build fiscal discipline into daily processes *from the beginning.* The best wisdom for developing resources is to construct stable funding streams from as many sources as are possible and productive.

Reclaiming Futures suggests the following ways to manage resources:[49]

- *Share resources.* – Every one of these models represented by many of their sites have some method of sharing resources under a philosophy of considering anything useful and "not nailed down." They share staff, equipment, supplies, transportation, and donations. Missouri Model officials wisely used existing buildings for their local residential facilities, including an old Catholic school that needed "just a little remodeling." Best of all, they were successful in designating significant Department of Corrections funding to build seven local cottages. They minimized construction costs wherever possible, which limited objections to the point monies were committed.

- *Identify new sources.* – Practitioners make it a point to try to have an active grant application in the pipeline as regularly as possible—continuously is the goal. Staff know that while grants are soft and unpredictable sources of money, one successful grant application breeds another. Foundations continue to look for good idea incubators that can help to multiply their funds. The Annie E. Casey Foundation's support of The Missouri Model and the Robert Wood Johnson Foundation's support of Reclaiming Futures provide examples of this. As an aside, the Reclaiming Futures site in Hocking, Ohio, makes sure that its treatment providers visit grantees to give them a vivid view of what their funds are accomplishing.

- *Be efficient.* – The best penny used is the one saved. Nothing goes to waste at these sites, and what is used is frugally employed. The meals at a VQ residence were mostly donated foods. Missouri Model early champions were successful in demonstrating that building five regional self-sustaining residential facilities was more effective and less expensive than having a large central facility.

- *Share staff.* – Functions can overlap for staff dedicated to completely different projects. Administrative staff, for example, can support several disparate projects.

- *Cross-train staff.* – Staff at these sites are jacks of all trades. A Reclaiming Futures site director often conducts group therapy then fits in her management and administrative duties around that. Whatever they do, all staff are actively engaged in goal-oriented work. If someone is gone even for a few hours, someone always fills in. The same goes for the inevitable job vacancy. The vision remains uninterrupted.

These sites struggle, but they maintain operational support through constant vigilance. The lesson is that they always operate within their means, sometimes on the edge, but still the bills are paid. Make sure that input always has a demonstrated profit in terms of goal accomplishment and cost effectiveness, both of which must be measured, tallied, and broadcast. Don't wait for the annual budget justification meeting to toot your horn, or it may be done for you and not how you would wish. This business is very much about survival, which is a daily concern; the best programs carefully plan from the very beginning and never stop.

Effective Practice

Conduct annual strategic planning devoted to sustaining resources, which include personnel, equipment and material, and funding streams with multiple goal-oriented purposes.

One of the better resources to gather ideas for planning is the Access to Recovery Implementation Toolkit (SAMHSA), which comes in three volumes.[50] As the name implies, its content is largely useful worksheets that can and should be tailored to local needs and are used as is by Reclaiming Futures sites. While the toolkit's focus is on the substance abuse and mental health system of care, it does explain the processes in terms of implementation, operations, and stabilizing a project when SAMHSA funds end. SAMHSA's toolkit is a complement to your overall effort to first build the capacity to deliver the suggested services and therapies. Its founding principles are consistent with the sustainability philosophies of these model programs. Specifically, the bedrock of these programs is, according to SAMHSA (2010), that they are client and outcome driven with an emphasis on capacity. SAMHSA also recognizes, correctly, that this work is less about aftercare than it is about systems change, which is another way to shift the focus toward sustaining services.

Choice leadership conducts annual strategic planning to ensure the continuation of resources. It goes further by designating a financial team to design the strategy, tactics, and processes before building those processes to carry out the plan. This program does not have to do personal fundraising because it's sponsored by the Shriver Center at the University of Maryland, Baltimore County (UMBC). However, it still must seek corporate, foundation, public, and private grants and business development. To demonstrate the necessarily diverse nature of this aspect of capacity building, the business they work with is a yogurt stand that's manned and largely run by its charges.

The Choice aftercare program philosophy of asking for money from donors demonstrates its ability to deliver on the "investment." Choice rarely approaches a sponsor for the full amount they need. A Choice representative asks for increasing amounts as its relationship with a funder matures. The wisdom of using development of resources as a major planning strategy is that differing aims between funders and stated program goals can be orchestrated to reach happy, communal accommodations. The first difference, for example, may be the need for funders to see results unrealistically soon by setting the expectation that realizing goals takes years. Discuss mutually agreed upon realistic goals, then pursue them. Remind your partners that "we" are attacking a municipal problem that's been festering for years—and your program is a long-term, realistic answer—and sometimes the only steadfast answer.

These programs give their funders little successes initially and a sense that funders are vital participants in the Movement. In time, you'll learn what your funders' interests are and why they wish to support a program that works. For example, when Choice leaders came to know the executives of a local bank, they discovered their interest was in literacy. It was then relatively simple to ask them to fund financial literacy classes for their program participants, again another win-win-win proposition. The program wins, the bank wins, and youngsters win. This is a sophisticated process of engendering mutual goals. Then, when it does come time for the check to be written, it's not a matter of if, but when, and perhaps how much. In the case of the bank executive, it was a $12,000 check to Choice. Significant money for a nonprofit.

You may be sure that the next request and subsequent check will be for just a little more because it will be a transaction among dear friends engaged in something worthy.

Reclaiming Futures in Hocking County, Ohio, has a remarkably simple solution to the conundrum of sustainability: Become incrementally permanent, one function at a time. Pick a key piece of your program to institutionalize—for example, screening and assessment. Another idea to enhance stability is to formalize strengths-based transitional programming.

> **Begin as soon as possible creating the infrastructure of stability by, for example, writing and rewriting policies, procedures, memos, letters of agreement, and duties and responsibilities.**

Begin as soon as possible creating the infrastructure of stability by, for example, writing and rewriting policies, procedures, memos, letters of agreement, and duties and responsibilities. This documentation will describe the proven processes of what staff do daily. It means regularity, which is another way of describing stability.

Also, get people in general talking about your program in favorable terms, the Reclaiming Futures site director councils. Map projects, befriend community stakeholders, enlist thought leaders such as a key judge or the sheriff, and attend as many local meetings of groups interested in aftercare as possible. Get supporters to start referring to themselves by your program name. For example, a judge enthusiastically claims to be a Reclaiming Futures judge because his court decisions support intensive, strengths-based juvenile aftercare.

While discussing this take on sustaining resources, I asked the Choice executive what could have gone better with resource development. The response was, "Be mindful of spending." While these model programs have learned to live within their means, they, too, got caught in what seemed to be endless budget cuts, which led to many programs losing much of their operating budgets. Funding, especially public funding, can whimsically disappear. Be prepared, because "There are no guarantees in this business," came the voice of experience from the Choice director. In other words, even aftercare demands financial risk management.

A Missouri Model official, when asked the same question, said the main obstacle to having a steady stream of resources is cultural. He said, "Make sure your frontline staff deeply understand the vision, because what they do is essential to a credible program worthy of funding." Even resource development is bottom up. All of this is to support your unique array of services.

6. Build Evidence-Based Services on an Evidence-Based Program and Processes.

A discussion of terms is in order. The rush to employ evidence in the public sector has inevitably led to the misunderstanding, misdirection, and misapplication of the use of evidence. The reality is that many programs are called evidence-based when they are not. Terms are used interchangeably, especially at the policy and agency levels, with the result that many opportunities to penetrate and institutionalize good ideas are lost. The danger is that these programs continue to be misperceived, fail, and blame this on a false promise. One failure makes it that much more difficult to start another good idea—or kills it outright.

While spending time with aftercare practitioners, one observes that evidence is employed in three ways: for a program, a process, and a practice, with important differences. To put the arguments to rest and facilitate a more helpful discussion, let's posit them as follows.

- *Program* – An evidence-based program is an entire entity of related projects that seek to resolve a specific problem and have a specific goal or strategic objective. For example, Rite of Passage concentrates on preparing youngsters for life after justice system involvement or law-violating behavior.

- *Process* – We drill down to a series of unified steps, tasks, or activities to realize a stated outcome. An evidence-based process is the flow of work toward goal accomplishment, which must be done efficiently. An example would be policies and procedures to do research-based screening and assessments according to evidence that supports a certain application of these tasks.

- *Practice* – Lastly, the most confusing term is evidence-based practice—the regular approaches, methods, and techniques of the staff. These are the therapies with a research basis that are determined to be the best interventions with proven improvements in the client. It bears repeating here that an evidence-based practice is erroneously conflated with best practice. Some make a good case that there's no such thing as a "best practice," as what works in one locale is no guarantee it will work in another. However, a best practice can be a point of departure in discovering what works in your municipality, with your resources, your politics, and your people.

Part of the confusion is that decision makers have the tendency to grasp at a few of the more popular therapies that come equipped with some evidence then call their entire effort evidence based. However, all three entities of capacity building—programs, processes, and practice—must work synergistically to become one seamless service delivery system over a lengthy passage of time. It's important to document the evidence to support the growth of your idea. An EPB is just an idea until it matures with every new application. Again, do not assume a great idea in one area will work in your area without much long-term work.

The practice is the least important of the three because its success is entirely dependent on the other two, that is, having a program and processes that are based on program-specific data and evidence. Practices at the local level demonstrate it's more important to understand how a program and processes can and should be evidence-based, as then and only then will a practice work.

The National Institute of Corrections (2004) makes further distinctions between effective and best practices and what works.[51] A *best practice* is largely experiential, reflecting "wisdom of the field" and are not scientifically examined. What works are ideas that are linked to outcomes but may not be linked to desired systems and community improvements. An *evidence-based practice* must have two qualifications: It must produce desired, measurable results consistently and be *realistic,* meaning practical to implement, even though difficult to achieve, yet essential to permanency. Thus, practitioners choose services for their relative ease of implementation and measurement, if they're measured at all. This isn't "wrong" if the chosen services produce sought-after results. Still, it is obviously better to have an array of services rather than be restricted to only those that have the great and rare fortune to have been scientifically evaluated.

Now, with these distinctions we proceed, if briefly, not with suggested therapies but much more importantly, with how to prepare for their successful, evidence-based implementation. Summarily, it is about developing local evidence that a chosen service is making a difference with the target population and with your community. This is how these sub-national/sub-state, decentralized local programs became evidence-based. Some would argue that to be truly evidence-based, a service must be subjected to a randomized, controlled experiment. That is just not practical. Remember the site that simply monitored a waiting list for their services to determine what, where, and how to expand? While that is not rigorous science, it worked. That's being realistic and practical—and successful. What matters is that local stakeholders can determine some effect on measures meaningful to them and their support groups.

The proof of effectiveness is in reclaimed lives. Let's consider if there are advantages to being decentralized and local.

The World Bank has been working to develop local education, businesses, and health delivery systems that mirror aftercare programs in principle and application.[52] Well run local programs, especially when they're comprehensively evidence-based (and especially if locally determined), enhance productivity, are more transparent, and enjoy more accountability than nonlocally run programs. Services are more responsive because efforts reflect local priorities set by local stakeholders with local resources. They encourage participation and eventually improve penetration to the target populations.[53] These findings are confirmed or even proven outright by these model capacity-built programs. They're cited for this model of aftercare effective practices that are enjoying these advantages listed by the World Bank.[54]

The lesson, whether for global development or your one-site aftercare enterprise, is that this work does make a big difference. It does take making complex systems work as one. It does take time to know your population and direct and conserve limited resources, according to The Hocking County, Ohio, Reclaiming Futures project director.

Models for Change begins with principles that guide the therapies they employ, systemically integrating evidence that's meaningful to stakeholders. In turn, stakeholders can manage and inform interdependent systems such as jobs, housing, and social and health services, which comprise the services array of an aftercare program.[55]

Effective Practice

Build an evidence-based program and processes to support your evidence-based practices.

Notice how Models for Change begins building a philosophy of change to guide that first group session.[56] This is also emblematic of what each of these models do— i.e., build structure around and in support of their therapeutic services as follows.[57]

- *Assess risk/needs using actuarial instruments.* – This is a weighting of various variables to assess risk and determine the services specific to an individual. Begin a relationship with a client by thoroughly knowing them through informal observation and interaction and formally by collecting risk, needs, and responsivity data. This means sitting down with clients for a conversation and comprehensive screening and assessment. Thus, you can determine a personal profile of strengths juxtaposed with needs, which will then be used to individually manage the case. An effective outcome cannot result without an effective sizing-up. Pair this data, the *what,* with detailed policies and procedures, the *how,* to ensure good case management *and* aftercare. The important thing here is to make aftercare the priority. Guide the comprehensive composition of supports and services for the *individual* rather than simply focus on just needs-determined therapies. The assessment instruments from SAMHSA are most helpful.[58]

- *Enhance intrinsic motivation.* – Staff who are skilled in motivational interviewing[59] enhance preparation for independence in the community. They strive to become attuned to the individual needs of clients. This new breed of strengths-based intensive care staff is realistic about what their charges can accomplish. Not surprisingly, initial expectations for troubled youth might consist of being able to get out of bed at the prescribed hour. The next step might be to straighten their room and learn proper hygiene—small, realistic steps first.

- *Target interventions.* – Focus is on the criminogenic factors of high-risk youth, who will need upwards of 70 percent structured time to integrate treatment with sentencing requirements. Basic to this is for staff to understand each client's certain mix of temperaments, learning style, and culture. High-risk offenders deliver the most return for effort and expense, because many of

> **Teach, practice, and reinforce pro-social behaviors. Affirm more than admonish—but meet a rules infraction with swift and increasing penalties.**

them, when treated appropriately, will not reoffend. If they are successful in the community, they can become independent of public support and free of further criminal justice system involvement. The process is all about "competency development," as with Models for Change in Pennsylvania.

- *Train skills through directed practice.* – Train all staff in cognitive-behavioral techniques, for example, that enhance protective factors. By training all staff, especially external staff such as probation officers, these skills can also be reinforced in the community and within the family.

- *Increase rewards and incentives.* – Teach, practice, and reinforce pro-social behaviors. Affirm more than admonish—but meet a rules infraction with swift and increasing penalties. Young clients do respond to rules, regulations, and strictness when caringly implemented and when a clear path is available for the client to return to their homes and communities.

- *Engage ongoing support in natural communities.* – Each juvenile from extremely high-risk populations has significant others. Strengthen their ties to them, especially family members.

- *Measure and document relevant processes and practices routinely.* – Measurement must take place on two levels: Regularly, if not continuously, assess youth progress and staff fidelity to the modality and process of the program. Stakeholders must have evidence that the client is developing skills for independence and that staff are maintaining services according to the delivery directives from the research. This is the basis of an evidence-based program. It will deliver desired outcomes only if applied following a strict research-supported protocol.

- *Use data for feedback and programming adjustments.* – This is quality assurance to make sure services are delivered with reliability and accountability for reaching staff and client goals, both programmatically and individually. People prefer to know how they are doing and will largely respond accordingly in these situations because their stake, their progress, increases with regular and productive critical advice.

This approach marks the shift in thinking from control and punishment to strengths building and outcomes for the individual, the agency, and the system.[60] Make no mistake that what is being prescribed—targeted and timely treatment—is a rigorous regimen tougher than "boot camp." By comparison, it is much simpler and quicker to return the young offender to jail; but the cycle just repeats, lives spiral downward, expenses mount up, and public support can't keep up. Practitioners interviewed continually commented that this is anything but "hug-a-thug" and is the real "tough on crime" policy. The greatest caution from practitioners is that becoming research-based is easily said and masks a basic truth from the field. The struggle program practitioners will have is with implementation. Get implementation right and your EBP will work. Clearly selecting an array of services to tailor to the individual is only part of a much larger equation that steers a wayward youth to success. A plan is necessary.

Effective Practice

Build a single plan for individualized, comprehensive treatment that focuses on post-program aftercare.

Planning done with capacity in mind assures that staff can focus on developing services. Deciding on a service depends on having in place:

- working and committed l*eadership,*
- a vision of *strengths-* and community-based comprehensive treatment and aftercare,
- an accurate assessment of *capabilities,*
- well-working quantitative and qualitative *analyses* of process efficiency and program effectiveness,
- reliable *political* support,
- a services selection process to *acquire* evidence-based services, and
- qualified staff who are believers in strengths-based programming and therapy.

When all of this is firmly in motion, even if it's not necessarily complete, a service with the following basic features can emerge from the planning[61] as exemplified by Pennsylvania's Models for Change. The planned program is best served by being:

- *Individualized* – Treatment must be tailored to every young client and, as much as possible, be comprised of family and intimates, which includes caregivers of the reforming youngster.

- *Prescriptive* – Detail what will be done for the client and how to do it. Emphasis should be on what happens after the program and sentence are completed if the justice system is involved. That includes reasonable independence seen in pursuit of further education and training, holding down a job, having a stable place to stay, and staying out of trouble and away from substance abuse. These are the goals and practical proof that your services are working.

- *Linked* – Linkages are the firm connections (established by monitoring results on a chain of outcomes) between program treatment and post-release goals.

These goals are usually for success in school or perhaps employment, suitable living arrangements, supports, and links to the community.

- *Continuously reviewed* – Processes must be established for continuous monitoring and subsequent adjustments to the treatment regimen.

- *Targeted* – The plan must be a mechanism, a tool by which key objectives are matched with specific activities to realize programmatic, process, and individual goals.

The individualized plan of treatment for the client is marked by continuous planning, action, analysis, modification, and planning again, only much more informed. Note the continuous cycle of action, analysis, decision, and informed action. When done correctly, you'll have minimal work with low-risk youth, maximized accountability with the highest-risk youth, and major services focused on medium and high-risk youngsters. This is where you will have the most impact. Also, the adoption of strategies, especially therapies that target delinquent behaviors, honors the uniqueness and responsiveness of each client.[62] This is another way of describing a change in culture from reacting to juvenile misbehavior to research that causes systemic reform with productive behavior outcomes. It defines the basic character of the movement to strengths-based aftercare from the systems control model of addressing juvenile delinquency and thus reentry to the community. All that remains now is to correctly choose evidence-based therapeutic practices you know work experientially for your unique program.

Choosing therapies is tricky. Most times, quickly importing a brand name idea such as Anger Management meets with considerable obstacles. So, what should programmers look for? Simply look for strict proof of the evidence that things are working, as many alternatives that may be considered are impostors. They may be measures that are merely convenient or, worse, do not measure goal accomplishment or improvements in the target population and community.

Practices in the realm of aftercare are considered evidence-based when they have a chain of measurable outcomes that assist a troubled youngster in making good life decisions, staying out of trouble and away from arrest, and growing in maturity toward independent living. So, what practices can work this alchemy? It is a matter of choosing wisely then integrating the quantitative with the qualitative effective practices according to the National Institute of Corrections, which suggests looking for the "Gold Standard" practice.[63]

Effective Practice

Collect data that support the evidence-based practices adopted.

Program staff need to adopt those therapies that have a history of consistently changing lives for the better in the business of aftercare across various settings. These form the infrastructure that helps deliver the practices you choose. Ultimately, move toward an idea that is proven via a good scientific investigation, sustained accomplishment of aftercare goals, the experience of replication, and strong evidence of improved subject behaviors.

These standards are why, for example, Parenting with Love and Limits and Functional Family Therapy are demonstrated effective therapies. Beyond that, scientific investigation suggests *who* should teach the therapy, *how* to conduct it, *how* to monitor it, and *how* to ensure fidelity. For example, VQ has the practice of having model (evidence-based practice) developers introduce, train, and monitor practice implementation and fidelity to vision, mission, and goals. Experience helped them develop better methods of training.

Functional Family Therapy began with only one week of classroom training, which is quite impractical. Now, it is taught in phases with the first phase consisting of

> **All these model programs have an intense and, where humanly possible, immediate critique of practice delivery.**

a week of basic training followed by practical field application; then phase II training and more practical field work happen before a budding therapist is put into a therapeutic situation. Training continues with coaching and mentoring. Notice how an EBP is ramped up, even modified to fit VQ as needs dictate.

Even the best selected idea is subject to the drift away from specified practices that will render it a waste of time. That is why all these model programs have an intense and, where humanly possible, immediate critique of practice delivery. Staff conducting a session may be videotaped for instant feedback on effectiveness and conformance to the precepts of the model. Other programs have a therapeutic process checklist that's ticked off after every session to monitor and assure delivery accuracy. Little is assumed according to program therapeutic staff, who also observe that this attention to detail develops "hardcore partners." VQ fidelity to the modality and process includes monthly reviews of outcome measures, matching of clinician performance to 20 benchmarks, and use of a fidelity checklist. Consultants get quarterly therapist-to-therapist comparisons and a review of their contribution to overall site measurements and performance. After a therapy session, the therapist or staffer conducting the session is coached by senior staff or trainers. Little is left to chance, staff are proud to say, because everyone is watching and learning, whether or not they're in a direct therapy role.

For example, parole officers begin to understand what these programs do and how they fit together. Services development is all about training stakeholders and establishing overall expectations for clients and their families, according to the VQ executive in charge of evidence-based practices. Also, by being strict, proven practices fit better into an array of selected services. The array includes not only support services but case management, individual, family, and group counseling, crisis prevention/intervention, and wraparound services, as practitioners do at Aspire. This paves the way for better implementation by maintaining program integrity and intervention fidelity.

What is happening here and what you want to promote is the idea of wraparound (holistic, comprehensive) services becoming stable on their way to being sustainable and then to calculated expansion. This is the process of closing the services-to-needs gap. Evidence is an essential key to reform.[64]

This leaves arguably the most important critical capacity building program element to discuss— staff—and how to plan for a goal-oriented driven team of believers.

7. Build Key Staff to Support and Deliver Strengths-Based Services

This section will be brief for two reasons: First, the information on what to do about staffing is abundant; secondly, it's more advantageous to understand the essence of how these model programs build their human capital (not human resources). The Choice executive director states that this program builds collaborative environments that attract truly unique people for this demanding business. Every model program investigated herein seemed to be staffed with people who are bound together— soldiers, friends, and fellow champions—engaged in noble work. How is this so similarly done across these exemplary programs? First, these programs are known for being highly successful for years and, in most cases, decades. They are the epitome of integrity. Good people are attracted to a well-run cause where staff are as qualified as they are intense, and they have a bit of fun, too. Vetting of good people is grounded in a penetrating sense of the mission. Little deviation in its understanding and inter-pretation at any level is evidenced. When a new hire must be made, staff look in a most rigorous way for people like themselves.

First, every effort is made to hire from within. Internal progression is fostered by a learning culture, team building, internal motivation, and a desire to do more and better. People involved in this work want to become their best—to be good and do good for the common good. Everyone can see, feel, and be part of what is bigger than any one individual. Everyone can see, feel, and be part of what becomes greater than the sum of the parts. It's more than motivating; it's inspiring if you can achieve it.

Executive and supervisory staff are continuously on the lookout for talent, that special desire to help, and the unique individual whose wish for recognition is to attach it to others. Interviews occur after a pool of qualified prospects develops. Naturally, there are educational, technical, and experiential requirements. Hopefuls usually are required to have a degree in the social sciences, possess therapeutic skills, be competent if not an expert with technology and data, and have some history in the mission of what the program is trying to achieve.

Interviews are meant to probe the intangibles of character, creativity, ingenuity, determination, perception, and the belief that this unique population of distracted youth can make a difference. It's a belief that most of these youth can raise themselves up with just an occasional nudge and encouragement to stay on track to success. A big intangible element about prospective staff is their willingness to learn. The key to having productive staff is to train, train, train, which is intense, according to the VQ chief for evidence-based services. A prospect must be steeled for never-ending and often intense training. It can be nearly minute-to-minute, sometimes under the dual lenses of expert eyes and perhaps a video camera to capture the many ways they must improve. It takes years to develop a competent person in this arena, especially if that person aims to be a program therapist and maintain fidelity.

When it comes to adopting an evidence-based practice, they should internalize that it may take years for their efforts to produce measurable results. Program staff are looking for those who are willing to commit to long hours and accept near daily disappointment and legendary low pay. While many do not make it past the interview and more soon wash out, those who make it past the rigors of becoming part of the team tend to stay. VQ, for example, enjoys the stability of most staff who have worked there for more than 10 years, and many for more than 20 years, because these practitioners concentrate on their personal growth. Once the hire is made, every effort goes to helping them become a team member. Every new VQ hire gets a senior-level mentor, which other programs provide as well. Staff are encouraged to take charge of their personal development on and off the job and encouraged to continue their education, technical training, and professional development. Team building becomes natural.

In other words, present staff are looking for a fellow wanderer to help them keep a holy grail of meaningful aftercare.

Effective Practice
Select staff with a multi-step vetting process.

The Choice executive director has devised a two-stage interview checklist based on characteristics of an ideal director of operations. See Round 1 Questions for Choice Director of Operations and Round 2 Questions for Choice Director of Operations on pages 105 through 109. The interview questionnaires take inspiration from *Good to Great* by Jim Collins,[65] which discusses desirable traits necessary to build a remarkable enterprise and includes applicable observations for this public sector work. Staff members are usually humble, calm, and prefer to lead and be led by reasonable and fair standards. They want the program to succeed but are quick to give others credit for successes. They focus on getting things done, appreciate a well thought-through and permanent program, are responsible, and rise to the challenge of a great vision and goals just out of reach.

These questionnaires occur in two phases for a reason. Leadership requires plenty of discussion in between. Some programs have a policy that *all* staff, and even clients, have a say in the hiring process. Each desired characteristic is succinctly defined to avoid misunderstanding about the defining traits as much as possible. Existing staff must be satisfied that each characteristic is real in potential hires and not "gamed" for the interview. Any doubt that even one is not met is a non-negotiable disqualifier. Do you see what is happening? Even the hiring process, beginning with the job posting, is training the individual to be an integral part of the team. This is the way someone new should be hired—by a deliberate process. After all, the relationship between the program and the new hire has the potential to last years, if not decades. Thus, the new hire becomes part of the family.

Consider the following job description. Note the range of probing, germane questions. Note also that the interview format gives plenty of time for the aspirant to engage. Realize also that this interview, about an hour, is to determine engaging someone you will be with perhaps for years. Ask relevant questions, clarify, and let them talk.

Position: Developer of people/staff

Attributes: Able to coach and develop strengths of staff. Savvy judge of character. Recognizes strengths and weaknesses while being able to foster specific behaviors to help staff be successful. Listens to others, asks the "right" questions to understand as well as learn from staff at all levels of the organization.

Interviewer question (Phase 1): Tell us about a supervisee from whom you've been demanding better performance. What did you do to help them be more effective?

Notice that the subsequent interview tests the same characteristics but with different questions. Read over again the initial question above meant to determine needed qualities and character, which in the second interview is worded as follows.

Interviewer question (Phase 2): Tell us the last time someone came to you and asked for your help in a critical and/or specific area. What was the situation and how did you help the person?

Program staff hire people who are not afraid to train a successor and are happy to see that person take their key duties, if not their job. Something else is happening here as an example of the many benefits of a deliberate process of acquiring new people. Succession is largely assured in these programs because the people who come on board, while ambitious, are ambitious regarding overarching goals, which are achieved by sharing and helping each other. The process and these questions allow a glimpse into the soul and heart. This goes much beyond the usual interview.

The process determines team-orientation, an entrepreneurial spirit, superior people skills, potential as a developer of people, facility with data for quality assurance, integrity, problem-solving ability, and planning. A potential employee is prequalified with the basics, subjected to two interviews, vetted by staff, imbued with vision and mission, and thoroughly oriented to duties, responsibilities, and expectations. By then, there's reasonable assurance that this person has the necessary qualifications to succeed. In addition, they probably have the more important intangibles such as being team oriented, and vision/mission directed. Existing staff are, after all, choosing a family member.

Next, let's consider more comprehensive two-round interview questionnaires for the Choice Program's director of operations.

Round One Questions for Choice Director of Operations

_____   _____
Name of Candidate   Name of Interviewer

Round 1: Questions for **Choice** Director of Operations

Characteristics of an Ideal Director of Operations for The Choice Program
Non-negotiable disqualifiers: Staff without the critical characteristics below are not suitable for the position in any way.

Team oriented: Candidate displays ability to extend full confidence in "the process" that engenders a spirit of collaboration when addressing organizational challenges. Non-authoritarian or secretive. Uses persuasion as a primary vehicle of influence. Pulls rather than pushes people.

1. Describe the last time you had "too much on your plate." How did you manage it and whom did you go to for help?

Entrepreneurial: Candidate must operate in a fast-paced mission-driven environment that stresses excellence while adhering to the bureaucratic structure of a large State institution. High level of flexibility and agility. Choice is a fast-paced organization and needs someone with high energy as well as a strong drive to achieve. Has a high level of confidence while also having humility.

2. Tell us about the last time that you were the only one willing to speak up and express a contrary view. How did you make your point?

Possesses superior people skills: Able to manage people in crisis, resolve complex and/or difficult situations. Cultivate internal and external stakeholder relationships. Needs to be customer oriented.

3. Tell us about the last person with whom you had a challenge working effectively. How did you work things out?

Excellent at developing people/staff: Able to coach and develop strengths of staff. Savvy judge of character. Recognizes strengths and weaknesses while being able to foster specific behaviors to help staff be successful. Listens to others and asks the "right" questions to understand as well as learn from staff at all levels of the organization.

4. Tell us about a supervisee from whom you have been demanding better performance. How did you help them become more effective?

Skilled at managing data for quality assurance: Able to collect and analyze data in a "meaningful way" and be able to devise short-term and long-term plans for improvement of systems or services.

5. What data do you currently use in your job to determine if your supervisees are doing a good job? What data tells you they are not? How do you use data?

Additional important characteristics:

Has high integrity: Must be trusted and perceived as direct, open, and truthful. Must be able to admit mistakes, protect confidentiality, and be a steward of the organization's resources. Ask how the candidate internalizes and projects integrity.

Proficient at solving problems: Solutions focused. Able to approach problems and issues with an open mind. Able to assess, prioritize, develop, plan, and implement solutions when multiple variables, conflicting inputs, and stakeholders to balance are involved. Must be able to step outside of self and see the big picture. Understands and handles organizational politics in a positive manner. Ask how the candidate solves problems.

Excellent at planning and designing: Able to develop plans and design creative initiatives that inspire confidence and competence in the organization's capacity to carry out the mission. Discuss how the candidate devises a plan of action.

Round Two Questions for Choice Director of Operations

_____   _____

Name of Candidate   Name of Interviewer

Round 2: Questions for **Choice** Director of Operations

Characteristics of an ideal Director of Operations for The Choice Program
Non-negotiable disqualifiers: Staff without the critical characteristics below are not suitable for the position in any way.

Team oriented: Candidate displays ability to extend full confidence in "the process" that engenders a spirit of collaboration when addressing organizational challenges. Non-authoritarian or secretive. Uses persuasion as a primary vehicle of influence. Pulls rather than pushes people.

1. Tell us about the last time you helped a team within your organization work together to overcome a challenge or difficult change. What was the primary conflict and how did you resolve the conflict?

Entrepreneurial: Candidate must operate in a fast-paced mission-driven environment that stresses excellence while adhering to the bureaucratic structure of a large State institution. High level of flexibility and agility. Choice is a fast-paced organization and needs someone with high energy as well as a strong drive to achieve. Has a high level of confidence while also having humility.

2. Describe the last time you had to change your management style to adjust to the people you were managing. How did you change your management style?

Possesses superior people skills: Able to manage people in crisis and resolve complex and/or difficult situations. Cultivate internal and external stakeholder relationships. Needs to be customer oriented.

3. When was the last time you had to tell a supervisor you were unhappy with a recent interaction you had with her/him or organizational development he/she was responsible for? How did you resolve your concern?

Excellent developer of people/staff: Able to coach and develop strengths of staff. Savvy judge of character. Recognizes strengths and weaknesses while being able to foster specific behaviors to help staff be successful. Listens to others, asks the "right" questions to understand as well as learn from staff at all levels of the organization.

4. Tell us the last time someone came to you and asked for your help in a critical and/or specific area. What was the situation and how did you help them?

Proficient at solving problems: Solutions focused. Able to approach problems and issues with an open mind. Able to assess, prioritize, develop, plan, and implement solutions when there are multiple variables, conflicting inputs, and stakeholders to balance. Must be able to step outside of self and see the big picture. Understands and handles organizational politics in a positive manner.

5. Tell us about the last time you implemented a project. What was the impact it had on other units of the organization? How did you go about it?

Skilled at managing data for quality assurance: Able to collect and analyze data in a "meaningful way" and be able to devise short-term and long-term plans for improvement of systems or services.

6. What system have you put in place in your current position to help improve the quality of services or maximize the efforts of your staff? How did you implement it?

Skilled in planning and designing: Able to develop plans and design creative initiatives that inspire confidence and competence in the organization's capacity to carry out the mission.

7. Describe the last time you launched a new idea, service, or process. How did you go about it? What was your greatest challenge in implementation and how did you handle it?

Has high integrity: Must be trusted and perceived as direct, open, and truthful. Able to admit when he or she has made a mistake, protect confidentiality, and be a steward of the organization's resources.

8. Tell us about a time when you made a mistake or lacked integrity. How did you resolve the situation?

Next, consider organizational structure for staff, which is flat, lean, and peopled with working supervisors and leaders. One of the first examples of a good leader is to exhibit good followership. Great leaders are humble and introspective, taking the blame if need be and giving the glory. Leadership and staff live the fact that *everyone* is a leader!

Effective Practice

Create an organizational structure that's lean and flat, in which everyone must be qualified and ready to deliver line services.

The "trenches" where clients are treated are the focus of organizational design, and rightly so. Line staff must be supported by supervisors, managers, and leaders, who are at the *bottom* of an organizational diagram. This is a complete reversal of the top-down diagrams we're accustomed to seeing. This is another interpretation of the bottom-up nature of capacity building. One program's executive director opined that they "lost their sense of community" when they experimented with outsiders who brought in top-down methods. Internal development is *the* proven effective practice.

Choice serves as an example of a lean and flat organization. No "fat" is evidenced by underutilized management types, and there are only a few levels from the executive director to line staff. Only five people are in leadership positions: the executive director, a director of operations, and a director for community partnerships, who has two assistant directors. The director of operations, through the assistant directors, manages eight service coordinators, who each direct the activities of three Ameri-Corps Fellows. The director of community partnerships supervises two main people, one each for personnel recruitment (because volunteer AmeriCorps Fellows cycle annually) and information systems, a position also responsible for quality assurance.[66] Notice another nuance here. Quality cannot be controlled; it can only be assured via trained and self-directed staff with introspective leadership.

This leaves the three senior "executives" free to ensure program integrity, performance, and expansion, while the remainder of staff delivers intensive, personal, in-home aftercare. Leaders exude the philosophy that "you (staff) will succeed, and we will help you." Forty-one people comprise the entire Choice effort in Maryland at the time of this writing. Line staff at the point of service delivery know they can ask for and will get assistance from every level. Communication flows up and down, ideas flourish, and the young clients, via caring with strictness, know they can do better.

Reclaiming Futures runs a bit differently from Choice but is certainly no less successful. We make the point again. The germ of an idea for aftercare presents no guarantee it can be successfully transferred to another site, even across town. It must be made to work. Note that all these model sites have the same goal—functioning youngsters doing well in the community—yet all are quite unique in how they get there.

Since Reclaiming Futures is a court-centric model, the emphasis is largely on what judges can do to see that sentences are carried out. The difference is that instead of focusing on intensive aftercare as Choice does, they put heavy emphasis on initial assessment and individualized, comprehensive services in preparation for independent living. Thus, they have functionally structured two teams, one for the drug court and one for Fellows.

The court team is comprised of court officials, from a judge who holds drug court to the probation officers who see that the court serves the public's need for safety and security while they broker service providers who help manage cases.

The Fellows, representing the court (a judge), treatment, juvenile justice, the community, and the project director, see that services are delivered. Reclaiming Futures, by being client centered and strengths-based, is a remarkable example of how a formerly top-down compliance-oriented agency can refocus and recreate a culture of caring but with client-centered rules—from the bottom up. These teams have enjoyed organizational stability for years since their initiation. All these programs in their own way are client centered, bottom up.

Many of these model programs build the human infrastructure around daily client-by-client "run downs." They discuss what happened the past few hours and what should happen next. This is shared case management, which simply wouldn't work in a traditional hierarchical control model because it's a culture of service and learning versus rote training and standards somewhat distantly contrived. Staff are free to own their personal development according to one Choice task team supervisor. This lean bottom-up philosophy of staffing is evidenced no matter how many people are being brought into a program. This is just one physical manifestation of efficiency and effectiveness. Transformation is a big word and appropriate. Children are transformed because these programs are built on people who *are* transformational.

Additional Thoughts on Planning and Implementation

Every interview ended with an open-ended discussion on how staff built their ideas to consequence and permanence. We talked about what was important, if not essential, to becoming a bottom-up and truly client-centric program. They explained their redefinition of how to deliver public services efficiently, effectively, successfully, sustainably—so the services would last as long as the problem they address lasts. Note that many problems of social dysfunction tackled at the local level of government are endemic, pervasive, and permanent. This doesn't mean you should throw up your hands in frustration and defeat; it's a call to build answers to combat these problems—reentry being one of them. This attitude of "come what may" resolution does, in fact, better the community one youngster at a time. The community is better for you having tried, and that is enough.

This redefinition of local public service is calculated, not haphazard. The practitioners' answers were simple and elegant.

- Create a process where people feel engaged.

- Avoid getting hamstrung by being unrealistically all-inclusive and indecisive about acting.

- Meet with stakeholders "with purpose in mind," and that purpose should be collaboration.

- Set goals with the neighborhood.

- Believe in your model. When it is successful, stakeholders will come and stay.

- Proceed methodically and not too quickly to expose an resolve unforeseen issues and challenges.

- Understand your youngsters through face-to-face interactions. It's *not* about, "You will *do* what I say" but "you will *want* to do what I *suggest.*"

- When you get a programming or funding offer, "no" is a good answer when things aren't right. Repeatedly, practitioners remember turning down the easy dollar because it didn't fit the model. But when it was right, they were ready to commit. Build your program on believers.

- Embrace evidence. "Evidence is a way of life" is the voice of experience from VQ practitioners.

- Pursue all resources relentlessly; what is beyond money makes the difference. Continuously make friends who are inspired to become partners.

- "Believe kids will succeed" is how the Choice director summed up the Movement. This also goes for their families. Fellowship is important. He also observed that being involved with wayward youth is the work of setting up *national* support networks. Strive

> Previously "throw-away kids" by the thousands are now returning to productivity, possibilities, and respect.

  for meaningful participation. When a troubled youth succeeds, the whole community is more wholesome and feels better about neighborliness. This is about how individuals get involved with schools, churches, families, providers, and agencies—anyone who has some meaningful connection and real contribution to youth success.

- Set expectations. And yes, our institutions are becoming part of the solution by realizing control is not the way; it's a "faceless" approach. What works is most personal. The new strengths-based model is the real safety net. Expectations and standards are exceptionally high—more so than ever before. The old model was largely about completing a court-ordered sentence. It was about "handling" a wayward youngster instead of seeing their potential. Now it's preparation for "fulfillment" and a seat at the family table. Previously "throw-away kids" by the thousands are now returning to productivity, possibilities, and respect.

Every interviewee ended our talks not by being discouraged by the odds but by being quite optimistic and encouraging. They *know* their work is making a difference.

Let's move on now to the next chapter on Operation and Stabilization—that crucial phase in which you put planning to work.

LIFE CYCLE PHASE II – OPERATE AND STABILIZE

Chapter 3

LIFE CYCLE PHASE II – OPERATE AND STABILIZE

Long-Range vision and strategic planning are great tools,
but we need to get some things done before lunch.
– Anonymous from the Pennsylvania Commission on Crime and Delinquency[67]

The Model for Juvenile Aftercare Services

The most important part of planning is operationalizing all the talk[68] Just how do you move your idea from the planning stage to the murky unknown of implementation? Operations are where the comfortable fuss of planning must become the necessarily risky business of doing of it.

While each major phase of the project life cycle has its defining criticality, which when neglected, usually leads to failure. During planning, it's simply the failure to plan properly—or at all. During operations, it's the failure to build the business to support services delivery. During stabilization, it's doing too much too soon. The saving grace is that the model programs in the juvenile aftercare reform movement have shown they can conquer the difficulties and barriers to implementation.

Again, for clarity's sake, the Movement described in this book and via the study sites marks a concerted effort to reform public sector services delivery from the bottom up. By approaching problem solving from where the problems originate via local networked solutions, services can be targeted to a specific need and even to specific individuals. This results in a much more efficient and effective distribution and use of very limited resources. State and federal resources then become part of the solution instead of attempting to be the solution as in the established top-down approach, which is less than efficient and effective. It's mostly because decision makers are arguably divested and distanced from the realities of the neighborhood. The whole bottom-up process becomes workably synergistic, multiplying the resources brought to bear on a problem. It's proving to be a cure for the problems of implementation in the public sector. Every action concerned with planning, operating, and stabilizing/expanding an idea must be made to work as one, even when fragmented agencies and disconnected services are concerned. The quantifiable subcomponents of implementation include: leadership, operationalizing the plan, being customer focused, being information and analysis driven, staffing, process management and building the business to deliver services.[70] The model of implementing a sound aftercare strategy explained in this book follows the path of these critical features.

The executive in charge of the Missouri Model understood these challenges of implementing and sustaining evidence-based and promising practices. The following was adapted from an in-house briefing paper for the Missouri Division of Youth Services.

- *Integrating practices* – Processes and service practices must be made to work within dynamic and evolving organizational and community frameworks. Staff must build some predictability in an unpredictable environment. For example, hiring, budgeting, and resources development need some sort of normalcy to productively and, in turn, help the program accomplish stated goals.

- *Maintaining accountability* – Leadership must be held to results-based accountability, even amid possible confounding, competing, and contrasting values and approaches. Standards and smoothly flowing processes keep personalities and unrealistic demands for premature results at bay as much as possible.

- *Encouraging culture change* – The environment must engender transformative culture change. It is a change from protecting turf to sharing it. All concerned need to feel motivated and inspired to do something worthy together. Productive change cannot be forced; it must be cultivated. This dictates a wholly different approach to how human capital is nurtured, whether that capital is staff or clientele. Yes, the clientele served are a big part of your partnership's success. Agencies have little motivation to develop human capital as well as they must with a bottom-up view of idea/project building. Thus, it's that much more difficult for public institutional agency staff to see the benefit of progress toward strength-based aftercare. This complicates needful reform and services delivery that effectively and permanently transition court-involved youth back to the community and productivity.

- *Sustaining change* – Structures and resources need to support participatory believers—over time. Building a project is done in unstable operating environments with competing priorities.[71] Your service project is not a priority with local government; you must make it so. This situation is especially endemic between agencies, sectors, and service providers with competing practices, variability of staff, and disconnected "silo" services. The work of sustaining depends on sustained commitment. That work depends on long-term friends, participants, and the matrix of services. For stabilization, therefore, design and build your program around the existing array of local (aftercare) services. Do we dare say, "Don't reinvent anything."

Once local advocates have decided to do something about the court-involved, at-risk youth in their communities and thoroughly

Working with children is a duty and has intergenerational implications.

understand the difficulties of implementation, they need to understand this arguably most difficult population. Because once the courts are involved, it's an indication of multiple and deep-seated problems. Although it's difficult to connect with them, it's vital—and critical to serve them. They comprise a very expensive group with which to try to work. Still, consider the downstream effect of keeping a child productive, motivated, and on his or her way to rewarding adulthood. His or her children will have a role model for the same. Working with children is a duty and has intergenerational implications.

Parenthetically, let's make an all-too-brief mention of what we would call rational altruism. We are naturally giving of our time and resources. It's how we progress as people. But the time and resources devoted to a difficult child are resources that cannot go to many children who just need a gentle nudge, a little encouragement to stay on the straight and narrow. We must always consider the rationality of what we do with our resources, especially the most dear—time.

Complicating the already complex work of bottom-up project development, the target population is quite demanding. Youth derailed from the mainstream have serious trouble socializing to good behaviors and at the same time have been socialized to bad behaviors.[72] These realities point to certain principles or smart things to do at this stage of initially operating an aftercare program:[73]

- *Progressive growth* – Aftercare is a maturational learning process. Your clients must be gradually prepared for full independence, which brings attendant responsibilities and accountability. Transitioning is a process; it's not a matter of completing the program while not recidivating and moving on to the next referral. This is about helping youth develop self-control for a lifetime rather than imposing controls for the few months of a sentence. The youth interviewed for this study were quite proud that they could make it through a program because "That's what the judge wants." However, the same youngsters are also searching for a way to do better. Help them to grow incrementally.

- *External support* – Connection to community support systems is vital and difficult, as many initial links may be weakly formed. Many youth advocates and aftercare staff have taken for granted a youngster's ability to interact productively with family, school, a job, church, organized activities, and groups of peers. We can't assume such connections. Such interaction is essential to a successful transition but difficult to comprehend for a disturbed, disconnected, and misdirected teen. These connections grow slowly and naturally with correct nurturing and are well worth the calculated effort, as lessons learned and life corrections foreshadow a successful adult.

- *Transition partners* – People in aftercare support roles are part of, if not essential to, shepherding a child back to the community. They must be targeted, recruited, and oriented/trained to be skilled masters, mentors, and models of good citizenry. Positive pro-social external bonding is an essential part of rebuilding a distracted young life. It takes work to assist their blossoming into responsible adults with real potential.

- *Development support* – These populations of court-involved youth, many of whom have special needs, require connection to job opportunities, training, education, and appropriate services and activities—beyond midnight basketball.

- *External control systems* – Each youngster in the program is best served by meeting expectations, conforming to certain rules of behavior and conduct, and being monitored. While building strengths for independent, crime-free living, they must have consequences for noncompliance. This is combined with individualized case management, therapies, and intensive supervision. This is the stick of behavioral expectations to the carrot of the generally nurturing environment of this new philosophy of aftercare.

You will happily find that many of these challenged and challenging children need only a nudge to learn to be productive and responsible. They want this type of rigor, discipline, and path to something better. Save the criminal justice system for those who truly warrant it.

These principles of growth, support, and control can be considered effective practices. They are proven by a history of successfully helping youth learn pro-social behaviors, have a lower likelihood of recidivism, and develop skills for a successful return to the community. The insight of these programs is that as the controls of the courts lessen, these models ramp up community involvement and support. Eventually, they leave most program graduates capable of making better decisions and becoming independent.

Contrast this with what are commonly called "reentry" programs that only begin the transitional process. Reclaiming Futures has thoroughly thought through what constitutes effective aftercare. Their website is a wealth of practical information that puts more flesh to the bones of these principles. Their model is a superior tool to guide implementation[74] by quantifying progress on 12 key activities, such as infrastructure development, coordination, and screening. The lesson from Reclaiming Futures is that many courts can design, conduct, and enforce a powerful bottom-up, long-term aftercare program while still carrying out their required duties and legal mandates of the court.

Each of these reform movement programs has detailed documents on critical aspects of an aftercare program that can be augmented by well recommended and experienced consultants or well selected (meaning evidenced-based), proven, practical literature. The Missouri Model for Change's *Risk Assessment in Juvenile Justice: A Guidebook for Implementation*[75] is a superior publication regarding the implementation of client assessment. It's full of insights gleaned from years of experimentation, practical learning, and subsequent effective application. Their eight steps, which discuss a few of the critical features of implementation, leadership, services, and staffing, are generalizable to program implementation as a whole:

- *Prepare staff.* – Staff must be qualified by assessment and work in a supportive learning environment.

- *Prepare buy-in.* – Approach only essential partners and collaborators. A critical failing is to try to be egalitarian by being all inclusive, which is practically impossible and leads to difficulties in meaningful action. Contrary to many public efforts that try to be all things to too many people, these programs are served best by including as *few* people as possible. Determine partners and collaborators by their ability to do long-term work for the aftercare project.

- *Prepare the risk assessment tool.* – A hallmark of aftercare programs with impact is immediate screening and assessment. All other treatment, transition, and aftercare services and planning follow from knowing in detail who the specific client is and what needs he or she has. This, in turn, determines what you need to do and how to proceed.

- *Prepare policies and procedures.* – Policies and procedures establish how project implementation happens. The basis of aftercare implementation must be data centric and on task to building permanency. Data determines if the program is working efficiently and, especially, effectively. All effort must eventually lead to the idea being self-perpetuating based on proven processes and procedures and a reliable stream of operational resources.

- *Prepare by training.* – Staff and stakeholder preparation and continued competency means training is continuous. Programs are constantly training the people associated with their aftercare effort, especially those administering and interpreting any risk assessment tool adopted. Don't forget that even clients must be trained as to how they fit in the success of your program.

- *Prepare by piloting.* – Try never to go live without testing what you intend to do, if possible. Conduct mock screening, for example, to make sure the protocol works. If not, fix it or toss it out for the next evidence-based screening tool.

- *Implement.* – Nothing happens without committing to the plan by obligating time and resources when you have consensus that it's time to put plans to work. Act you must! People always ask, "Well, when do you know it's time to act?" The answer is: when principal participants of your project or action item are mostly sure the time is right. Never perfect, just right. Plan until you have a consensus, a feeling really, that it's time to do something. Little happens when people try to be 100 percent sure. That's analysis paralysis. One hundred percent consensus never happens in this work. Only action will tell you if you're right and how to get it right—or even shrug and say, "Well, what should we try next?" Even that is progress.

- *Prepare for sustainability.* – Maintain adherence to the proven processes that determine the evidence-based practice. Always glance at that vision just over the horizon.

Implanting risk assessments as an evidence-based practice in a program exemplifies what should be done for all effective, evidence-based practices. Practitioners advise that each approach to aftercare should be eclectic and borrow the most applicable ideas and activities from each of these models according to what suits them and their town best. These models are critical to your planning because they have solved the tangled Gordian Knot that is implementation.

Little happens when people try to be 100 percent sure. That's analysis paralysis.

Operationalize the Plan

It helps to begin at the end.[77] Imagine an independent, competent young adult risen from desperate circumstances. He or she is the happy result of a seamless, comprehensive program that links program and community services and does not let that youngster fall behind. This new way of thinking about reentry based on nurturing yet strict aftercare is a system in which everyone is intimately involved in the life of the teen. In some programs it's 24-7. Nurturing aftercare is where agency staff, especially parole officers, are continuously and progressively trained in treatment delivery and practice the new *normal* of implementation progress.

See Figure 4, which follows. It's a most helpful example from the Reclaiming Futures Implementation Index Summary.[78] An explanation and brief instructions follow the chart.

Figure 4. Reclaiming Futures Implementation Index Summary

A. Overarching Systems		
A.1	System ensures consent and confidentiality of all youth and guards against self-incrimination across all steps of the program.	0
A.2	All written policy/protocols and training materials incorporate language and practice that ensures cultural, gender, and racial appropriateness, inclusiveness, and equitability.	0
A.3	Implementation team meets on a regular basis for ongoing assessment of process and outcomes for the purpose of performance improvement.	0
A.4	Data is systematically collected, readily accessible, and used routinely by implementation team for performance improvement and reporting.	0
A.5	Formal communication and documentation exist to track youth through the entire process and is used routinely by the implementation team for performance improvement and reporting.	0
A.6	Identifiable leadership advocates and sustains the focus on implementing the RF model.	0
A.7	A governance structure guides collaborative leadership work and decision making.	0
A.8	A comprehensive process improvement effort is in place, uses rapid cycle testing to improve the movement of youth through the steps of the RF model, and uses resources and toolkits (e.g., NIATx) with treatment agencies that provide services to youth in the justice system to improve client retention and agency fiscal solidity.	0
	Overarching Systems	0.00
1. Initial Screening		
1.1	Written policy exists for initial screening of youth eligible for treatment or supervision in the community.	0
1.2	Written procedures/protocols exist for initial screening of youth eligible for treatment or supervision in the community.	0

1.3	Evidence-based, standardized screening tool is used to evaluate youth referred for screening.	0
1.4	All staff are trained in intake, referral, and initial screening procedures.	0
1.5	Information systems exist to provide readily accessible information about referral and completed screening rates.	0
1.6	Formal communication channels and documentation exist to track youth through the referral and screening process.	0
	Initial Screening	0.00

2. Assessment

2.1	Written policy exists for assessment of youth eligible for treatment or supervision in the community.	0
2.2	Written procedures/protocols exist for assessment and treatment matching of youth eligible for treatment or supervision in the community.	0
2.3	Standardized assessment tool is used to evaluate youth referred for assessment.	0
2.4	All staff are trained in intake, referral, and assessment procedures.	0
2.5	Information systems exist to provide readily accessible information about completed assessment rates.	0
2.6	Formal communication channels and documentation exist to track youth through the assessment and treatment referral process.	0
2.7	Data on parent and family involvement in the assessment and treatment referral process are documented and accessible.	0
	Assessment	0.00

3. Service Coordination

3.1	Written policy exists for service coordination of youth eligible for treatment or supervision in the community.	0
3.2	Written procedures/protocols exist for service coordination of youth eligible for treatment or supervision in the community.	0

3.3	Service coordination includes documented participation of all service coordination team members.	0
3.4	All staff are trained in service coordination procedures.	0
3.5	Information systems exist to provide readily accessible information about service coordination.	0
3.6	Formal communication channels and documentation exist to track youth through the service coordination process.	0
3.7	Data on service coordination are used routinely by the implementation team for performance improvement and reporting.	0
	Service Coordination	0.00

4. Initiation

4.1	Written policy exists for initiation of youth eligible for treatment or supervision in the community.	0
4.2	Written procedures/protocols exist for initiation of youth eligible for treatment or supervision in the community.	0
4.3	Time between service planning and initiation is monitored and managed to ensure timely initiation.	0
4.4	All staff are trained in initiation procedures.	0
4.5	Information systems exist to provide readily accessible information about initiation.	0
4.6	Data on initiation are used routinely by the implementation team for performance improvement and reporting.	0
4.7	Data on parent and family involvement in the initiation process are documented and accessible.	0
	Initiation	0.00

5. Engagement

5.1	Written policy exists for engagement of youth eligible for treatment or supervision in the community.	0

5.2	Written procedures/protocols exist for engagement of youth eligible for treatment or supervision in the community.	0
5.3	Information systems exist to provide readily accessible information related to engagement.	0
5.4	All staff are trained in engagement procedures.	0
5.5	Data on engagement are used routinely by the implementation team for performance improvement and reporting.	0
5.6	Engagement is monitored according to the service plan to measure both consistency and satisfaction.	0
5.7	Data on parent and family involvement in the engagement process are documented and accessible.	0
	Engagement	0.00

6. Transition

6.1	Written policy exists for transition of youth eligible for treatment or supervision in the community.	0
6.2	Written procedures/protocols exist for transition of youth eligible for treatment or supervision in the community.	0
6.3	Information systems exist to provide readily accessible information related to transition.	0
6.4	All staff are trained in transition procedures.	0
6.5	Data on transition are used routinely by the implementation team for performance improvement and reporting.	0
6.6	Transition is monitored according to the service plan to measure both consistency and satisfaction.	0
6.7	Data on parent and family involvement in the transition process are documented and accessible.	0
6.8	The transition process provides youth individually developed recovery supports and/or connects youth to a reentry network for long-term support.	0
	Transition	0.00

	B. Community Involvement	
B.1	Community Fellows are actively involved in Reclaiming Futures implementation.	0
B.2	The range of community partnerships is sufficient to meet the service needs for all youth in the program.	
B.3	Community partners represent a range of youth development options and opportunities for youth in the program.	0
B.4	All team members are trained in youth development strategies.	0
B.5	Transition has a built-in post-intervention follow-up to ensure that community engagement continues.	0
B.6	Family and youth have a clear voice in service planning and community engagement strategies to meet the needs of youth.	0
	Community Involvement	0.00
	C. Sustainability	
C.1	An ongoing effort exists to incorporate Reclaiming Futures into jurisdictional-level policies to ensure the institutionalization of the six steps of the RF model.	0
C.2	Funding mechanisms exist to fully support the institutionalization and maintenance of the RF model as a standard practice.	0
C.3	Ongoing communications efforts (media, events, training) about Reclaiming Futures exist to raise awareness and support for Reclaiming Futures.	0
C.4	Data on the efficacy of Reclaiming Futures is reported to the community, stakeholders, and decision makers on a regular basis.	0
C.5	Designated staff has authority to spearhead sustainability efforts, with sustainability-related performance outcomes.	0
	Sustainability	0.00

The value of this tool is that it allows program staff to objectify the subjective. Look for a tool that gives clear examples of what each criterion of readiness expresses. Note that any tool is merely a suggested guide, not all items are applicable, and any other item deemed necessary for the project at hand by project staff should be added. What matters most is that this tool gets you thinking about sustainability.

The tool should have numerical ratings for each item to quantify level of readiness and then track implementation progress. The quantification scheme for the Reclaiming Futures tool above can be on a scale from 1-10 for each item, one being no readiness or progress on the item to 10 being completely ready or 100 percent complete. Progress through such a checklist should also suggest how to accomplish each criterion, which is preferably stated as an action item. You must employ any and every way you can to compel thoughtful action. Because of completing each applicable item, the program has the potential to be operated as efficiently and effectively as possible.

Take "A. Overarching Systems," for example, where you have decided that written documentation needs to be in place, and it needs to be reviewed for efficiency and effectiveness. This item would be rated at different levels based on available evidence that readiness or progress is: minimal; there's some demonstration of progress; it's in consistent practice; or it's institutionalized. Each level of accomplishment would have a numerical rating. Each criterion can be acceptably ready with specifics of who needs to do what by a specific date. An overall composite score compared to the maximum possible score offers an idea of program readiness for operations. You may even wish to give yourself a grade for another way to rate efficiency, effectiveness, and progress.

This tool is much more than a readiness indicator; it's a process of implementation, which must be well planned and will be your most difficult task of sustaining the delivery of reentry aftercare services. Effective implementation puts the proper emphasis on capacity while recognizing where services fit. Another reminder: Services are not a goal in themselves; they're only part of what makes an idea an accepted, productive practice.

Caution: These readiness indicators or implementation checklists tend to focus only on getting a specific service ready to deliver. Much, much more needs to be considered. A service is only one small part of the array of services required for comprehensive aftercare. Let alone building the business of capacity building to support any services. Plus, services are only one of 10 critical features of the project life cycle, from the conception of the idea to when it's a routine part of the municipal services fabric. The Reclaiming Futures Implementation Index hints at what full implementation entails by including community involvement and sustainability. This is why the discussion in this book takes the broader view of implementation for Capacity Building.[80]

We begin implementing the plan with a discussion of leadership.

8. Develop Leadership for Citizen Engagement.

This section will try to capture the energy, talent, philosophies, and ideas of those who are reshaping juvenile aftercare and, in the process, reshaping our criminal justice systems. These key people involved with high-functioning, measurably effective, sustained reform projects do many things right. What sets them apart from more common top-down agency-based service providers is that they embody the collective effort where the whole is greater than the sum of its parts.

However, I hope to convey an appreciation for the intangibles that compel a person to succeed at juvenile aftercare where others fail. It's not just about doing a service but how these people shape themselves and consequently their programs.

Many times, the people in key positions in this work are ex officio, assigned a duty in an aftercare program by virtue of their position. A judge begins a drug court and, as an aside, is asked to work on a juvenile aftercare program because he or she is the judge. What works is when that same judge is inspired to be the prime mover in juvenile aftercare.

How leaders conduct themselves in a sustained, impactful project is more important than who they may be or what their position may be. Just talk to judges from around the country who have started Reclaiming Futures drug courts with juvenile aftercare as the primary focus. They don't try to administer to all criminal matters largely resulting from substance abuse. They embody boundless faith, they are *the* motivating factor in establishing the aftercare idea in their communities, and they were the ones ordained to make a difference. Attitude is everything. They express the belief that too much is at stake by ignoring another generation of juveniles who run afoul of the criminal justice system; they *had* to do something. Judges are the epitome of being overwhelmed with the demands of the job compounded by iterations of more work born of sustaining a new idea. They struggle with attempting to control a new system that defies control, because no longer can they just rule that an action will be done. They are compelled to use their position and power to see that a young life is returned to community and family as a valued member.

The people starting a nurturing-based aftercare program must *want* to intensely invest themselves in the lives of difficult, even belligerent delinquents. They must want to encourage the development of aftercare programming determined to return a wayward child to the community. This is a great departure from what they might have been doing by dictating how these struggling young adults must act or suffer a wrathful bench. Judges must apportion their time to court duties and the strategic and tactical intricacies of building a new concept that dictates a new culture. We reiterate, this is not "hug a thug." It is tough for all, especially young charges. They have to know people care and it is "up or out." Or in this case, back to detention or jail.

Attention must swing from the established order of the court to the disorderliness of managing the networks of disconnected service providers used to doing things their way. This work must be done conversely to the top-down system they're used to. They must now view actions as evolving from the bottom-up and then back down in a virtuous cycle of testing and improving ideas and processes. Judges and aftercare service providers are more accountable than ever before because they know the failure of the idea means the death of possibilities for so many youngsters. This new reality of conviction regarding the cause and commitment of time and effort reflects the position and disposition of key people in every one of these reform movement ideas.

Leadership in the forward-thinking aftercare business *seems* the same as observed in any well-working enterprise, but it is not. My discussions with program officials about the qualities of leadership were lengthy and revealing, because energetic, properly focused leadership pervades every critical feature of capacity building. Everyone in these programs is a leader and exercises their sphere of leadership in some way.

The director of the Missouri Division of Youth Services lent insight into how he, as the chief official for aftercare programming in the state, perceived, designed, and led the effort. The first quality he emphasized for people in leadership or supervisory positions was to be sincerely responsive to partners, staff, and the young adults in the program. Conducting business while expanding the idea to more locations and markets to reach more troubled youth has requirements. Executives at all levels need to be engaged—not micro-managing but paying careful attention to details up and down the organizational chart and especially at the line level.

> Judges and aftercare service providers are more accountable than ever before because they know the failure of the idea means the death of possibilities for so many youngsters.

Responsiveness here means to be available for requests and needs, which is easily said but tough to do. The goal is to create a culture that grows intrinsic motivation—first in program personnel then in the youth they serve. This takes a lot of hands-on oversight in the field. It's not uncommon for executives to know the names of all the youngsters in a program, because their service-level involvement is intense. Management is not a sterile entity in a remote office. Managers are physically engaged by being in the field—present in group sessions and residences and when reviewing cases. This physical presence exemplifies the vision that every child can have a fulfilling life and speaks volumes to staff throughout the program about priorities and goals. Leadership is focused on developing people wherever in their programs an attentive ear can be found.

Effective Practice

Practice hands-on developmental leadership and train to sustain.

This pulling, pushing, and inspiring people to do more largely depends on the teachable moment that presents an opportunity to make a particular point. One moment a key staffer may be participating in a group therapy session; the next, they may be building relationships with officials, potential funders, and families. Each requires an adjustment to what people want to do, must do, can do, then what they will do. The leader of the moment must inspire if not goad a person to do more than he/she thought possible. *All* program staff individually and collectively are responsible for measurable, meaningful outcomes. All outcomes are defined first by what is meaningful to the intended target population/individual, and the vision, mission, and goals. Realism is the watchword.

Staff learn to work with the positives and negatives of people, their personalities and politics, because all can see the impact of being part of something meaningful. Something worth the sweat. Over time, everyone evolves to be better and better at delivering nurturing but strictly defined, delivered, and disciplined services; they prefer having clear responsibilities and being accountable for their contributions and overall program success. The expectation is for people to exercise their creative juices to conduct daily business, to be flexible in dealing with the vicissitudes of working with youth in transition and to adapt as the situation demands. This allows a systematization of staff development. People are trained to sustain the program because members *want* this way of working. Hence grows a healthy work environment where goals matter and experimentation is encouraged. Obstacles are seen as opportunities. Mistakes are opportunities to make things better. People don't fear the day. They know problems will arise, *but* they also know they have the intestinal fortitude and experience to solve them and learn. The project gets better and more and more institutionalized.

When a program operationalizes the philosophy of training staff, who, in turn, sustain programming, policies, and procedures, it shows a real "investment" in all people and their potential as leaders. Thus observed the Missouri Model chief executive. Succession training, that is, ensuring the technical and professional competency of staff, is on-going. Program staff learn new concepts and skills, leadership development classes are common, and the use of data is paramount. Anyone associated with these forward-thinking aftercare programs understands how new ideas are planned and implemented with the emphasis on the model's *processes*. Movement must mean something.

A constant stream of new ideas moves talk to action, where coaching is continuous, germane, and ample. Coaching at these programs is ingrained because of leadership by example. Leaders in this program are constantly on the lookout for a moment to teach anyone close at hand. This type of active leadership cascades down even to line staff who teach each other something they learned or a little better way to do daily work. This way of doing business is vital in the Choice program, where a new crop of community Fellows cycles through the program every year. While the Fellows do have extensive introductory training, they learn a great deal on the job by watching and working with more seasoned staff. What better way to learn? Every situation can be a teachable moment if staff are on the lookout for the occasion.

Leaders in the Missouri Model pair practice change with leadership. They may begin a new idea or introduce a better way to do therapy by supporting the idea. In some cases, they may teach a technique then follow up to see that the new idea is imbedded in practice and policy, perhaps with its own standard operating procedure. Then the new idea endures, improves, and proliferates.

Family engagement in the Missouri Model deserved a handbook to lead therapy, so it was drafted then became policy. An idea becomes part of the culture in cases where staff develop competencies with the new way of doing things—in this case with the therapy handbook. Relevant roles, duties, responsibilities and, most important, expectations are codified. All the while they monitor it to make sure the new practice ties to existing practices. The idea becomes the proving ground for succeeding generations of supervisors, managers, and directors. This is an example of the way good change is institutionalized and strengthens their model of aftercare. It's one of the reasons these programs endure. Idea development continually renews the life cycle of project development while nourishing staff by supporting their creativity and sense of accomplishment. They can see that *their* ideas make real differences and *their* work matters.

Staff imbued with the life-cycle development model learn to pay attention to details and all-important processes, because efficient and effective processes are the foundation upon which an idea can be established. They learn to continually ask how an idea is doing. What is going well, what is not? How can it be done better and what are the next steps? How does it relate to the client? To core beliefs, the vision and mission? Does it help the program evolve and adapt? According to the Missouri Model executive, they take to heart the do-what-it-takes philosophy of hard heads (strictness and discipline) and soft hearts (empathy and nurturing).

> **If the community is not involved, good ideas rarely get a good beginning and struggle to sustain.**

Put another way, staff are persistent and demand goal-oriented results of themselves and those around them. They're proud but hopeful and chronically dissatisfied with how things are because they constantly wonder how things can be made better. This is not to say they adopt the lot of the galley centurion whose purpose is to demoralize and dominate while beating out a drumbeat to follow. Daily work is guided by the philosophy that if we're not going forward, we're falling behind. This dissatisfaction is a celebration of the need to improve. Evolution is not a problem in Movement Models, which are continuously getting better and rationally expanding.

This mentality extends to necessarily engaging the wider citizenry, vital to every stage of the program life cycle. If the community is not involved, good ideas rarely get a good beginning and struggle to sustain.

Effective Practice
Continuously engage the citizens.

Citizen engagement is another unique feature of these Movement Models, as exemplified by the Missouri Model. They don't have leadership boards so much as they have advisory boards. There's a difference. Stereotypically, leadership boards are purely in the policy and decision-making role and very top-down. Members are ex officio and see themselves as little more than visionaries, which tends to make them aloof from operational processes and short lived with the program. That mentality is, "Let's see what others need to do (because *I know,* and I'm moving on)." Instead, the appropriate attitude is, "Let's see what I can do (and please put me to work; I'm here for the duration)." Line-level awareness and participation are rare in the ex-officio board unless the members are committed to a long-term working relationship. The tenure of largely appointed leadership boards is usually not long-term, which would be required to groom them over the years it takes to grow an idea and sustain it. They tend not to be hired to do project work such as developing money, drawing up a charter, or helping to design duties and responsibilities. Rarely do they get to know the client. On the other hand, advisory boards in these programs are marked by bi-partisanship and common expectations for near-term development and long-term program sustainability.

Right-minded directors are involved without micro-managing and see themselves as facilitators of policy rather than policy directors. The Missouri Model advocacy board, for example, is composed of members of both parties, the citizenry, and clients. Members have specific talents and a worker mentality. Typically, these advisory councils so composed don't have the instability often seen during a change of administration. They are bi-partisan and on a renewable three-year appointment cycle designed to dovetail with the gubernatorial cycle. They're involved for nearly as long as they want. Thus, they can focus on program strengthening with, for example, their biannual report.

The biannual snapshot of the Missouri program to the legislature reports on how the program is working, the good and the bad. They couch the report in terms that elaborate on the struggles and successes of the troubled youth they serve. Board members are candid and transparent about operations without bringing up the hard cases in terms that may be interpreted as overly dramatic. Data and truth telling are paramount. They stick to the facts and state positions meaningful to elected officials, especially by making cost-effectiveness (again, not cost-benefit) and trade-off arguments. This apolitical leadership structure occurs at least at the state and local levels. A similar philosophy for composing leadership bodies extends to community liaison councils found at the municipal level.

Community liaison councils are another way that VQ program officials enlist local leadership with a vested interest in juvenile aftercare work. These councils are bodies of advisors/advocates usually made up of local leaders who have a stake in juvenile reentry that focuses on aftercare. One of their primary functions is to engage volunteers. These local leaders are quite active in their communities at the municipal level according to VQ practitioners. This means they are very concerned about program performance, building an evidence base, and maintaining practice fidelity. They help the community with impressions about how kids can and should be perceived as capable and not bothersome delinquents, for example. In fact, legislators are invited to be part of these local councils. This is another take on developing believers who, although external to the municipality of the program, are essential to the local site.

Effective Practice

Engage collaborative leadership skills, especially with external change agents.

A perpetual difficulty for juvenile aftercare programming is to engage external organizations. The reason is they're quite engaged with their own work and have scarce money and resources to assume new or expanded commitments. Movement Model executives are always looking for ways to engage external organizations because they're important, if not vital, to working with the youthful target population. An answer to this recruitment problem is to develop collaborative skills among program staff so they have the knowledge base to approach prospective partners and collaborators (note matrix building) at a service agency. This involves learning how to connect to the various systems such as the health or educational systems or agencies, for example, that can contribute to aftercare. There's no authority to compel cooperation or collaboration, yet these relationships are essential to a worthy aftercare program. How does a Division of Youth Services that sponsors aftercare influence the Department of Mental Health to steer its resources to aftercare? Forging a working relationship between agencies is indeed the complex work of years.

If only a start, one answer these programs use is fostering a learning environment. Staff are encouraged to learn how essential agencies work to find ways to collaborate. Cross-familiarizing oneself with a partner agency, if you will, is especially useful when dealing with public careerists. Many times, such people are a significant obstacle to a program that changes their comfortable business as usual. Some of them have instinctive resistance to cross-participation, a perceived threat to their fiefdom. It's the nature of bureaucrats to avoid risks and resist change. According to a senior Missouri Model executive, they're used to keeping their heads down when a new idea comes along. Reform Movement Models are cautious about offending agency careerists because these people are operational leaders, managers, and supervisors who are vital to juvenile aftercare. However, they must be made part of the team to be able to participate.

Building a team of essential partners is the long-term work of teaching them how intensive aftercare can help *them* with their jobs. They're also taught how *they* can overcome some of the inertia of working in a bureaucracy, which is another major obstacle to reform. With rational explanation and time, people in the health and mental services, for example, can see that keeping a child out of their systems is a way to potentially decrease caseloads, even dramatically so. Furthermore, people working in established agencies see that aftercare is the right thing to do; they just need a mutually beneficial way to participate.

The key to this engagement is imbedding like-minded change agents in a program, according to the Missouri Model senior executive. He councils the necessity of courting then teaching key change agents in and around the program. The purpose is keeping little ideas going that collectively mean so much to an agency's functioning continuously a little better daily. This is another theme of these Reform Movement Models: Little steps matter.

Movement leaders build a program worthy of presenting and then communicate the good news to potential partners. They begin with data as a basic communication and teaching tool. The right and compelling facts are important. It takes only two or three measures to make a point. These savvy leaders can see what is working well, keep it going, and build on it.

Compelling data provide the common denominator for decisive discussion. Everyone understands when the numbers look good or look bad. Remember to convert these numbers to cost-effectiveness then trade-off numbers, as discussed in this

> **People working in established agencies see that aftercare is the right thing to do; they just need a mutually beneficial way to participate.**

Capacity Building series. Once done, it becomes routine and gets more and more compelling over time. Just a few numbers are needed, provided they show program performance, preferably in dollars and cents. Your program is now cost effective and vital to the community because everyone can understand money, especially how to conserve it. Take recidivism, for example, because it can easily translate into dollars saved in institutional involvement. And focusing on that number and savings rather than people, partners, employees, or clients, is unthreatening and can lead to solutions. Numbers-driven, cost-effective progress and goal accomplishment teach key operational people they are part of something successful.

When working well, these people practice the leadership mantra of *"Each one teach one."* Communicating progress, yes, and the battles and setbacks too, is done via training, meeting, working, planning, dreaming, and even commiserating together.

Program staff, especially senior officials, are careful not to oversell evidence-based practices, a surprising number of which are not actually evidence based nor practical.

The VQ director of operations observed that career parole officers often don't understand what an evidence-based practice really is. They certainly can't practice it if asked to do so. For example, a college tour, which is an evidence-based practice, with students who are *not* college bound makes no sense. VQ officials are very persuasive with the argument, properly and persistently put, that the only thing worse than parole is more parole, which is proving to be criminogenic and complicates the work of old-school parole officers. Yes, parole has its purpose, but it's punitive, and it masks what can be done to improve undesirable behaviors. VQ court officials are encouraged to monitor aftercare services according to data-based results; the numbers do the rest of the persuasion. Their work is affirmed as never before; VQ practitioners assert that they learn to love evidence-based case management. When approached about the virtues and results of intensive aftercare, these representatives of the system become some of the best advocates of the Movement.

Ideally and over time, external partners become accountable and collaboratively, productively interdependent with primary aftercare staff by being integrated and vested in mutual success. They become imbedded change agents themselves given time for perspectives to evolve. They become kinsmen who do not do well with obstructionism that their own organizations may present—but in fairness, may not even be aware is happening. When discussing these programs, the word "participation" is heard frequently. It's not a palliative. A virtuous cycle of commitment exists in which ideas cascade up and down the organization. Leadership then flows naturally to assessing and operationalizing the capacity to deliver. The progress of these reform movement programs is agonizing and takes decades of work, yet progress they do.

9. Assess Capacity for Readiness and Cost Effectiveness.

Let's resume the discussion of capacity assessment introduced in Planning. When it's operationalized, it must evolve. What is the purpose of capacity assessment? You're encouraged to pause and think about what it may mean relative to building capacity for permanency no matter what your service program or idea may be.

The director of operations for VQ has an insightful perspective on understanding just how much and what a program can sustain, which is another view of capacity. He suggests that defining the limits of deliverability is to identify then remove systemic and demographic barriers. Systemic refers to the difficulties of bureaucracies, and demographic barriers are the underlying forces of risk and resiliency associated with high-needs youth who can benefit from intensive aftercare. This is one of the insights that come from experience operating a youth-oriented aftercare

> **Good aftercare is only the start; it must put the young client in the frame of mind and mentality to pursue a meaningful career.**

program. An interpretation of this perspective is that capacity assessment is not merely understanding how *little* can be delivered and *done well*, but understanding the *limits* of systems to identify obstacles that can be more realistically wrestled to submission.

Courts, for example, have sway over program youth only for the duration of the court order and parole. But the success of aftercare is determined long after the courts have moved on to the large stream of youth processing through the court turnstiles. Youth who respond well during supervision and learn pro-social decision making and behavior may not have the capacity for post-secondary education; thus, a little technical training for a semi-skilled job is a reasonable expectation for them. Ask, how can we meet the needs of that type of youngster now and as they progress to meaningful productivity in the community? Capacity assessment in this context helps practitioners see how aftercare practices can be accomplished.[81] It also helps answer the question: Compared to what?[82] Assessing capacity is yet another way to ensure that daily program functions match the vision and purpose of the program.

Never forget that the ultimate purpose of juvenile aftercare is to help prepare our youth to be a productive part of their communities with a meaningful career that supports independence. Good aftercare is only the start; it must put the young client in the frame of mind and mentality to pursue a meaningful career. This means much more individual work following aftercare. Few of us are destined for college to prepare for a life-sustaining career, and it's desperately difficult to earn a decent wage even with post-secondary education. Also, check out the salary and career potential of an HVAC technician, a plumber, a small appliance repair man! Now back to the topic at hand.

Just what is capacity assessment then? In simple juvenile reentry terms, it is the number of available staff and the size of the caseload they can handle compared to the stream of referrals to the program. Circumstances of resources, especially human, to satisfy demand determine what is done. Movement Models assess capacity for their far-flung multi-state operations; individual sites do it to justify existing staff. For example, Local VQ staff track the numbers of cases that are under supervision. This helps them know how many clients they can take and adjust workflow as referrals increase. Program staff also include a pre-test of risk and needs as an initial indicator or baseline for appropriate service delivery. For example, new clients could be prescribed Aggression Replacement Training, an evidence-based practice. If delivery quality falls off as seen by an increase of behavioral problems with clients, staff ask if the therapeutic modality is being done properly. Or, if it is right for the program at all.

Understanding referral flow, the life blood of aftercare work, directly affects capacity by helping staff understand demands for staffing. Monitoring referral flow is an intricate part of daily aftercare business operations. Choice staff use capacity assessment to adjust human resources, for example, by sending counselors to various sites as needed. They also continually court new partners, especially service partners, according to anticipated modality need and demand.

Reclaiming Futures has a variation of this theme. They continually track every youth through every phase of treatment and report quarterly the numbers of clients served. Yes, numbers matter at first, especially if they hint at or prove progress is being made in young lives. They can predict the resources needed within 100 clients of approximately 2,000 who are being served annually at the time of this writing.

The staff at the Pennsylvania Division of Youth Services Models for Change have put a lot of thought into understanding capacity and, by extension, readiness. Understanding capacity is basic to incrementally building resources to satisfy an assessed demand such as transitioning court-involved and at-risk youth back into the community. It's most important to continually match capacity to demand to deliver a quality "product." When discussing a well-working operation, staff also allude to the elements of capacity, which include the following:

- *Information flow* – easy, accurate, timely
- *Common motivation* – to share rewarding work while being recognized for it
- *Worthy goals* – to accomplish as a team
- *Leadership* – inspired, tireless level-five leadership, demonstrating humility with the will to achieve meaningful success

The Pennsylvania Juvenile Justice System Enhancement Strategy[83] demonstrates how a program progresses to readiness. A program usually begins with inertia where most people are content with the way things are. Inertia is followed by some discontent with a few individuals, perhaps thinking things could be better. Or, they may hear of a new way to attack an old problem, say, confronting a failing reentry effort with intensive aftercare. Inertia happens: the initial few who would like to do something to answer their discontent may be timid to act or they're able to see only a hazy way forward. Perhaps they have no defined purpose or leadership. This initial group of the discontented gathers more people to the budding cause and begins to coalesce around the problem; possibly they propose a direction forward. Perhaps a leader emerges. They start to search for information and try to answer what can be done with this new idea. They gather more information about the problem area, which paves the way to a feeling for what needs to be done and how to muster commensurate resources, especially human resources. A nascent project begins to blossom.

The idea is then set on a path of years of successes and failures, of progress and reversals, toward full maturation as an accepted practice. During that time, documentation such as policies and procedures may be drafted to formalize and institutionalize the maturing idea. The search for stable operational aftercare resources begins in earnest. Energy builds. Beliefs, vision, and mission emerge. Comfort grows with all concerned that the idea *could* work. The new idea becomes the norm with a remarkable amount of work over several years and a little luck. But people working on juvenile aftercare tend to persist. The idea stabilizes and ultimately earns the mantle of being worthy of export to other programs, internal and external; it penetrates and proliferates. After years of persistence, it finally becomes the new normal. Understanding capacity during this process is paramount, as capacity determines readiness even to take the first client—and everyone thereafter.

Effective Practice

Understand programming readiness to help determine capacity to deliver defined services.

Each stage of readiness presents opportunities to develop strategies and activities to build, and especially sustain, the aftercare practice idea.[84] The value of putting program stakeholders through even a rudimentary readiness assessment is that a functional understanding of what needs to be delivered will result. Then the how of making it happen becomes more apparent. The critical functions of the life cycle take shape. The initial leaders can recruit, train, and operationalize talent, who can be assigned tasks. They can procure the necessities of delivery, choose services, and tailor them to the intended recipients. Operational capacity assessment is meant to dovetail with the capacity assessment done during planning. Trade-offs will happen between unanchored expectations for new practices and those that can be implemented. Those decisions are best made on the cost-effectiveness calculations that should be part of meaningful capacity assessment. Capacity assessment and readiness make those trade-off decisions more visible and the resultant decisions less difficult. After defining and understanding just what services can be adopted, it's also helpful to understand the details of what they will cost outright in hard dollars and what sacrifice of scarce resources will result. That is, doing these social programs is always a trade-off between what staff choose to develop and other worthy ideas that will never be entertained. Worse yet is making a wrong, expensive decision at the cost of the better decision. It's called a trade-off calculation. Doing something always comes at the expense of not being able to do another, especially in the public sector.

How you determine costs is important. It's compelling if your idea makes money or saves money. That money can then be used for more of your program or something else the town counselors may want. Such a case also burnishes your luster as a team player.

The hierarchy of costs is helpful to know, as it can assist in justifying initial operational funding, continued support, and expansion. Pay particular attention to your unintended consequences, as these are most times startling and, if good, are compelling come budget time:

- *Direct costs* – Costs directly tied to production. Salaries.

- *Indirect costs* – Costs not directly tied to production. Delivery.

- *Cost benefit* – Direct expenses of the undertaking and the value rendered.

- *Cost effectiveness* – The value of an undertaking for the money paid.
  This is the "profit" of a project. This measure demonstrates the monetary advantages of your effort and is a strong defense during a budget meeting.

- *Hidden costs* – Obscured costs, usually revealed *after* expenses have been incurred.

- *Unintended consequences* – The unforeseen. Arguably the most expensive. Not part of the original purpose. Beneficial or harmful. Usually the *most* important "cost" to define when making your case. Negative unintended consequences of *not* doing your program are compelling.

Field experience demonstrates that calculating cost effectiveness is much easier and especially much more practical than doing cost benefit, which is somewhat about smoky accounting practices. Cost effectiveness essentially says for X overall cost you get Y benefit. One dollar means $1.29 returned. It is relatively easy to do and much easier to communicate, especially in the public sector, where services are quite dear. Determining costs and subsequent benefits resulting from resources invested is a theme throughout these models. Don't forget to tout what you can do with the "profit."

Cost-*benefit* analysis, done right, is prohibitively complex and laborious. The term is carelessly tossed about as if it can be done quickly, but the true cost of delivering a service needs to be periodically updated as fresh data develops more accurate numbers on what things demand from the public or nonprofit checkbook. Again, it is easier to update cost effectiveness rather than cost benefit. There are so many hidden expenses only revealed by experience. Following the money to calculate cost-benefit requires a certain trained skillset and man hours devoted to the laborious task, which takes time away from the intensive face-to-face experience that good aftercare demands. Something must give, and it is usually the work of determining the precise cost of what you are attempting to do, and thus cost-benefit is never calculated the way it should be. The tendency is to botch this work; after all it is monotonous and especially superfluous when a youngster is acting out just down the hall. Even if cost accounting to determine if your program has a cost-effective benefit, the complex process and result may still not help justify your program, which should easily demonstrate that more money is saved via aftercare than without it.

A suggested way to proceed is to simplify the accounting process by coming up with a cost-effectiveness statement, which is the cost per unit of production. In this case, the unit of production is a child who completes the program and avoids the costs of another trip through the criminal justice system and/or the attendant public services. This is relatively easy to compute and more important, as it makes sense to the people concerned with the results of your work. At the risk of oversimplifying, take all program costs for personnel and operation and divide that by the number of graduates for the cost per unit of production. This number can then easily be compared to the alternatives to your program. These include deeper penetration into the criminal justice system, associated costs of crime and victimization, and the loss of the production of a young citizen.

The comparison costs will dwarf your programming costs. The case can be compelling, especially when the cost of incarceration or detention is compared to the pure costs of an evidence-based therapy.

Effective Practice

Extend capacity assessment into a statement of cost effectiveness.

Thoroughly understanding what you and your external stakeholders are getting from dwindling dollars is the foundational work of your sustainability effort.[85] Those outcomes alone mandate building cost-effectiveness into your daily work routine. An analysis of costs needs to be constantly refreshed with new and developing data. The obstructions that the calculations reveal will in turn attach to cost savings once those difficulties are solved. Hence, offer more program justification beyond huge initial savings, which are seen in *all* the featured reform movement aftercare models. Models for Change, just one model aftercare experiment, exemplifies what can be investigated according to cost:[86]

- *Details of what it takes* – A cost-effectiveness analysis is one of the best ways to fully understand what lies ahead in terms of the commitment of hard dollars and what those investments accomplish. Understanding costs is another mechanism to illuminate more and finer details of required work processes and staffing.

- *Depth of required internal and external buy-in* – The costing process will bring you in touch with needful connections to service providers and people who can help with resources. It provides a way to approach them for what they can and must contribute to the establishment of aftercare in your community. One aftercare official reported that a benefactor reached for his checkbook before the cost effectiveness case was made.

- *The criticality of right timing* – You gain a greater appreciation for when things must be done. More importantly, understanding how cost-effective your program is helps staff commit to appropriate action. The efficiency and effectiveness of process is another way to gain buy-in.

- *Appreciation for the required hard goods to do the work* – Costing capacity defines and justifies essential operational requirements for space, supplies, and equipment and subsequent increases.

- *Honing results according to client and stakeholder needs* – There's nothing like attaching a cost to a product to crystallize the worthiness of producing it.

Cost-effectiveness determines if a practice or resource, whether it's a therapy or a van to shuttle students, should be eliminated. There's no room for niceties; just about everything and everyone must have a purpose and show a profit—that is, a quantifiable contribution to cost-effectiveness.

- *Discovering hidden advantages* – Shadow positives (and negatives) are always taking shape or waiting to be discovered. We are talking again about unintended, usually surprisingly good, consequences. For example, realizing a worthy benefit to local employers, who may want to connect to qualified, motivated program graduates.

- *An understanding of commitments of time and conserving it* – Time takes money. Unexpected efficiencies will come from understanding costs.

Appreciating and computing cost-effectiveness is all part of arranging the constellation of people and things with the intent of preserving the idea.

The director of the Missouri Division of Youth Services, who oversees the Missouri Model, spoke of reframing the organization in terms of capacity assessment. Frames, which discuss leadership styles, are also a useful way to conceptualize and communicate the subjective, amorphous concept and practice of aftercare. The director refers to the book *Reframing Organizations: Artistry and Choice and Leadership* (4th ed.) by Bolmant and Deal,[87] in which the authors describe an organization in four frames. These frames are structural, human resources, political, and symbolic. The approach is another way of categorizing, describing, then fathoming the multidimensionality of capacity:

- *Structural* – The structure of an organization describes how program purposes mesh with people.

- *Human Resources* – This frame is concerned with motivating participants.

- *Political* – The power dynamics of the organization, this frame describes how people cope with stress.

- *Symbolic* – This describes the organizational core culture, which we hope evolves to be one of strict nurturing in the case of aftercare.

The Missouri director maintained that the structure of these frames and an understanding of capacity enable leaders to become more focused, empowering, persuasive, and communicative while building the organization around the idea. The Missouri official further recommended Bolman and Deal's book as essential reading for aftercare practitioners, whatever their level may be within the organization.

Understanding organizational frames has implications for how an organization ought to operate, while providing a common language to describe what happens, especially when considering capacity. For example, staff at the Missouri Model preface an interaction by saying, "Let's put this in the structural frame." Practitioners might use frames when discussing goals, building relationships, detailing duties and responsibilities, or perhaps when writing a standard operating procedure. The language of frames can become a handy way to communicate the messages of capacity assessment.

Capacity assessment builds comfort with the means of services delivery while opening opportunities for problem solving and improvement. Staff can see the end goal and thus can better understand the ways to achieve program goals within it. Missouri Model staff comment that daily meetings are peppered with references to how a certain action can be accommodated. Meetings become more meaningful. The day becomes more meaningful. The project becomes more and more meaningful. Terms of capacity become the lexicon, the "coin of the realm," of the high performing organization. It's one more mechanism from which ideas for efficiency and effectiveness emerge.

One Movement Model program conducts surveys of employee engagement every 18 months, asking employees how they feel about being associated with their program. Leaders use results for relatively immediate feedback on how staff are doing individually and how the organization as a whole is faring. The feedback is helpful for regular reporting to all management and leadership. One more mark of a progressive program.

> The language of frames can become a handy way to communicate the messages of capacity assessment.

Capacity assessment determines how to tackle other critical capacity building functions.[88] For example, understanding a program's capacity makes it possible for leadership to make better decisions on developing proper amounts of resources. Along with analysis and evaluation, capacity assessment helps determine if services are contributing to helping clients become independent adults. Staff are better able to see where the project is going and make their individual contribution to that progress. With a good understanding of capacity, problems are more likely to be anticipated and avoided because the focus is on process not people. This fits ever so nicely with determining the scope of what you must do versus what you can do to close the services-to-needs gap.

10. Monitor and Limit Scope Creep.

Determining scope, again, how much you can do while doing it well without sacrificing quality, program impact, and longevity, is challenging. Yet it can be done practically and productively while learning to do it relatively easily. Don't let your scope creep to demands and responsibilities you're unable to fulfill—and worse yet, keep creeping. It's great to say, "Yeah, we can do that." Then you leave that meeting with the sinking feeling of wondering how to do the impossible.

Know what you can provide and the limits of delivering it—especially by knowing in detail what you can't do and why. Know you're on the way to creating a program that does good things and lasts. Know your idea, your program is a *permanent solution to a permanent problem.*

There's nothing wrong with saying, "We're not ready to tackle that one. However, give us till the next committee meeting. Then we can tell you that by D date we can deliver E, so you can decide what you (e.g., the town council) can and will support." This gives you the magic of time to cool the heat of the moment. You can then come up with a compelling case for what you can do on your terms that also serves the governing body or sponsor and those you serve.

By having your scope and vision, mission, goals, and values written down, your project is attacking a major threat to project success: insidiously expanding scope. Most insidious of all are unrealistic expectations of evidence-based practices. Therapeutic modalities and claims of their achievements and supposed ease of acquisition sometimes take on mythic proportions, according to VQ staff. The task is to manage your scope and keep it from overextending your unique capacities. Practitioners I spoke with were concerned with not doing too much too fast while still challenging staff to do more client and support services within the program as well as judiciously expand the program idea to other sites.

This tension between what was being done and what staff wished to do in these reform movement programs was controlled as much as possible by having a good sense of scope and constantly revisiting it. Here, tension was not a bad thing, as it motivated staff to always do a bit more. If scope is planned well, documented well, and part of the process of operation, most of the critical work of scoping is done. It just needs to be periodically, perhaps annually, revisited.

Effective Practice

Carefully limit project scope to keep from overextending service delivery capacity.

This effective practice is about taking on too much, risking program goals and longevity. The natural tendency in delivering social, mental, and health services is to want to do more and more because the need for these services is obvious and unfilled. And you know you can do something about it. The tendency goes treacherously unnoticed by program staff until they are stretched or overwhelmed, the latter usually being when the program is in danger of failing.

One of the worst symptoms of reaching too far is your charges become experiments. Therapists try to bend them to the newest best thing or put youngsters in the wrong therapeutic settings.

Some struggling programs grasp for pseudo programs that merely sound good, such as college visitations for kids who are *not* college bound. This experience will most likely frustrate them and deter them from more appropriate paths. Interest in data continues to dwindle when scope creeps. You don't even have time to acknowledge the warning signs. For example, referrals may dip below a program-sustaining level. You may be unaware that your effort is failing or, at the very least, you may miss opportunities to strengthen your program. Not understanding scope is at the root of many of the symptoms of program decay.

These Movement programs seek to limit insidious demands in creative ways. The Missouri Division of Youth Services (DYS), which runs the Missouri Model, works to keep as many juveniles as possible out of their programs in the first place. They partner with juvenile court day treatment as an alternative program to their primary aftercare program. Day treatment has the advantage of taking high-needs youth *before* they are court involved. It keeps them out of the justice system and further delinquency yet puts them in the population needing aftercare. Prevention: A very wise approach.

Notice how scope creep is prevented via the Missouri Model. They argue that prevention costs about $1,200 per youth per year and criminal system involvement can

> **Not understanding scope is at the root of many of the symptoms of program decay.**

cost up to $40,000 per year according to the Missouri Model chief executive. This is a dramatic cost-effectiveness statement. It's compelling, even eyepopping. So simple, so effective. This justifies money and support but only for a designated number of referrals, because they know how much each referral will cost to treat. The basics of data analysis are in place to provide rationale for smart policy to control the clients in their programs by referring some potential clients to day treatment programs and taking only the number of clients they can serve well. Smart.

Next, Missouri Model staff work hard not to "bounce" the youth from program to program. When a client becomes involved in the juvenile justice system, the tendency is to shuffle some of them from program to program. This usually means deeper penetration into the system rather than working to graduate the youth to community independence. Some make the discouraging point that a youngster can become more even undisciplined and even criminalized. Missouri Model staff place a referral in a group with a team. The team's purpose is to keep the child till graduation and then transfer him/her to proper aftercare, thereby avoiding bouncing the child from agency to agency. Another technique to control bounce and achieve a better result is working with small groups of clients. Smart again.

The Missouri Model has gravitated to groups of 10 clients, who get intensive 24/7 treatment in local residential settings. This helps reduce the cycle of recidivism by nurturing better behavior while teaching skills for independence. Never-ending control in large residential settings has given way to strengths-based therapies delivered to small groups of youth, which result in their permanent return to the community. Once again, smart.

Let's focus on a few overarching priorities to limit scope. The main guiding priority taken to heart by the staff of the Missouri Model is the Missouri governor's vision based on the epiphany that all children served by the Division of Youth Services (DYS) can be successful, productive citizens. This vision defines the Missouri DYS, according to its director. How does this daring statement translate to reality? Missouri Model staff *know* that most troubled young adults can have a family and be accepted in the community. Better still, they can be happy and productive.

Value statements such as believing that every young person wants to and can succeed then become the lens for every decision. They are posted on walls, talked about in conversations, and become standards for conduct. Values do not permit a youngster to be blamed for problems or failures during the process of learning responsibility and being accountable for becoming productive. A bold vision tempered by realistic operational scope and meaningful goals becomes a reality check for over-wrought or misdirected ambitions, according to the DYS director. This discussion is about balance, both on the job and in life.

Some of my most informative discussions occurred with the director of the Missouri Model. Leaders of these Movement ideas are always concerned about not only doing things well, but about doing the right things well. Doing what is productive is another variation on getting scope right. It is about teaching how to live a balanced life well, a theme recounted during many of my interviews. How sensible. He recounted a story for me that was originally told in Stephen Covey's book, *First Things First*, Habit 3 – Put First Things First. It bears repeating. Here is the story of "Big Rocks"[89] (italics are mine).

In the middle of a seminar on time management, recalls Covey in his book, *First Things First*, the lecturer said, "Okay, it's time for a quiz." Reaching under the table he pulled out a wide mouthed gallon jar and set it on the table next to a platter covered with fist-sized rocks. "How many of these rocks do you think we can get in the jar?" he asked the audience.

After the students made their guesses, the seminar leader said, "Okay, let's find out." He put one rock in the jar, then another, then another—until no more rocks would fit. Then he asked, "Is the jar full?"

Everybody could see that not one more of the rocks would fit, so they said, "yes."

"Not so fast," he cautioned. From under that table, he lifted out a bucket of gravel, dumped it in the jar, and shook it. The gravel slid into all the little spaces left by the big rocks. Grinning, the seminar leader asked once more, "Is the jar full?"

A little wiser by now, the students responded, "Probably not."

"Good," the teacher said. Then he reached under the table to bring up a bucket of sand. He started dumping the sand in the jar. While the students watched, the sand filled in the little spaces left by the rocks and gravel. Once more he looked at the class and said, "Now, is the jar full?"

"No," everyone shouted back.

"Good!" said the seminar leader, who then grabbed a pitcher of water and began to pour it into the jar. He got something like a quart of water into that jar before he said, "Ladies and gentlemen, the jar is now full. Can anybody tell me the lesson you can learn from this? What's my point?"

An eager participant spoke up: "Well, there are gaps in your schedule. And if you really work at it, you can always fit more into your life."

"No," the leader said. "That's not the point. The point is this: *If I hadn't put those big rocks in first, I would never have gotten them in.*"

In both our business and personal lives, we have big rocks, gravel, sand, and water. The natural tendency seems to favor the latter three elements, leaving little space for the big rocks. In an effort to respond to the urgent, the chaos of crisis management, the important is sometimes set aside.

What are the "big rocks" in your life? A large project? Spending time with your family? Your health? Your finances? Your faith? Your personal development? Your dreams?

Make a list of your big rocks. Then plan to ensure that you put your big rocks first. Block out time in your schedule for those activities. Amazingly, the other stuff still gets done.

Periodically reflect on how you're doing. Are you putting your big rocks first, or does gravel, sand, and water dominate your life? If the big rocks aren't getting in, what will have to happen so they do?

When you're planning your month, your week, or your day, and even when you're making specific decisions during the day, refer to your list of big rocks. Then, work them. It is more than the "rocks" of work. Plan time for friends, a hobby, family and the children—great training for becoming a grandparent, too.

While the people I interviewed were overworked and stressed as this work commands, it was with good work and the excitement of leaving a legacy. They were whole people with pursuits and lives beyond work. They didn't forget to first put in the big rocks of a life well lived.

Now, with scope planned and operating with limits, we turn the discussion to evaluation and analysis.

11. Put the Components of Evaluation and Analysis in Place.

Before you can evaluate or analyze the efficiency and effectiveness of your program, you're well advised to have quantitative analytical capacity. This means the capacity to generate performance numbers understood by all that compel productive action and planning. Your program must be ready to support data manipulation before you can become evidence based. The major task, then, is to build the evaluation and analysis data machine, which includes the tools, processes, and procedures of investigation.

The parts of aftercare services you are building must be useful and sustainable and add overall value to the entire effort in goal accomplishment and cost-effectiveness. To repeat an important point: Do not confuse this with cost-benefit, which is the domain of accountants. Effectiveness is your goal. If you aren't effective, you will dwindle away. Effectiveness means you are changing lives for the better, and it makes economic sense to continue your work. Dollars invested means a profit, a return on that investment in improved, productive, contributing lives. Determining usefulness means that data processing must be simple enough for staff with only a basic knowledge of evaluation to use every day. You may need to offer a brief professional development workshop to get all staff up to speed. It's not wise to bury your analysis function in an office, the responsibility of one person detached from what matters. People delivering your service need to enter their data and see the effect of their work.

The simplicity of data points examined is essential to sustaining analysis. Dare I say again, less is more. This implies that data must be easily recognized, digitized, analyzed, reported, and distributed in terms intended audiences understand and can use to justify action. Main groups of users are clients, program staff, budgeteers, and supporters, mainly in the community. Lastly, data must materially contribute to the program by improving processes, supporting goal attainment, and developing new ideas the program can employ. This latter purpose, one of innovation, is done to great advantage in these Movement programs. Evaluation (of process *efficiency*) and analysis (of results and impact *effectiveness*) are the backbone of becoming performance-based, thus are the most essential on-the-job tools that ensure the health and survival of your program.

First, it helps to have an operational understanding of what evaluation and analysis are doing in tandem. This means comparing them, herein interpreted as quantitative evaluation (process) and qualitative monitoring (results).

Some of the best programs have all staff involved, physically, materially in telling their stories of success—by the numbers. Being close to the action, front-line staff can best document and tell the program story. Yes, you'll encounter resistance and "That's not my job." Show them what it means to their pay-

> It's not wise to bury your analysis function in an office, the responsibility of one person detached from what matters. People delivering your service need to enter their data and see the effect of their work.

checks, however, and enthusiasm blossoms. They know what they're doing! Help them do it. Let's establish a rudimentary, common understanding of analysis in the form of evaluation and monitoring. Please refer to Figure 3, which follows, for a comparison between the two processes. This chart essentially evaluates effectiveness outcomes and monitors the efficiency of operational processes.

Figure 3. Comparison Between Monitoring and Evaluation

Characteristics	Evaluation	Monitoring
Subject	Usually focuses on strategic aspects	Addresses operational management issues
Character	Incidental, flexible subject and methods	Continuous, regular, systematic
Primary client	Stakeholders and externa audience	Program managementl
Approach	Objectivity, transparency	Utility
Methodology	Rigorous research methodologies, sophisticated tools	Rapid appraisal methods
Primary focus	Relevancy, outcomes, impact, and sustainability	Operational efficiency and effectiveness
Objectives	To check outcomes/impact and verify developmental hypothesis	To identify and resolve implementation problems

This table graphically represents how these two aspects of analysis are interdependent. Efficiency is about how processes are done. Effectiveness considers how well processes accomplish stated purposes. Working together, they strengthen processes and procedures and enhance goal accomplishment. Monitoring program processes helps determine if the collective effort is making a difference or having impact that can be quantified. This is important because some measures can be merely for convenience or a bit abstract. For example, program compliance and attendance can be enforced while the client is under court order; but compliance and attendance do not measure how much the youth is learning about being self-reliant. Nor do they indicate how much the individual is turning away from crime and not recidivating.

Parenthetically, if you can't connect a measure directly to a client's improvement that can then be converted to economic benefit, you should consider abandoning the measure. Although that measure may be good to see materialize, it probably doesn't contribute to the mission. Moreover, it probably doesn't contribute to the cost-effectiveness trade-off statement for your budgeteers and supporters. Note here that private businesses understand cost-effectiveness/profit and can write a check immediately.

The test of program effectiveness, then, is determined by how many graduates are not recidivating long *after* court supervision is complete and direct program influence is gone. This is extremely difficult, yet vital, to track—*and* it's the justification for an extended period of aftercare. Even directly after graduation, graduates of these programs are very difficult to track, let alone for a few years to truly test the effects of therapy and aftercare. This hints at the justification for a reasonable extended period of aftercare. It's natural to wonder what truly happens to graduates of these aftercare programs. Have they left crime behind? Do they really become productive citizens? Have they landed a career instead of a terminal job? Do they have a rewarding family and social life? Practitioners suspect that this population of misdirected youth continues to struggle on the edges of society as adults. This is justification for an extended period of aftercare to effect better and better transitions to the promised fulfillment. The reform Movement would be well served by a study of its long-term effects. Presently, capacity building aftercare programming remains a very smart thing to do.

Monitoring program processes for efficiency is relatively simpler than calculating impact. So, monitoring process is necessary and an introduction to the more difficult work of making the vital statements about how well program staff are doing. It may be more realistic to track a few long-term graduates whose story will add a face and depth to program needs, especially for funding and staffing. Suggest this continued connection to a few students. Enough will want to stay in contact and thus provide a better assessment of behavior improvement. Even one or two encouraging firsthand testimonies will be compelling come budget time.

The fact is that meaningful results won't happen without goal-oriented work. Understand what the chart above depicts: results-oriented processes determined by impact evaluation and process monitoring encourage results-oriented management and administration.[90] This, in turn, encourages the growth of results-oriented cultures and results-oriented learning, and creative idea development and implementation. This further encourages results-oriented services programming (evidence-based therapies), which also encourages your program officers to doggedly pursue meaningful impact. That's what is analyzed and makes good things happen. All enhance the chances of solidifying the idea in the municipality, its government, and community.

When done properly, evaluation and analysis is essentially about the much larger and vital work of idea development and figuring out implementation. In other words, evaluation and impact analysis help make your idea and project achieve goals, become permanent, and work toward successfully transitioning youth. Movement models demonstrate that the most difficult part of becoming data-based is to begin monitoring processes for efficiency and evaluating the program for a chain of results. Again, small steps are advised. Start from the moment your service idea takes shape.

Wisely, personnel working within the movement caution to start simply, especially if your model is a standalone project with little connection to a statewide or national effort. Don't despair at that reality. I can personally speak to the good work of many ideas unfettered by bureaucracy and interest areas from above that are quite removed from what it takes to make a program work. Work on making one essential process work well, documenting at least one primary indicator of results, and then build this into daily routines for making data work for you. Do it as if your program depends on it—because it does.

Just how does data become operationalized? It begins with the foundational work of planning a logic model, which traces the chain of outcomes from inputs to results. From that will come a vision, mission, and goals. Then develop goal-directed processes, procedures, interventions, and resources. Preferably, continue that momentum to develop a statement of values, which proves exceedingly valuable with this type of work. Values such as safety, trustworthiness, choice, collaboration, and empowerment are considered the nuts and bolts of the Missouri Model. Now put together sources of data and the tools of measurement; then follow up to see that analysis-evaluation are operationalized.[91]

Effective Practice

Become data driven by putting the components of evidence gathering in place.

Start with a few meaningful measures. Note how this *less is more* theme weaves throughout capacity building. Prove your processes gradually, then layer on as your data points become clearer. You will need relevant data, the tools of analysis, and a means to disseminate the information.[92]

First, understand who will want the results of evaluation and analysis and design reports to suit their needs. Both internal and external individuals and groups have a need to know how their interests are faring. Effectiveness, that is good results, will be difficult to achieve unless your operation is efficient.

Your first data consumers will be *staff,* who need to know they are working well and are contributing to program success. Most of their information will be on whether the processes of daily work are efficient, simply making sure time is being used well. I emphasize again how vital well-working processes are to goal accomplishment and the attainment of meaningful results. The program hierarchy from the line level up need to know that resources are not being squandered and the program is on track Never forget to keep program *participants,* their *families,* and external supporters informed with regular communication. External data consumers will be the many program partners and supporters. These are the people controlling your program's political support and financial and operational resources. The Choice program provides a great example of how to work the data with external stakeholders.

Their supporting foundation wanted rather grandiose target measures like the number of arrests and school expulsions—dramatic but not realistically actionable. Choice program officers used the request as an opportunity to supplement those reports with data on family engagement, attendance, and graduation, among other measures. Then they reported on client arrests and expulsions. Naturally, the results were monetized with a "profit" statement for additional program support. The foundation now has a new appreciation for what Choice can accomplish besides simply reducing a client's likelihood of arrest. This, however, doesn't ask or answer the question, "What led to the arrest in the first place?" Be prepared for some disappointments, but even disappointments inform what you are doing and how you do it.

> **Never forget to keep program *participants,* their *families,* and external supporters informed with regular communication.**

Some federal agencies wanted full-time teen employment tracked as a prerequisite for discretionary funds. This number will always be low since full-time employment is unrealistic for all teens, let alone those who are system-involved. Such measures lead to reporting complacency and can lead to the degradation of practice fidelity, or delivering it as intended—especially when pushing for certain numbers means the processes that determine effectiveness are pushed aside.

This is an example of top-down convenience data gathering to show some gains in popular measures. What matters to positive behavioral change includes, for example, attending class, not being disruptive, and being prepared to learn. One intrepid counselor took to patrolling the streets to find truants and personally put them in class. However, any intervention—even magic—can't help those who aren't willing to take their seat.

The perspective on evaluation and analysis from aftercare stakeholders is quite interesting and as usual, insightful. The director of the Missouri Model observed that its measures evolved according to challenges and the programmatic purpose of focusing beyond reentry to aftercare. The governor of Missouri, recognizing that generations of youth are being lost to juvenile delinquency and unfulfilling lives, challenged juvenile services professionals by stating that *all* children deserve better. This blossomed into programming to develop graduates free from crime and with skills for responsible living beyond court supervision. The pronouncement also means the recognition that youngsters do make bad choices and still can learn to make good ones. Juvenile lack of judgment and bad decisions are, for most, the process of growing up; most teens will mature to be responsible, accountable, and productive. Many just need guidance and perhaps some incentives, along the way. The challenge is to initially measure realistic progress, the result being the collection of data that reflect students returning to public school ready to learn and graduate while being free from mischief and crime *after* graduation.

Missouri Model staff directed their attention to the challenge of treating all children. Therefore, smaller local community sites were built that enabled young adults to remain closer to their homes and parents, which is important to the process of learning independence. Treating all troubled teens suggested the local, small-group, nurturing, residential treatment model, which allowed 24/7 attention. All but a few of the most violent and incorrigible young adults were accepted into these homey residential settings, with notable progress for most of them. Money well spent. Targeting matters. Starting small but doable matters—no, it's vital!

It also became easier to measure how the family progressed to more responsible living, as they had to be part of the aftercare process with their child. Quite smart, so basic. The obvious insight is that if a young adult's home life continued to be dysfunctional, most of the work done by the program was easily undone. I have also been privy to involving home and family in school safety programming. A wholistic view and practices work.

Program staff track recidivism during and after program enrollment when they can, noting the difficulty of doing so. But tracking recidivism is worth the effort because evidence beyond an aftercare program about how a young life is returned to home and community is compelling justification for intensive aftercare. Program staff track family engagement, productive involvement in evidence-based therapies, and utilization of day treatment. To these practitioners, just knowing that the numbers are demonstrable, though challenging to gather, keeps them motivated in difficult work. At the time of this writing, Missouri Model sites experienced a 24 percent high school or GED completion rate. Since it was double the national rate, they could have rested at that level. But staff persisted and raised the graduation/GED completion rate to 46 percent because their initial goal was a challenging 50 percent—and even that will improve over time. Fifty percent is just out of reach, a stretch goal, which challenges the best in people. And they deliver. Difficult-to-obtain results are possible in a bottom-up, community-based aftercare program.

Staff advise a detailed review of daily work routines to choose which are most relevant to process implementation. This advice comes from decades of experience operating the Missouri Model. For example, staff sift through diverse sources of information such as meeting minutes, grants, and perhaps analytical reports for bits of the process picture. They also go through reports from external sources. This includes the courts, their municipalities, the local medical and mental health departments, service partners, fellow granting agencies, and especially the regular schools for information about program participants. In addition, they delve into their everyday processes.

They analyze the delivery of a therapy for fidelity by video recording therapy sessions to ensure the evidence-based elements are being practiced as intended. Obviously, this provides immediate critiques, which are most helpful, and records a history of how the practice is being improved. People are great sources of information.[93] Look to relevant people, from program participants to the most senior executives, for their views and recommendations for data sources. Look to sister sites, even though they may be in other states; someone may have blazed this trail before you. A national sponsor of aftercare, the Annie E. Casey Foundation, is a wealth of information backed by years of experience and exceptionally sound transferable action research.

Model sites spend a remarkable amount of time observing and critiquing processes and each other. They continually ask, what is the best way of doing this task? It's part of being discontented and not fearing a bit of creative disruption. After meetings, they may simply ask how things went, what was learned, and if they have spent time productively. Pre- and post-tests are given to program graduates; peer reviews and document analysis prove quite helpful. Ultimately, intense case management offers a wealth of information from having a demographic summary of the court experience and a psychological assessment. This type of documentation lends itself to information technology for meaningful data gathering, analysis, and dissemination. Much data processing and analysis can be and is done on a simple spreadsheet.

The yield of this work will be feedback about the therapeutic and essential work processes. Solutions for efficiencies will be quite evident and nearly automatic to implement, as many little changes can be made on the fly. Since process and performance are synergistic, justification will arise to improve an idea, continue processes and programming, or sometimes more important, cut what is inefficient, ineffective, or just indifferent. This is the definition of innovation. Implementing a good data basis for your program depends on staff adopting the processes to inculcate it, having solid capacity to gather, understand, and disseminate the subsequent information, and sustaining the use of it.[94]

Once your program is data-based, you'll gain insights into unique and powerful uses of the results of data collection and interpretation. Something that begins dry and sterile becomes interesting, even energizing. The Montgomery County, Ohio Reclaiming Futures staff noticed that girls didn't have enough substance abuse therapy to be assured they would stay drug free prior to out-of-program placement. They piloted an alcohol and drug therapy modeled after Functional Family Therapy, which they had been successfully implementing for eight years for other purposes. During that time, the girls had shown notable improvement in staying away from abusing substances. They took those lessons learned and translated them into a program for boys, then grew the program from 150 to 400 graduates, one client at a doable time. At the heart of this success is strong data gathering, assimilation, and use of it to improve therapy delivery. Everybody wins.

Effective Practice
Develop a dashboard of results-based accountability.

Movement Model programs develop a "dashboard" of measures. When automated by spreadsheets and analytical tools, it presents an on-the-fly status of program performance. Imagine getting near instant feedback! What better way to see the problem and its answer quickly when right action matters. Measures must be selected to tell the story of program progress and be meaningful to stakeholders, know what they need, and deliver truthfully.

For example, a few measures on The Missouri Model's dashboard include: high school and GED graduation rates, educational progress in core subjects, client involvement in programming, residential length of stay, day treatment, and family therapy participation. If setting this up seems daunting, the continuous admonition applies—start small and increase measures incrementally with proof of progress. Decide on the few most important measures to you and to your supporters and begin the processes of collecting data and the stories they relate. It's all about processes. Get them right first and the quality of the task at hand will always improve. Expand the infrastructure of the function—in this case, the hardware, software, and procedures— and comfort with that expansion will grow as it evolves in its usefulness. Data gathering and interpretation are the basis of becoming evidence based. Any evidence-based practice or therapy will not work well without the numbers and the narratives of success.

Let's return to evidence-based practices, referring to evidence-based therapies versus evidence-based programs or processes. Same theme, slightly different approaches. The important difference is that therapies that improve behaviors are built on a solid program that comprises the capacity to deliver the therapy. Pause and contemplate the difference. The best therapies are marginalized and certainly not sustainable if they aren't supported by the infrastructure that makes them possible. Therefore, build adequate program structure before therapies are practiced. Capacity to deliver must match demand.

> **Reform movement programs persist with evidence-based therapies because, overall, young charges do respond to them.**

A VQ executive warns to be realistic about what it takes to make evidence-based therapy work. Just because it worked in one location is no guarantee it will work in another. One executive was fond of saying, "Things are different in Lizard Lick, North Carolina, say, from New York City." How true. Consider the therapies; they are the life blood of program effectiveness, yet they are wickedly difficult to fund, implement, measure, and sustain. They're also time-consuming. Realistic expectations of what they can accomplish are amorphous. Even when they're up and running, it's maddening to sustain their gains because therapy fidelity, or how to deliver the modality as designed, takes constant vigilance. I have witnessed a therapist deliver an evidence-based, recommended therapy that had deteriorated into a question-and-answer group session, which couldn't be further from its original intentions. Despite all this, reform movement programs persist with evidence-based therapies because, overall, young charges do respond to them.

Staff make these therapies work in creative ways. VQ, for example, has case managers working hand-in-glove with therapists from a program called Parenting with Love and Limits. Thus, they augment therapeutic progress by developing direct contacts and leads for housing and employment for attendees and families. The evidence-based practice itself is both short and long term goal oriented. Results are normalized by comparing them to similar programs in and out of state. Therapists can see data collection and analysis that depict how they are doing individually and compared to other therapists using the same model or doing the same work. Objective data also ensure fairness in comparing therapists and maintaining practice fidelity.

Hopefully your selected practice will come with a data package that solves the important issues of how to automate data collection and manipulation and what indicators need to be tracked. Automation makes it convenient to measure by benchmarks. VQ uses the following:

- *Cost reimbursement* – The number of clients served, an initial output[95] on the chain of outcomes, is divided into total program cost to determine cost per student served. This number can then be compared to the cost of other programming or alternatives to aftercare. A better extension of determining costs is to calculate cost effectiveness as a basis of the argument for your program in monetary terms. The good sense of doing your project is made dramatically simple, plain, and compelling.

- *Contracted services* – Contractor hours are monitored because they augment the work of fulltime staff and demonstrate a wise, if not cost-effective, allocation of resources.

- *Client wait time* – How long a client waits for programming to commence is important, as delay affects program results. It also is an indicator of process efficiency or lack thereof.

- *Participation* – Attendance rates indicate participation, which enhances the prospects of graduation with better behaviors and coping skills.

- *Behavior changes* – Actual behavioral changes and improvements, such as school and program attendance and staying drug free, are obvious measurements of program effectiveness.

Note how these measures fit on a chain of outcomes. They also hint at a client being ready for program graduation and a better chance of succeeding independently. Measuring variables like these helps Movement programs in their reform efforts by redefining stereotypes. Victims, troubled kids, "problems" to be punished, or criminals become young adults with strengths and abilities to become someone much better.

12. Build Resource Streams by Keeping Broad-Based Constituents/Believers Informed.

Developing resources to run your program during operations is a matter of seeking and maintaining support for a well-working program. Therefore, you need to demonstrate programmatic stability and strengths to key stakeholders, groups, and individuals. Operationalizing resources development means building believers, according to Movement Model staff. Of course, this implies that the driving focus is on making young clients whole, wholesome, able, and on the way to autonomy.

This concept of building believers is elegant and yet not easy to do. It's as simple as communicating the status and successes of your program but is made difficult by the consuming detail and time commitments this work requires. Ask what your stakeholders want and then deliver it.[96]

> The problem of having someone not accept your program is more than likely a problem of them not being informed.

Bond with need-to-know individuals and groups, be regular and frequent with visits to communicate positive and negative information about the program. Don't oversell what you're accomplishing, yet be humbly proud of justified progress. Building program permanence is not guaranteed and many children still fail at maturing to productive adults. Tell the truth about the struggles you're having but always with a statement about how, with collaborative effort, difficulties can be overcome. More important, stress that this work is worthy even if a few young lives are improved. They have many, many good, productive years to "repay" this investment and faith in them.

First, consider the categories in which your believers find themselves. Internally, you have staff, clients, and families. Externally, you have stakeholders in attendant local communities, elected officials, and partners, who consist of service providers and people who bring money, goods and services, and expertise to the project.

Effective Practice

Maintain resources by keeping stakeholders informed.

The problem of having someone not accept your program is more than likely a problem of them not being informed. This is usually because they haven't received targeted, regular, continual contact. A good program director gives good briefings as convenient. A great executive director attends the meetings of supporters, attends their functions, knows them, and knows what is important to them. A lack of information flow risks your program being pigeonholed as the program du jour and becoming trivialized when compared to other pressing or better justified needs for local goods and services. Maintaining resources, according to the Missouri Model statewide director, is a matter of keeping stakeholder groups informed about how well the program is working and communicating that fact in their words. The Missouri Model has strategies to do this:

- *Share continuous improvement* – If you're not growing, you're dying, according to Missouri Model senior staff. Stakeholders gravitate to dynamism. It's great to have announcements of large successes, but they are infrequent and just momentarily persuasive. Successful persuasion is a continuous drumbeat. People want to know what is being done for them *today*. Far more compelling are the little wins along the way, which rightly foster the real mystique of success, so share how you are continuously improving (see the next bullet).

- *Develop constituency supporters by demonstrating outcomes.* – Your multi-dimensional, multi-sector constituents need to understand your program from the bottom up, according to Movement Model staff. Get your elected officials, including your general assembly member, to visit. Have a flyer handy. Attend county and city meetings, applicable social groups, and select non-governmental organizations. Include clients and families in what they are accomplishing by giving them the same printed material you're using to publicize the good news about program successes. Parents are one of your most impactful sources of cheerleading. Most important, make believers of staff by celebrating daily successes. The program has many and various levels of constituents, beginning with clients and families.

One of the continuing themes about developing any program that survives implementation is to cultivate multiple streams of revenue from perhaps municipal funds, Medicaid, private insurance, donations, and planned giving, to mention a few sources of revenue. Do not depend on only one or two sources of operational funding, especially grants, which are terminal and bothersome to manage. Furthermore, winning a grant is mostly a matter of luck! Plus, any grant comes with mighty strings attached.

> **Successful persuasion is a continuous drumbeat. People want to know what is being done for them *today*.**

In the case of these programs exemplified by the Missouri Model, they tap the monies that follow the population of youth targeted by aftercare.

Effective Practice

Have the money follow youth targeted by aftercare.

This effective practice seems simple, but it isn't, according to practitioners. Movement Models have been working on stabilizing funding for decades. The Missouri Model works to secure several major categories of funds for operations.

- *General assembly* – First, their general assembly contributes general revenues, even though this source is unpredictable due to the vicissitudes of an elected body and a volatile economy.

- *Medicaid* – Funds for direct treatment are a significant source of money.

- *Missouri DPI* – The program gets average daily attendance monies from the Missouri Department of Public Instruction, which credits schools for keeping children in class.

- *Property taxes* – The program bills local schools for services that are paid for from local property taxes.

- *USDA* – Federal departmental monies are the smallest streams, but some funds come from the U.S. Department of Agriculture for free and assisted breakfast and lunch, which helps pay for program subsistence.

- *Lottery* – A little assistance derives from gaming dollars, which come through the juvenile court diversion program.

- *Department of Juvenile Services* – These funds filter through the Schriver Center.

- *Foundations* – These are a source of a considerable percentage of operational means.

- *Volunteers* – A large Choice resource is not monetary but comes in the form of volunteers. Choice is purposefully located at the University of Maryland, Baltimore County campus to take advantage of the stream of AmeriCorps volunteers on whom the program relies. It gets a huge value added from these volunteers as service with Choice also trains a significant cadre of the next generation of social change agents.

Note that the above are formal agency agreements, probably forged over the years. Any single source can't cover expenses, but together they can. Note the length, width, and breadth of these sources. The advantage is they establish a history of funding and thus are somewhat stable and can sustain a program. A disadvantage is they need to be justified annually. Don't forget to consider the many other sources of dollars, such as donations, fundraisers, and events. The message is evident that, with creativity and persistence, any good idea well run and justified can develop funding streams. An annual bake sale, car wash, and raffle establish predictable funding streams given enough time.

Even with this impressive array of operational funding, constant vigilance is necessary to anticipate wild swings in amounts that reach the program. Raising money is a constant drain on personnel and progress because it leaves little time to work out processes and problem resolutions before the next budgetary cycle or crisis. Staff lament that what suffers most is implementation.

Leadership must truly agonize about accepting more responsibilities or expanding. Be prepared for the vagaries of funding and be flexible. When funding is cut, have staff cross-trained or moved to other functions or locations. In a worst-case scenario, staff are let go. The point here is to continuously sell what you are doing to your supporters. Aftercare is a struggle for money, yet a growing number of these programs last and flourish. Describing these models via capacity building captures how they are doing it. This idea for service is proven to work and be good, so be determined to make it work for you.

The interviews about funding during operations turned to the question of how to keep the long-term commitment you anticipated and promised in the planning stage. It's about doing a lot of little things the right way over many years. Concentrate on quality, genuineness, and credibility and be known for it. Credibility means that when, not if, something goes wrong, own it and set about creating a plan to correct it and make it better than before. You will be known for living your truth and be trusted.

The Missouri Model began in the early 1970s as a service to help struggling students get a GED, and it worked very well. They grew that reputation to what it is today, a statewide program with national implications. Multiply given resources by making sure processes are efficient and the program offers value for the investment of time, money, and resources—then deliver on promises. If you do well, senior staff observe, you will deliver more aftercare services and begin to close the services-to-needs gap, your vision all along.

13. Design Services That Emphasize Skills for Independent Living.

The heart of aftercare services is recognizing that young adults are not *yet* adults. The corollary to that is that they are on a path to maturity. The task, then, is to tactfully, firmly guide that process. Since we now have grounding in how to build a good program by planning it well and carrying out the plan, this section will describe the characteristics of services without listing specific services or research-based practices.

First, we begin with the programming. We recognize that troubled youth are not fully mature adults and admit to the need for a real change in their culture from one of delinquency and perhaps crime to one of strengths, potential, and determination to do and be better. Incrementally, much is possible. When seen from that perspective, the nature and purpose of programming and services become clearer. Services don't narrow to the hardest of cases but expand to accommodate the best of this target group.

Programming needs to be youth-centric by focusing on guiding youth to their potential and not systems-directed in which the tendency is to offer relatively short-term programs. This puts the emphasis beyond reentry and on true aftercare that lasts long after youth fulfill the requirements of the court.

Services then need to be aimed at resolving the effects of trauma and perhaps substance abuse, while building self-sufficiency skills based on natural resiliency and strengths. Youth also need pro-social connections in their communities and as much support from their families as possible. Families, in turn, may be ushered into therapy when they realize how they figured into the troubles of their children and further realize how they can make amends. Firsthand experience with these Movement Models reveals that expectations are high and standards are strict, with consequences when expectations aren't met. In fact, a client can be expelled from a program and returned to the criminal justice system. Relatively few are. Therefore, programming must be a continuum in which reentry isn't an end but prepares the teen for the real work of remaining independent. This is about reforming juvenile aftercare.[97]

The reform is summarized in emerging practices for juvenile reentry and aftercare services that do the following:[98]

- *Integrate science* – The juvenile brain is simply not fully developed until the mid-20s. That is a neurological fact. Cognitive therapies, such as the popular evidence-based practice of Cognitive Behavioral Therapy, work best for this population. This practice recognizes the primary function of the family in the transition process and the importance of pro-social connections to peers, school, and work.

- *Build strengths* – Each maturing young adult is a mix of risks, strengths, and potentialities. It's proving to be much more productive to focus on nurturing strengths than curing deficits. Intuitive! This also recognizes that

> Therapy, counseling, and medical/mental health treatments are not enough. You need to offer preparation for further education and training in employment skills as well.

the process of transition is much longer and complex than previously thought—way beyond reentry and through a lengthy aftercare. Intensive case management is advisable from the initial risk and resiliency assessment to individually designed therapies through post-program follow-up. Yes, this is outside what public agencies can provide. However, it's quite realistic when public agencies collaborate with local public and private providers.

- *Engage families* – Families and communities must be part of the solution, which usually means many families participate in their own therapy and follow their child's progress. Rebuilding becomes a family affair. Again, intuitive. This is another reform movement change in culture, from one where the offender alone was dealt with to one in which the family unit is encouraged to grow. From a problem to potentialities. It's most helpful if communities supply nurturing peer and adult relationships via mentors as part of specialized aftercare services.

- *Focus on the essentials of reentry* – Therapy, counseling, and medical/mental health treatments are not enough. You need to offer preparation for further education and training in employment skills as well. Housing providers, educators, and employers must also be part of the transitional team.

- *Support transition* – Maturing into an adult is ultimately an individual process. For troubled youth, this process arguably takes much longer. Experience demonstrates that high-needs youth largely need specialized and intensive guidance to mature. This is why reform models are gravitating to round-the-clock residential programming for small classes of clients. The newly independent youth learn to put down the roots of gainful employment, independent living, and family relationships. They need to be motivated to plan and work toward a successful future.

The importance of this strategy is growing as it appears to be more realistic and effective in keeping this target population on track and away from unproductive, anti-social, or criminal behavior. The Federal Office of Juvenile Justice and Delinquency Prevention (OJJDP) Model Programs Guide for aftercare makes the well-researched point that no protective supervision is statistically better than having protective supervision. In other words, the conventional model of parole is not as effective in reducing recidivism and encouraging productive behaviors as these new models of post-release programming. Prevention is always preferred. It's morally sound and makes eminent sense monetarily. So, the earlier the intervention in the chain of dysfunction or even criminality the better.

The OJJDP also makes the point that aftercare is still in an evolutionary, developmental phase. We need more understanding, especially about the application of evidence-based practices and how they fit with a program that rests on effective processes. Ultimately, we need to make the correct mix of individualized care more permanent by teaching the individual to seek, procure, and maintain their own array of supports. Successful independence is the very possible-to-reach goal. I will explain how to best do this kind of aftercare that's emerging from and being proven by reform Movement Models.

Effective Practice

Have the aftercare services continuum emphasize capability for independent living.

Prior to the reforms suggested by bottom-up community-based strengths versus top-down controlled aftercare, the continuum of care stressed justice system interventions. These include mainly sanctions, confinement, secure corrections, and weakly defined aftercare, all of which are largely a function of the criminal justice system. The basic flaw to this modality is that something has to go wrong for the system to act. The justice system doesn't consider prevention and intervention. These sanctions are arguably ponderous and expensive and have questionable results when compared to strengths-based action. Yet they were considered necessary to "handle" our difficult citizens, although most are just wayward. When sanctions or a sentence end, so does "aftercare," practically and functionally. Matching programming, therapy, and services can be highly effective, but it's unfair to ask our criminal justice system to create and administer programming to teach skills of adult independent living. Its mission and purpose are control oriented and punitive, and yes, society needs what it has designed these systems to do. However, this system must work with strengths-based programs as a follow-up in the chain of outcomes in youth development to adulthood.

The most intensive and lengthy programming is channeled toward the more serious, highest-risk offenders. Thus, these programs of extended aftercare stand to yield the highest return for effort and money expended when they break the cycle of criminal reoffending.[99] Aside from prescribing evidence-based therapies for the highest-risk youth to reduce recidivism, doubt is cast on the efficacy of institutional control of delinquent and crime-prone youth.

A publication of the Center for Juvenile Justice Reform presents a meta-analysis that enhances our understanding of preferable evidence-based practices.[100] This meta-analysis of 548 formally evaluated programs makes an excellent case for the types of reforms the Movement Models are practicing. The measure used of the effect of good aftercare was recidivism, an important measure to institutional officials but only an initial measure to determine programming efficacy seen in individual improvement. Still, it's a good start to begin a continuum of client-centered actionable results, as the following hints. Recidivism improved when:

> **Nurturing with expectations works much better than commanding change by implied or real threat.**

- *Resources were focused on the highest-risk, most troublesome youth.* – Initial screening for risk, strengths, and needs helped channel limited resources to where they would do the most good. Opposing that is the recognition that lower-risk youth don't need as many services nor for as long. Individual, detailed, concentrated case management matters. This is also true for individually designed case actions, which is better accomplished with local aftercare.

- *Therapy was emphasized over the control philosophy.* – Nurturing the natural tendency to desist from bad choices is more effective than trying to demand change. Indeed, skill building is better at reducing recidivism, and by extension, preparing for productive living, than scared straight programs, for example, delivered during incarceration. Nurturing with expectations works much better than commanding change by implied or real threat.

- *Generic and embedded programs together were more effective.* – Combine group settings with an evidence-based therapy for better results at modifying bad behavior. Small residential settings matter.

- *The amount and quality of services matter.* – Continuous, intense, case-managed attention is effective, and it must follow the child long after release from incarceration and court supervision. Contact hours delivering therapies as intended (fidelity) matter. Aftercare is the key to completing the work merely begun via reentry programs.

The authors of the publication for the Center for Juvenile Justice Reform[101] have described our reform Movement Models. The better programming is restorative, builds skills for independent adult living, and is based in proven counseling. It's best delivered in the community near the child's home and family by mustering multiple coordinated services. The implications are common sense:

- *Serve target populations.* – Target the most at-risk and delinquent populations of youngsters.

- *Emphasize personal development.* – Constructive personal development is highly productive at reforming misdirected youth.

- *Prove with evidence, evidence, evidence.* – Use evidence-based practices in nurturing settings.

- *Adhere to strict service delivery.* – Deliver services as intended with the proper duration and contact hours.

Essentially, match a risk-and-needs assessment with the appropriate duration of services guided by individual case management. In fact, this rational approach has been recognized formally since 1993 when James Howell proposed a Comprehensive Strategy for Serious, Violent, and Chronic Juvenile Offenders.[102] So what is taking so long? Resistance to change.[103]

Our entire approach to confronting juvenile delinquency and crime is singularly about a philosophy and a huge infrastructure based on institutionalized control. Careers are thus built. Careerists endure and rise with their ideas and ways. We should keep the institutions we've built, because some youngsters are just incorrigible. They need "the system." But the focus must incorporate these common-sense lessons we've learned.

Post-release is where healing and reconstructing a young deserving life begins. Therein is the thesis of this book: Bottom-up collaboration of public-private resources developed by building services delivery capacity holds the best chance to improve the lot of at-risk and most criminally involved youth.

The North Carolina Department of Public Safety Division of Juvenile Justice suggests Service Plan Protocols (see Figure 5, which follows). All suggestions for services assume the supporting programs are established and working well. This continuum of domains is an excellent context for developing individualized service combinations and a great framework for case management with emphasis on intensive aftercare[104] Furthermore, it serves as a general guide for capacity building by deciding on and understanding just what services an entity will provide. The staff can then work backward through all the critical features of planning to check and strengthen general program stability and continuance.

Figure 5. Service Plan Domains and Focus Areas[105]

Service Plan Domains	Focus Areas
Safety	Responses Stability of Youth's Environment
Personal Accountability	Reparation of Harm Personal Responsibility
Family Functioning	Home Environment Family Management
Health	Substance Use Mental Health Risky Behavior and Aggression Physical Health
Education/Vocation	School Behavior School Participation Vocational Development
Social Competency	Self-Management Interpersonal Skills Independent Living Skills
Support Network	Peer Relationships Adult Relationships and/or Community Ties Use of Free Time

The service mix for each juvenile begins with screening for needs, which leads to a service plan for which only the most essential focus areas should receive resources. Experience demonstrates that it's much better to deliver fewer but well conducted services rather than overwhelm the client and program capacity by being expansive. Less is more—again. Monitoring and evaluation are also built into the plan. Each focus area includes further details of how to go about building an individualized plan. The Protocol suggests data sources, goals, behaviors to modify, services, and measures to use. This type of intensive case management is critical.

Reform Movement Models demonstrate that case management ought to be redefined to emphasize transitional supports such as family, peers, and community, and especially skills for independence.[106] This implies the dovetailing of court supervised systemic services and post-release community sponsorship of the newly autonomous young adult. This is critical and is actually an extension of our major institutional services, as it will ultimately determine the success of the emerging adult. Transition has been defined in terms of reintegration from the criminal justice system to the community[107] as the youngster transitions from a control to a strengths-based, nurturing environment.

Only the most essential focus areas should receive resources.

- *The Services* – Services need to be comprehensive, continuous, integrated, coordinated, and *client centered*. The ideal service should be evidence-based, active, problem/goal purposed, and measurable, and effect rather rapid behavioral change (OJJDP Model Programs Guide).

- *The System* – The system of services and their delivery should be based on mutual respect between institutional and community-based services, with shared accountability and responsibility.

- *The Family* – The family unit must be materially involved in defining and assisting with their child's process of rebuilding and perhaps seek their own therapies as well. First, they must be helped to recognize the failings of their family unit, how they are complicit, and naturally, how they can work to become better.

- *Outcomes* – Action should be outcomes-based and defined in terms of measurable cost-effective benefits to the individual, the family, and the community. This takes measurement way beyond charting recidivism.

- *The Problems* – Problems are viewed as opportunities for inventive resolution, not as obstacles presented by the delinquent that must be controlled and reformed.

These characteristics of reintegration point us in the correct direction to community-based services and supports of permanent community and family assimilation.[108] The highest-risk juveniles are best prioritized, so all youth coming into the criminal justice system require risk assessment for the entirety of aftercare to work.[109] It's the right thing to do, and it's the overriding necessity to conserve limited resources, especially time, human resources, and money.

Risk assessment determines the chances of further criminality and thus more accurate programming possibilities.[110] These possibilities need to be defined by emphasizing first the youth then family and community and determining how to measure/monitor progress on the prescribed path for all concerned. It's necessary to blend with court supervision, which comes with sanctions and enforcement. Relatively few are incorrigible and need a firm hand. However, treatment and service selection and provision are redefined to emphasize the development of mental attitude, behavioral maturity, skills, and support for independent, productive, and fulfilling living.

This further implies that the criminal justice system and its professionals should modify their responsibilities to be brokers of the community-based means of independent living. While this sounds good, it's more than that. It's not naïve to obstacles that are a constant blight to this nascent idea of true aftercare. After all, this idea is a radical change from thinking about and carrying out punishment that has evolved over centuries to its present state.

Experience demonstrates that obstacles to this relatively new thinking about aftercare also present solutions. These solutions reflect some of the character of the cultural change that must occur for post-release services to develop at all. The public system of services is not set up for intensive aftercare. Funding has been limited even before the historic austerity of recent years, which promises to continue as the new economic reality. Staff are loaded with cases, most times to a ridiculous degree, at the sacrifice of needed individual attention. Just who oversees aftercare has not been firmly established. We have as many different takes on what these services should be as we have locations attempting this new model. Logistics, that is assembling all the relevant people, material, supplies, office space, and business infrastructure, plays a part—or at least the lack of it does.

We still have too many centrally located facilities, even though research suggests that small, local residential facilities are far more rehabilitative and cost effective. Monitoring progress is difficult, thus the systems and automation for case management need to be in place. This leaves aftercare providers to navigate untested waters. Aftercare providers as they stand now may not be involved throughout the process as they should be. They need to be involved from the outset. Likewise, it's tough to accomplish the detailed coordination of aftercare while the young adult is under court supervision. Ideally, coordination between the institution and the community should begin at intake and continue for perhaps years, as the young adult and the metamorphosed adult who rises from these programs may remain at risk for years. The same holds true for the family, with a different set of difficulties, as historically, the family has barely been involved.

Movement Models naturally have a unique take on lifting a fully functioning youth from a bad start and bad choices. Most models focus on consistency by keeping the same case manager throughout the whole process of aftercare. They also have multiple separate treatment programs from which the family unit chooses and tailors programming and services to their needs. This begins the real bottom-up partnership so vital for long-term success.

VQ has a Youth Services Advisory Board and Choice has Intensive Advocacy Teams, both data driven, to ensure that youth and their families have a say in their treatment regimen. The Missouri Model, for example, tries to put a conduit for life-long services in place well beyond aftercare. Now that's forward thinking! This is a take on imbuing youth with the skills to pursue and preserve their own means to independence.

Reform aftercare assumes the family unit is equipped for success; blame never enters the equation in these Movement Models. The mechanics of this is their handbook/workbook, which is a self-help comprehensive guide to aftercare for independent living and even community leadership, geared to the family unit. Further, this is a great statement of what Capacity Building does no matter the local service. The practitioners exemplified by the Missouri Model are focused to obsession on honing the *processes* of program operation, as they have discovered by difficult failure that implementation is where good ideas usually go to die.

Cultural change, meaning overcoming inertia, will take a lot of time, perhaps decades, before intensive juvenile aftercare realizes its promise. We have a natural institutional resistance to it and continuous diversion of funds for other "priorities." Promoting and facilitating cultural change is the job of reform, which now has a strong beginning in science and especially in practice. It's staff, the last critical capacity-building feature, who make aftercare happen.

14. Motivate Key Staff Intrinsically and Plan Personnel Succession.

The structure for creating a team of believers is designed during planning. Vision, mission, and values guide the search, selection, onboarding, and career development plans for this, the life blood of reform aftercare. Leaders, according to VQ executives, realize that maintaining a high level of training is exceedingly difficult and thus will need constant, concentrated, consistent, creative leadership, time, and single-mindedness. Planning ensures a multi-step staff vetting process. It also ensures that your organization is as hierarchically *flat* as possible by minimizing levels of supervision and leadership and as *lean* as practicable by having a productive, qualified workforce. Choice, for example, has just three levels of oversight, with three individuals at the top, two middle managers, and line service coordinators. Each level has specific duties to prod just a bit—the work with AmeriCorps volunteers.

Staff are paramount. They are cross-trained, for example. All program staff work in various capacities with their AmeriCorps charges. They deliver their successful brand of intensive advocacy, which is another example of congruency of purpose and execution. Ideally, program staff search, vet, and hire to retain employees, are in tune with employee wants and needs, and strive to deliver a superior work environment.[111] Operationalizing staffing is creating a workplace where challenge is part of the rewards of success. Those successes are celebrated by the team. Each member is guided to value their collective and individual contributions by constant feedback about each staffer's performance and project accomplishments. Engendering a sense of true belonging is paramount. Happily, in the public sector, progressive career development and meaningful work can be made to replace the flashier environments of notable private workplaces.

> A near-magical moment happens when the team realizes that the whole is greater than the sum of its parts, and they are integral to something worth doing.

Again, one of the enduring themes of Capacity Building is this: A near-magical moment happens when the team realizes that the whole is greater than the sum of its parts, and they are integral to something worth doing. People want to be involved in public service, and much more so with an organization that sees, develops, and encourages a collaborative team doing big and valuable things. Quitting time comes quickly, and morning can't come soon enough.

Operationalizing staffing is twofold work: first, create a workplace where people feel valued, and second, grow and perpetuate the working body of employees. You must create follower leaders. Workforce stability is a constant concern, so succession planning is a big part of operations. Ideally, as witnessed in Movement Models, expansion will happen, especially as this new brand of aftercare begins to proliferate.

The literature takes a rather simpler view of how to staff these specialized service ideas. It narrowly focuses on what it takes to man attendant services instead of also developing employees to produce program performance, stability, and growth. Thus, the body of knowledge is largely given to attracting and training the people who deliver services, in particular evidence-based practices rather than staff who can also broker services. What about the armies of people it takes to run the program? These support people need to be trained, guided, and developed to be competent and confident enough to respond both collectively and independently to the vision and mission. These are some of the broker roles.

Staff at each one of these Movement Models work especially hard at creating a learning/teaching environment where skills are constantly being tweaked, according to a Choice program executive. You can't assume that initial training and perhaps the occasional conference are all you need, as in many top-down approaches. Training, education, and professional development are comprehensive, cumulative, and continuous. Knowledge is rightly a grail. As said by the Missouri Model chief executive, the employees who endure do so because they're qualified and want to be part of a movement. They feel they're part of a family. They enjoy the camaraderie; they like the work and the people that surround them, and they feel a kinship with blossoming young adults.

Excitement at and with work is more meaningful to these people than a splendid private salary with perks.[112] Since compensation can't be controlled in the public sector, the working environment needs to help motivate and keep good people. It's been noted that the following benefits keep an employee at the job:[113]

- Career development
- Exciting, challenging work
- Work that truly makes a difference
- Great co-workers
- Being part of a team
- Having a great boss
- Having fun at work

- Feeling autonomous and in control
- Flexible working hours and other policies (e.g., dress code)
- Compensation package that's fair and competitive
- Inspiring leadership

It's all about staff who actualize by doing something worthy.

Notice these are vital intangibles much, much beyond a paycheck and health benefits. It's telling that career development is given as the top priority. This list is most reassuring because Movement programs work on each of these factors of program growth and prosperity while emphasizing that aftercare work is a good career. It's encouraging that it's not about the money if the work offers a living wage with reasonable benefits; it's all about staff who actualize by doing something worthy. Note: My observation of numerous successful local service projects over more than 20 years indicates this kind of leadership is often closer to the top of the list of sought-after work dynamics than the bottom. Line-level staff know that they lead also.

Effective Practice
Create a workplace to tap intrinsic motivation.

Staffing is the primary concern of Movement Models. Little can be done without the right people, and little compared to the potential is what's often done in most public endeavors. I have sat in on many job interviews during which the interviewer, the "boss," did most if not all of the talking, and we never got to know the applicant.

The Missouri Model combines continuous competency-based training and professional development, which flows throughout the organization. The Missouri director said that human capacity development, not "human resources," is seen as a lifestyle. It defines who staff want to be collectively and individually on the path to that ideal of professional and, more importantly, personal growth. Leadership want staff to be similarly successful during and after the workday. This staff development is aligned with beliefs and policies aimed at implementing, strengthening, and perpetuating the Missouri Model. They steer away from the one-time workshop, class, or conference. This is a holistic approach that honors mission values while equipping staff for the job in which the focus is always the young adult seen through competent, caring, yet strong eyes. Any training experience needs to contribute to building the competent employee, if not the whole person.

Embracing this philosophy of human *capacity* development means practicing leadership by example, from the bottom up. Two aspects apply: When something goes right, ask, "What did I do to bring this about?" and capitalize on it. Seeing and understanding what works sets up the next, quintessential question, which is much more important in moving an idea forward. When things go wrong, ask, "What did I do to cause this?" If you ask this question again and again, you'll find you're at the tangled roots of the issue. Accept the fact, sometimes publicly but certainly humbly, and make real changes in yourself before you change others or the system. Why is it that something this obvious, this essential, this effective is so difficult to accomplish?! But it is done by our best leaders. This topic of leadership by example needs to take up a large space on your bookshelf; biographies of the greats will shape and improve you. The greatest among us are the most humble and introspective. Yet not meek, not timid. Just how do these people lead by example in our model of capacity building local service ideas?

Top executives recognize that things get done at the line level. They attend the same training and learn from the same professional development experiences as line staff. Then they use experiences to help develop on-the-job expertise, sell programs, and discuss program development, especially implementation. The first rule of good leadership is demonstrating humility and introspection with integrity.

Leadership in these exemplary programs is congruent. What you see is what you get. Those in positions of authority say what they mean, do what they say, and are believable. Duties and responsibilities are constantly refined for the job, with regular input from evaluations and performance data. When someone transitions to a new project or job, new expectations are written for any new approaches. Plenty of cross-training duties are also written in job descriptions. People rotate in and out of other tasks and jobs or even to other locations, wherever the need may be. This builds model integrity, individual confidence, and competence. The whole operation is in a continuous state of strengthening. The last thing staff in general and especially senior staff want to hear is, "It's not my job." In high functioning, high performing local services, this is just not heard. The next model of public services implementation demonstrates that performance-enhancing teamwork succeeds. It's very doable, necessary, and worth the work as it becomes institutionalized rapidly. The correct work about the correct vision is self-fulfilling; it is simply a matter of building the habit of excellence. The high performance transformational coaching model[114] is the Missouri Model centerpiece training modality. It describes reform Movement Models. These simple-to-state, vital-to-establish principles include the following:

- *Set expectations high.* – Expectations are indeed high. In many cases, they're just a little excitingly, motivationally out of reach enough to be a genuine challenge and worthy of noting when achieved. Celebrations of achievement are meaningful and thus fulfilling and communally self-perpetuating. Staff take care not to overshoot a vision, mission, or goal by inflating it for effect, as those attempts are stillborn. Care is also taken to match truly inspirational, involved leadership with challenges. These challenges compel collaboration of talents and intentions.

- *Establish a learning environment.* – An environment of discussion-critique-action-discussion encourages continuous learning where people are supported and act free from acrimony if they fail. Again, it's the virtuous cycle of top-down, bottom-up, and top-down in an upward trajectory of continuous betterment. Decisions are collective, then decisive by leadership, as only action proves the viability of an idea and how to persist, modify, or ax it. The most adroit leaders also encourage personal development focused on reading, study, and personal growth.

- *Take the time to get to know one another.* – Staff take time to get to know one another as individuals. Building a working, synergistic, energized community requires true teambuilding, which does not degenerate to an easy afternoon off.

- *Develop mutual appreciation for fellow staff.* – Staff work on understanding one another's jobs to be able to step in when needed. They offer timely, accurate, kind, necessary, and mutually appreciated critique focused on performance, not personalities. They critique the system and how to improve it.

This environment of nurturing the potential of staff characterizes Movement Model staff development. It's marked by leadership that takes time, and plenty of it, to be with fellow staff and deliberately train and encourage team members to be better. It also works for Choice, where AmeriCorps service is limited to three years. Every year a new cohort cycles in as the old one moves on to seek a permanent career. Human capacity development must be paramount. A bit of magic materializes when it's working right.

There emerges an environment of mutuality, sharing, and caring where "each one teaches one," which was also observed in model *adult* aftercare programs. Everything is intentional because there's not a moment to spare in the juvenile aftercare business. Naturally, human capacity development, differentiated again from human resources management, is based on a stream of good information. This perspective belongs to the organization, not to another department.

What is one of the foundational aspects of this seemingly illusive, productive, challenging, and rewarding workplace? Data! Yes, you can measure behavior quantitatively and especially qualitatively. Part of knowing the work is valuable is to get constant feedback about how everyone is doing and how the project is returning youngsters to a worthy life. According to a site director, records and data at these sites are constantly being input and tallied, all aimed at strengthening the team, shaping skills, and facilitating meaningful change.

These Movement programs have regular, even daily, meetings to get updates and feedback on work while it's still "hot" and resolve impediments, thus making progress palpable. New hires are on-boarded with the intention of making them immediately part of the common cause. Senior people, perhaps founding members, constantly mentor and take the many teachable moments in a day to improve the simple things. Missouri Model senior staff have gone away from traditional top-down individual teaching by modules to train bottom-up as a team where they can try out real-world scenarios. I observed one case where a lead staffer did impromptu role reversals, asking even entry-level people fresh out of college how they would handle a real executive action—past or yet to come.

Employees, partners really, are made to feel they do have a say in their destiny at work and by extension in their personal lives. I observed real ownership and mutual care at these sites. Every effort is made to offer a decent wage. And as always, people have fun. Many meetings begin with light, witty but intimate repartee that strengthens working bonds, which quickly become meaningful friendships. This lays the foundation for taming turnover and succession planning.

Effective Practice

Tame turnover by managing employee and leadership succession.

Staff stability is a creature of planning. Staff are groomed for and by the program. Further, in the Choice program, AmeriCorps volunteers are shaped as future public servant-citizens by emphasizing their strengths as the next generation of change agents wherever their careers may take them. This strengths-based approach to staff development is an emphatic statement of programs that are congruent in their emphasis on nurturing. This mix of nurturing and high expectations with a positive philosophy of the human condition are highly motivational. So much so that in growing numbers, troubled youth do achieve productive, responsible, rewarding adulthood. Plus, the AmeriCorps staff, not much older than the clients they serve, grow as adults by understanding the worth of serving.

Note also that this current cohort of change agents will live routinely to be 100! Still vital and vigorous, age appropriately. Imagine their lives well lived with consequence into the next century! This work then becomes intergenerational with young lives, both staff and charges.

Witness the young adults who transition successfully, and AmeriCorps volunteers go on to significant careers as doctors, lawyers, and business owners or perhaps careers in the military. Who knows? What a great example for how to tap youthful energy, creativity, and intrinsic motivation.

Here we can take lessons from the private sector. A study of best-practice organizations revealed that the most successful succession planning has the following characteristics and application in the aftercare environment.[115] Note that "succession" planning is for the sustainability of the program and for young adults who progress to meaningful, productive careers. Human capacity development at a well-working, performance-oriented local service organization can be characterized as follows:

- *Simple* – Concentrate on building a well-working program that engenders pride. Then have a career development plan for everyone. This plan can outline skills training, formal classroom education, or the pursuit of a degree and professional development by attending conferences and workshops. Don't forget the vital pursuit of personal well-being. Some managers are fearful of training people to move on, but that is just what an enlightened leader wants. This means that working in a capacity-built service has upward mobility and thus attracts better candidates and keeps them.

- *Process oriented* – Underpinning the stories of success are well-run processes that handle intake of incoming clients, prescribe their plan of action, and anticipate after-program care. Clients receive assigned mentors. Staff need to know through their clients that they are accomplishing personal and programmatic goals. They are imbued with a feeling of purpose in a day spent with a client.

- *Defined in an overall strategy* – Succession, that is readying staff for increased responsibilities and longevity, must be specifically defined as a fundamental part of the program. The goal should be growth as a whole person on and off the job. Be realistic. Succession planning is not for senior executive positions. It's for entry level line staff to progress to the next and subsequent levels. The attitude is that career progression is linked to progressing in life.

- *Has senior leadership support* – Senior program people must live employee development by monitoring and fully supporting staff growth. This means monitoring the progression of individual and collective education, training, and professional development with on-the-job training.

The lesson from Movement Models is that succession planning does not emerge easily or fully formed. The best example of this is VQ, which began with the founder and 14 troubled youth to what it is today: a large, formal firm with residential campuses and hundreds of employees nationwide. This took decades, and it began with the vision to do so.

Many startup ideas begin with a burst of possibilities then dwindle. There seems to be little time for these very long-term nearly-out-of-context issues of capacity building and systems reform. Getting through the work of the day is all consuming, there's little time to anticipate what the future can be; and the stream of referrals is never ending. But senior staff encouraged the long-term focus and aggressive pursuit of personalized plans of staff and future leaders, usually with the backing of a board of directors. They coached and mentored them and gave them a chance to work on challenging projects.[116] It's not uncommon to see staff with decades of experience in this field and in these programs who were encouraged every inch of the way.

So far, the discussion has been about the intangibles of creating an intrinsically motivating workplace. Also consider some of the mechanics of stabilizing staff in their jobs to reduce turnover.

The mechanics, the infrastructure, of staffing, that follows the philosophy of nurturing human capacity are the documents and policies that define and perpetuate how this critical feature is carried out. These programs are big on developing, codifying, and regularly revisiting standard operational procedures that detail such things as how the new hire is made part of the team. This is way beyond "onboarding." Ideally, each new employee is assigned a mentor and gets a detailed personal and professional development plan. Each has a detailed explanation of duties, responsibilities, and expectations so they can see how they fit within the organization and their meaningful contributions to it. Everyone's job description is periodically updated, which is necessitated by the dynamic nature of what is being done. When someone labors on a new responsibility, the road traveled is ordered, although augmented by informally documenting what's done and how it's done. Training is intimately connected to getting implementation right.

Senior staff work all the shifts to truly know how training is or is not effective. Multi-tasking is commonplace; these programs could not survive if people were pure specialists. It's not uncommon, for example, for a Reclaiming Futures executive director to also be a therapist, to help screen candidates, and make home visits. As part of human capacity development, Missouri Model staff are encouraged to develop relationships with the courts, neighbors, and partners. Leadership is chronically dissatisfied in a way that's constructive. Challenges are energizing. Could this be the creative destruction hailed by our captains of industry? Staff are imbued with this restlessness to be their best and thus do more for the common good. The people observed at these Movement sites are not mere caretakers of an unearned bequest; they know they are involved in a higher calling.

> **Senior staff work all the shifts to truly know how training is or is not effective.**

15. Plan Facilities, Recordkeeping, Automation, and Marketing.

Site interviews concluded with discussions on the infrastructure and business capacity of delivering services unique to juvenile aftercare. Processes need infrastructure beyond vision and policy. This includes, for example, facilities, logistics, recordkeeping, automation, communication channels, and marketing. Reclaiming Futures puts facilities in the community, available for the client in a family unit. One of the most striking findings from the Movement Models is that centrally located control-oriented facilities don't work as well as small local facilities for most youth who are in the critical initial process of desisting from bad behaviors. Simply, centrally located facilities are top-down, control oriented, distanced, and impersonal, which makes it difficult to connect with youth as intensively as needed to change behaviors enough to begin the work of transitioning to independence.

Most dramatically, the Missouri Model closed its old-style reform schools and built, rebuilt, or leased small, local, homey places where they could focus on unique client therapeutic development for independent adult living. These homes away from home are very presentable dormitories with nicely decorated and appointed living rooms, high quality classrooms, and bright colors. They created a warm and friendly yet structured environment. Many times, this is the best, and often the only, physically supportive environment these struggling youngsters have known. Facilities managers keep the dorms lively, fresh, and inspirational by decorating the walls with art done by clients. The sofas are made of comfortable fabric, not plastic. Group work happens in a shared space only after a youth's room is cleaned and organized, ready for inspection by staff—and their mom when she drops by.

What a change from a few square feet of cement block walls and a WWII era barracks-style bed usually associated with a central facility. This philosophy of building a homey, strengths-based, nurturing place is shared by all Movement Models. It's especially true of VQ, which has a similarly appointed main campus and burgeoning sites around the country. Staff office space is minimized to save money and send the message that the goal is supporting services and being with clients.

Recordkeeping systems maintain consistency, according to many of those interviewed. While these data automation systems are not up to the minute, the latest versions of hardware and software, they are quite functional and growing in sophistication. They address needs for keeping base records, including the historical and demographic information that describe clients, staff development through training, performance and process data, and support tools. Those support tools are the documentation that operationalizes the processes and fidelity standards of evidence-based practices. These are the records that impact core practices, according to the director of the Missouri Model.

Their automation focuses on the classroom to supplement learning, which is technologically rich. This further emphasizes the correct priority of limited resources to the client served. They even experiment with tele-psychiatry where, if appropriate face-to-face contact isn't feasible, the medical professional is transported electronically to the client at the dormitory. Automation also allows a surprising amount of teleconferencing and training, such as onsite webinars. This keeps staff from having to travel to training as frequently. Subsequently, they have more time to focus on everyone in every cohort of students. Reports are automated with as much real-time data as possible to track, such as client length of stay, year-on-year graphs of production and performance numbers, charted trends to mark individual and program progress or lack thereof, and benchmark tracking of teachers. VQ even has real-time documentation during the counseling or group experience. It's not a monthly recounting of a few data points but real time data that's quite usable. Staff have plenty of time to do it because it's built into the model; it's a habit. These programs are following advancements in electronics that make efficiency and effectiveness dynamic, ever improving. Communication is just as vital.

Each one of the Movement Models had established lines of communication that enable information to move up, down, and up again in the organizational structure.

This is one of the mechanics of dynamic, action-oriented, practical use of information for informed decision making and programming.

Take the Missouri Model, for example. Communication is essential also to marketing, because it sells sincere hope for better futures grounded in a program with a history of meaningful success, decades in the making. The advisory board, community liaisons, and local staff focus on advancing the program and getting referrals. Videos are produced for specific engagements. Any materials aimed at third parties, perhaps local businesses that have an interest in aftercare, are transparent and data rich. They have flyers for any occasion and seek information distribution opportunities whenever possible. The article "Metamorphosis: How Missouri Rehabilitates Juvenile Offenders" by Jennifer Dubin is genuinely splendid and would be worth a momentary detour from this reading.[117] She explains in detail how attending to the root causes of delinquency help wayward youth to become a vital part of community, where they contribute well to schools, home, and the neighborhood. The message here is that these programs are quite forward thinking. A productive child influences others and their children and so on.

Naturally, the closure of interviews brought much reflection and introspection.

16. Recognize the Triumphs and Trials and the Necessity of Perseverance.

The good news is it seems that aftercare as the vital continuation of reentry is gaining recognition. The bad news is aftercare is gaining recognition. This is how the Models for Change executive in charge of evidence-based practices used this dichotomy to begin his introspection of program operations.

The bottom-up, strengths-based and community-focused model for aftercare is significantly beyond theory and is proliferating, with decades of bruises and lumps to validate the Movement. Now, what is to be done about it? The Movement will accelerate its success even more at the pivotal moment when the people in our public service agencies realize their purpose. That purpose is to support community capacity and individual independence and not assume responsibility for doling out a brand of services they think are needed for inadequate, terminal dollars. With that realization, which comes from reason and witnessing the success of a new way of doing things—these Models begin to change the system. They will do this by changing not the *what* but the *how* of their business—from control to brokering services defined by community need. The correct answer to *how* compels action. People in our agencies, systems, and the therapeutic communities are part of the solution, which takes the long view of building the aftercare idea to stability then proliferating it.

Program staff comment that bottom-up must work before top-down *can* work.

Experience illuminates a few ways of seeing operations through to stability. An agency cannot do this kind of reform without repurposing itself. It needs to support the local effort and learn to suggest to the community what it needs, what it should do, or what it should be and, again—how to do it. Aftercare staff have a unique leadership role by being able to best improve the problem of post-release juveniles, which bedevils nearly every locality. Program staff comment that bottom-up must work before top-down *can* work. In other words, reform happens by building effective practices, evidence-based processes, standards of programming fidelity, policy statements in and with the community in mind, and with the client as paramount. It also requires redirecting funding away from the control model to bottom-up, local capacity-built aftercare to get it all done.

Let's review some key elements of this overall approach to effective aftercare.

- *Measurement* – Make sure you measure what you want to accomplish. What you measure will be institutionalized. This implies that essentials of processes are evaluated to a fine degree. What you're measuring is the child's capacity, and to some extent the family unit's, to be productive, not just to stay out of trouble or simply to graduate or stay out of the criminal justice system. These are, at best, only an immediate measure of effect. They need to be connected to long-term success at independent living, permanently released from public support services.

- *Growth* – Meaningful growth happens at the grassroots level. The best champions of this work are the staff in direct contact with young clients. They drive the organization. Principles of reform should be exemplified, taught, and measured at the community level. Theory must result in practice. Growth also means that attitudes about young people change from one where they are trouble to be dealt with to individuals who have good intentions for themselves and others and just need a little guidance at a critical time.

- *Feedback* – Inculcating new ideas and processes takes constant communication up and down the organization and back again. No productive detail is too insignificant; meaning and implication for action exist in every little discovery about what works.

- *Brokering* – People involved in working with delinquent youth, especially those in our criminal justice system, need to be agents of change. They need to broker a range of aftercare-pertinent services instead of merely decreeing one or two top-down orders. Parole officers, for example, can learn to be mentors. They can become competent in evidenced-based practices such as motivational interviewing techniques. They need to catch young adults doing something *good* to reward rather than looking for reasons to reprove, revoke, and remand them. The suggested reform from surveillance to strengths-based behavioral modification will uplevel our institutional response to juvenile delinquency, criminalization, and crime. It will transform provider services from those usually associated with agencies and control to collaborating with those services that build life skills. The strengths-based approach is a critical part of an overall municipal strategy to address reentry because it's largely preventive. This strategy must be a continuum of services that extend way beyond release from dependency on public resources, especially the criminal justice system.

- *Taking it slow* – Note that growth is small and incremental over a long time. Cultural change takes more training, skills, and procedural modification than can happen via a proclamation and a prescribed annual conference. Change is about going slow to be able to go fast, as one insightful practitioner put it. People do, after all, usually want to improve. The long trek is painful, but the legacy is enduring.

- *Roles* – Reform cannot happen in a vacuum. Know who your cheerleaders are and who needs to have a say or just needs a friendly prod to make that annual donation. A critical role for leadership is to keep staff from getting distracted by the crisis of the moment and focus on high impact and strategic activity no matter how much the phone yammers.

- *Flexibility* – Rigidity of the kind experienced in bureaucracies hamstrings any reform effort. Practitioners must be supported in their struggles and permitted their vital stumbles that illuminate necessary adjustments and the way forward.

- *Fun* – This work is marked by a sense of productive playfulness. Oh yes, it's deadly serious work; but rarely do staff at any level miss an opportunity to laugh. The Choice program schedules semi-annual "play-work" training, where the order of the day is to learn to have fun at work. They have summertime "Choice Day," when teams compete on the sporting field, and quarterly "Reflections" on service experiences. "The glass is always half full" is a familiar refrain.

Social transformation is about doing things right and engaging clients in the treatment process. These models are the *only* long-term conduit to services for this target population, and rightly so. Movement reform is changing the culture of dependency to one of independence, where service providers, family, and community share responsibility for young people. This is the capability effect where a common goal musters talent and resources to achieve more than thought possible. Punishment is a very last resort for a recalcitrant few. Professionals in our systems are seeing there is a better way.

Practitioners are making strengths-based aftercare work. This is good for so many reasons but most of all to Model success. People in the community have been searching for a way to reconnect with their misguided children. Young adults want to be productively involved. In transforming themselves, a client and family can transform their little piece of the neighborhood. A successful youngster is an intergenerational triumph. Any intervention is only the beginning in the life of a child and their family, insightfully stated by the Missouri Model chief executive. A life-long virtuous cycle begins when ties to these programs formally end. Ultimately, this social transformation will result in ending suspicions that most of our youth are discipline problems that must be dealt with and not the individuals with potential that they are.

These pages are deservedly sanguine about this new take on aftercare, so it's appropriate to take a moment to reflect on reality. Any plan can be stopped in its tracks by a critical word from a well-placed doubter at the presentation of the idea. Imagine the devastating

> **In transforming themselves, a client and family can transform their little piece of the neighborhood.**

effect of potential lost. Yes, these programs are changing the world of juvenile reentry and aftercare—but it takes its toll. Between the satisfaction and smiles of making a real difference lurk frustration, disappointment, exhaustion, and burnout.

As the interviews progressed to deeper and deeper layers of how these programs came about and function, respondents told of resistance that came from all quarters— public, private, and private nonprofit sectors. Some came from people who it seemed said no just because they could. Control is comfortable: People don't want to let go of the way things are. There's no lack of nitpickers to attack this work because it threatens their status quo or even shows their own view of taming juvenile misbehavior is questionable. Woe to the program that suffers a setback to give these critics ammunition. Still, the practitioners in these reform Models convinced doubters that the Movement is the way to return wayward youth to fulfillment. Aftercare practitioners told of 50 percent staff turnover or having to release people who couldn't transition from top-down control to bottom-up strengths-based behavior modification. Some demanded training that threatened the existence of a program. But loyal staff still found or convinced just enough people who are passionate about youth and motivated by the mission to make halting progress to significance and permanency. Yes, the road to the current successes of juvenile post-release aftercare has and will continue to be difficult. Tenacity matters in this work.

> These aftercare visionaries are proving they must be revolutionary before they can be evolutionary.

Other fundamental difficulties need to be worked out during operations as well. Evidence-based practices are devilish because they don't automatically transfer from site to site well. Yes, the idea and the process of capacity building transfers, but each locale is maddeningly, wonderfully unique. Still, program staff stuck with the concepts until these ideas and practices worked as designed and proven. VQ, for example, was prepared to lose money for months until *their* reform idea began to work. Notice the concept of a strengths-based theme is universal and yet VQ made it theirs.

Communication is complicated. How do these organizations make sure messages are clear, concise, and convincing with the sender's intention, especially when the organization is far flung, whether across town or on the other side of the nation? These aftercare visionaries are proving they must be revolutionary before they can be evolutionary. There have been budget shortfalls that led to mass dismissals of staff who still became friends. No one wants to take a chance on something that challenges the status quo. But program leaders convinced just a few who would. In the end, observes the Missouri Model director, Movement program staff have faith that significant systems reform is happening and will continue to happen.

Well, you have planned with intention, and you have operations up and running. Leaders are engaged with clients and the citizenry. Staff have a good understanding of readiness capacity that's cost effective. Scope creep is under control. Evaluation and analysis guide program operations and services delivery. You've garnered steady streams of funding. Services are geared to teaching the skills of independent living.

Key staff are intrinsically motivated. Your program should feel somewhat stable except for the worthy discontent that there must be more. You're ready to expand to begin to close the services-to-needs gap locally and by penetrating other locations. This is what you've been working to achieve. Now it's time to consider Phase III of the program's life cycle: Sustainability and Expansion.

Chapter 4

LIFE CYCLE PHASE III – SUSTAIN AND EXPAND

Chapter 4

LIFE CYCLE PHASE III – SUSTAIN AND EXPAND

The truth of the matter is that you always know the right thing to do.
The hard part is doing it.
– H. Norman Schwarzkopf

This chapter begins the discussion of the real task of systems reform. Your idea is no longer an ethereal concept or something you heard about at a conference; it's brick and mortar, built to last. It's staffed by committed and trained people who are inspired and inspiring. Policies and procedures are documented, efficient, effective, and enduring. Now you can begin to close your services-to-needs gap.

Realizing Juvenile Aftercare

Your idea is established as part of the array of municipal services as a day program, a residential program, or both. You are now seeing the fruits of a good reentry-aftercare effort. Graduates are independent, even wholesome, young adults making good decisions and beginning to make their way as good citizens. Cultural change in your local public agencies is beginning to take root; people in the top-down systems are becoming bottom up. They're beginning to broker services and encourage the sensibility of intensive therapy in a home-like setting in the community. There, wayward youth have the guidance and freedom to reinvent themselves and become productive with the possibility of designing a happy life.

Why is this phase of the project life cycle—sustain and expand—so important? Because it's the most difficult and most *promising* era in the life of your idea. It's when you begin to make a real difference—when you begin to reform the system, the community, and the individual. But along with the hope and promise, we must interject a dose of realism.

The objections to anything this new are shrill. Our institutions and the genuinely valuable services they provide come with their prejudices and cultures that have taken decades to evolve. People have made huge investments in dollars and reputations in keeping things just as they are or by trying to do reentry without extensive aftercare—their way. However, what this reform philosophy of tough nurturing suggests is not a complete change to our systems. Rather, it suggests a recognition that the best juvenile aftercare is accomplished collaboratively, as proven by the programs highlighted in these pages.

Take comfort in the fact that this path to a new way of approaching juvenile reentry-aftercare has been paved. A big part of expanding your idea will be continuing to persuade the people involved in your local criminal justice system and social services agencies that nurturing aftercare is *not* another soft-on-crime experiment. It's *anything but that.* These programs are more regimented and demanding than a prison regimen! It's not uncommon for a program attendee to elect to go back to incarceration to finish a sentence rather than complete one of these aftercare programs.

VQ and the Missouri Model, for example, demonstrate that most difficult juveniles in the programs can eschew mischief, crime, and drugs and make good choices; the criminal justice system, however, tends to enable youth to continue delinquent or criminal ways. But let's be fair. Our criminal justice system is necessary for the more incorrigible, serious, or violent offenders. The system is vital to our way of life and is doing just what it's designed to do—keep law and order and carry out a sentence. Neither our systems nor the community can go it alone; we must have collaboration!

To be clear, in this reformed system, there's no top-down alone; there's no community struggling to develop adequate and quality services alone. It involves collective, mutual decision making and resource allocation *and* the clients and their families taking responsibility for their actions and future. As witnessed at these Movement sites, the whole of reentry-aftercare accomplished with networked matrix services is measurably greater than the sum of its parts. This can be seen by reliably plummeting recidivism rates and troubled youths turning themselves around. Still, these programs struggle when they shouldn't have to struggle.

Naysayers claim that nurturing-but-strict aftercare simply will not work. A well-timed word from an influential mayor or a powerful county commissioner can easily halt forward movement. Just saying no, however, is being uninformed. Movement programs have established a history of success that makes a remarkable argument for strengths-based aftercare. It demands that you *involve the naysayers*. Invite them to take part in the progress of a proven communal idea. Many will become valued partners and participants.

Too expensive, some will say. Understand the polarizing, charged arguments against it and make the case that, in fact, it makes remarkable economic sense. Take recidivism, for example. These programs dramatically reduce the revolving door to incarceration—some to single digits. Whereas, keeping a youthful offender under lock and key for a year can cost, just in direct costs, nearly the inclusive expenses of a Harvard education! The Justice Policy Institute (2023) reports that secure confinement for a young offender costs $588 a day or $214,620 a *year*—with a 44 percent increase in about 10 years and accelerating. This doesn't even include the significant costs of public programs and criminal system involvement leading up to incarceration. Furthermore, there's a pattern of criminality resulting in more arrests and being incarcerated for ever-more-lengthy sentences. On top of this, consider the lifetime costs of failure to launch. Harvard now costs only about $334,152, a bargain by comparison. Everyone benefits when a child is guided to being productive and away from crime, substance abuse, and a lifetime of failure.

> *Involve the naysayers.* Invite them to take part in the progress of a proven communal idea. Many will become valued partners and participants.

We also hear the argument that we have no resources, no manpower, and especially no time for a good reentry-aftercare program. Yet we spend whatever resources and time it takes to recycle the same marginalized youth repeatedly through our courts and correctional systems to end up where the youngster began—making bad decisions and being locked up.

You probably didn't get this far without having some justification for entering the aftercare fray. Having a local reentry and community-based aftercare program does make monetary and common sense, even moral sense, after all. The agency-based model of reentry alone doesn't work. Agency-based reentry is meant to be punitive, not restorative; it's largely designed to have an immediate effect: reducing recidivism *during* supervision alone. It is meant for the incorrigible, not the multitude of young-sters that can correct their faults with guidance. Conversely, a well-managed aftercare program that finishes the work begun with agency-based reentry has a longer-term goal to rehabilitate the youngster permanently. Yes, it's being done famously.

Young program clients largely do complete therapy and programming, they stay out of trouble, have coping skills, and are working toward a job. Most are on their way to completing their secondary education or continuing beyond high school. These Movement models are amassing compelling data about reducing recidivism, completing school, and staying away from crime. All of this indicates that the process works, the therapies work, decentralized community facilities work, and sustained programs work. They live the Capacity Building mantra of *Permanent Solutions to Permanent Problems.*

Since this idea arose, these permanent Movement models have been in the crucible of operation for decades. Community-based aftercare is highly replicable. If starting a reentry-aftercare program is purely an economic issue, these Movement models provide a precedent that just about any community can develop multiple streams of funding from insurance, state and local support, and grants, for example. We remind you that an annual bake sale and car wash provide funding streams when done regularly. More than a few programs have planned giving as a priority. Many people are looking for a way to will their assets to a good idea. At the time of this writing, Baby Boomers will transfer $50,000,000,000 (yes trillion, a number which increases nearly daily) to heirs and causes. It's a great way to "pay it forward."

The judges who began Reclaiming Futures courts started with no money. Money would have been nice, the judges say, but it comes in time. Indeed, for these judges, the egg of funding came before the chicken of a viable aftercare program, though not without serious struggle. Once gains in turning around wayward youth were documented, the funding streams from federal programs, local budgets, and state legislated funds, insurance, and systems-sharing resources began to flow. Business owners saw the economic advantage to productivity of getting and keeping youth. They needed good employees.

Financial support for Reclaiming Futures was a trickle at first, but a stream in time, nonetheless. Government institutions are "show me first" creatures. They are the product of many failures. These streams allowed statewide then multi-state expansions for the Movement models. The hardest part was starting the aftercare program. The process, the road traveled, becomes a virtuous progression from idea to idea, from site to site.

The VQ director of evidence-based services shared advice. Make sure that any move to expand laterally to another site or vertically to increase enrollments and commensurate services is based on transportability and readiness to expand. This means you complete your due diligence about preparing your program for expansion. In fact, it's built into your implementation plan before you saw your first charge:

- *Stakeholder support* – Make sure that stakeholders are of one accord.

- *Referrals to justify sunk costs* – Be confident that the stream of referrals will justify a certain level of service capacity sunk costs. Expenses such as staff, office space, and transportation will have to be met even with the ebb and flow of youth, funds, and the pains of growing anything worthy in the public sector.

- *Logistics* – See that you have funding streams, qualified staff, a place to conduct business, administrative support, and the local political will to see the project expansion through to stability.

- *Fidelity to the Model* – Stick with the strengths-based model of rigorous requirements, caring relationships, and meaningful commitment, especially from family.

Most times, it's very difficult to feel progress, but if this type of strengths-based programming is *not* done, children will continue to be lost in the steady decline of this experiment, according to the Rite of Passage director of Student Services. A significant worry is that this reform can be undone by politics.[118] It just may be more expedient, at least dramatic, to build more courthouses and jails. It has happened before; it's happening now. As you travel to or through a new town, scan the skyline. Many times, one of the biggest buildings is the jail! You'll know this monolith by its lack of windows. The only answer to that tragic reversal of the Movement is to give the community enough say in the use of resources to make sure that the political expedient is not the dominant one.

The Urban Institute has captured the purpose and direction of this aftercare reform Movement:[119]

- *Reorientation to reintegration* – Professionals and practitioners of our public systems need to understand and act upon the fact that attempting to reform a young teen during incarceration does not serve the individual nor the greater good. Much more needs to be done to help them overcome obstacles of poor circumstances, perhaps drug and gang involvement, and poor coping skills.

- *Focusing on youth strengths-based development* – Teenagers are not adults; they all need guidance. Many of them are receptive to strengths-based programs and nurturing by strict adults that help with their development to maturity. Youth who are taken into these aftercare programs respond in-kind to welcoming rehabilitative local group settings.

- *Being inclusionary* – The community of local service providers seem to know best how to serve this population of troubled youth in concert with our public institutions.

- *Making aftercare a national priority* – Actually, little is known about transitioning people, especially youth, back home. It will take sustained attention and resources at the highest levels to see these formative ideas of aftercare through to prominence in the scheme of local services delivery.

Every community has issues with reentry, especially for youth. These programs, though they have decades of success, struggle to survive. National institutional systems and public agencies must help build local aftercare infrastructure that can survive on its own. For the movement to be institutionalized, aftercare capacity must be built from the bottom up to endure as long as this crisis of our youth endures. Let's consider stabilization as a means to sustainability.

17. Stabilize/Sustain Operations via Brokered Services and Mapped Service Systems.

Stabilizing your operations is when your project begins to close the services-to-needs gap and you have the capacity, will, and means, to continually refine your model.[120] Your program should have maximum effect on your intended populations, but incremental changes are required to increase efficiencies and effectiveness. At this point, your program has earned a well-deserved place in the local hierarchy and array of services programming. It now has a place in juvenile probation, the local juvenile justice system, schools, for-profit and nonprofit service providers, local funding agencies, and perhaps state and local politics. All of this helps support your strategy for this quintessential phase of your project's life cycle.

A good strategy for solidifying your program is to target a close-to-home expansion, which is another way to think small and doable. Bite off too much and you risk overall failure. Try to keep your expansion efforts within the county where the best chances of successful replication lie. As obvious as it is, the first thing to do, according to the Choice director of Community Partnerships, and the Rite of Passage director of Student Services, is to narrow your focus on the delinquent child involved with the juvenile justice system or the ones that are on the brink of getting thrown out of school. Work on a three-way plan to do the following:

- *Divert* the wayward youth with potential for reform from the juvenile justice system.

- *Stop* further penetration into the system if they are court involved.

- *Reintegrate* them after their court experience.

Get intensively involved in their lives. Design and use the aftercare model lessons learned to stabilize the client and family in the community by helping to divert them from court involvement and detention in the first place. If they are involved, Movement Models apply specific programming such as a 24/7 structured environment and evidence-based therapies to change behavior. Take care, though, when you choose how you will treat young clients.

A good strategy for solidifying your program is to target a close-to-home expansion.

The tendency in the aftercare business is to employ a best practice because it's popular, convenient, or both, then wonder why a touted program doesn't graduate youngsters ready to make independent decisions. The task is to implement evidence-based practices and make them your own, tailored to your unique locale. Blueprints, for example, are wickedly difficult to transfer from site to site. Keeping the fidelity of an evidence-based practice is equally difficult. So, when you choose, select services according to your youth population's needs, not the needs of the standard public system. The latter may espouse certain practices without fully understanding the difficulties of adopting service choices. The system tends to overreach to appear to become evidence-based, thus effective, or remain mired in the inertia of bureaucracy, enforcement, and unacceptably high recidivism rates—which produces what? More of the same.

Youngsters need attention and services that are needs-, strengths- and interest-based. Popular therapies may or may not work. Multi Systemic Therapy may be too clinical for some clients and Functional Family Therapy done without fidelity doesn't work, according to Movement model practitioners. Guiding youth into a structured program, teaching them to be accountable for a clean, orderly room and how to show respect, then keeping them interested and on the task of behavior change and skill building is vital.

Effective Practice

Stabilize the brokerage of services.

It's a careful, if not artful, dance to balance the systemic needs of the juvenile justice system to reform a delinquent youth while honoring the child's need for development. This balancing is maddening because of the lack of material connection between our public agencies and community aftercare; but take heart. Productive connections are still being made by these Model programs.

This is the work of syncing the sometimes-opposing tasks of advocating for public safety while providing and brokering community services in a virtuous cycle—one success leads to two and so on. An example is a school that reduces arrests, suspensions, and expulsions by referring a child who's acting out to an aftercare program before taking extreme measures. Problem solved because the problem is gone. Model programming can respond in two ways: direct intervention and brokering services.

Brokering aftercare services means that people working in our public service agencies, such as judges, court counselors, and probation officers, look for ways to

Probably one of the biggest brokerage services is connecting youth to a job.

combine agency and private efforts. They overtly support community-based aftercare and take every opportunity to match a young offender to those services. Choice, for example, provides a school principal with an alternative to getting rid of problem students through arrest. Choice staff respond to a child who is on the brink of expulsion with coaching, tutoring, mentoring, and monitoring to see that the child stays in school. A child teetering on the brink of being undisciplined or worse is guided away from a justice system response and toward responsibility in school and then to a better chance of success in the community. This saves the justice system for the truly incorrigible. Coordination with the school is done while community services are brokered for the child. Probably one of the biggest brokerage services is connecting youth to a job.

The Virginia Commonwealth, for example, has online courses for job skills development and "Ready by 21" to prevent foster children from becoming homeless when foster care ends at age 21. Choice staff and Fellows broker job readiness training, internships, and job placement in program-supported employment where support is slowly withdrawn to encourage independence and the maturation of positive skills. Progress is closely monitored and analyzed. Skills development, information flow, and attitude and behavior changes are tracked and compared before and after the individually designed intensive plan of therapeutic action completes. Little of the progress a child may make is left to chance. Choice Fellows are with each student multiple times during the day in their homes and where they hang out to answer questions. They are *there* clearing obstacles and sometimes even waking their charges up to get them to class or group. It's no wonder Choice's success in this work is remarkable. These are extraordinary measures that lead to extraordinary ends. It's the epitome of the community being community. The commitment and time are worth it, staff reflect.

Missouri Model staff have a process for stabilizing services and eventually expanding them after proof of concept and complete capacity support is manifest. No knee-jerk, jack-rabbit action without the following hard justification processes:

- *Assess delivery capacity* – Note that this is the priority. It comes with a caution: Know exactly what you're delivering and everything it takes to deliver it—including the politics of it.

- *Assess the system* – This process hints at the need to map all services offered, both via public agencies and especially those that are community-based. This physical map graphically shouts strengths and weaknesses and thus where to place emphasis. Make a nice, regularly updated graphic and mount it on a "performance" wall.

- *Plan for positive youth development* – Every program and service must be strengths based to reduce risky behaviors and nurture the innate strengths a youngster may have. One evidence-based practice is not enough. There needs to be a core group of fully functioning, goal-producing practices done with fidelity, that is, done as they were designed to be done.

- *Train staff from top to bottom and back again* – This includes senior executives. They can best learn how to deliver the service by participating in it and to champion the vision for the program and service in question if they're based in front-line realities. This is leadership in action. It's guidance from the head and heart, intellectually and with intrinsic enthusiasm, which is very different from leading with the "fist," so to speak.

Philosophically, training gives staff a way to change from ordering its young clients about to helping them discover how they can make their own way. An example of insightful staff training aimed at breaking down apathy is Rite of Passage, where they take the time to train *kitchen staff* in the principles of Crisis Prevention Intervention. They realize that even kitchen staff may be called upon to intervene in crises and are part of an evidence-based practice. What prescience of leadership to see the vital value of this opportunity to create previously untapped therapeutic team members and program believers. A flash of genius. Kitchen staff, now part of the Movement, feed their students more than lunch by being able to guide them through a tough moment.

- *Pilot the process* – Incremental steps in program development win the day. Resist the temptation to grow too fast or too far away. Rigorous planning, followed by an equally rigorous and methodical startup, guards against a new service, another idea, or the next site retreating to the old control way of doing business.

- *Follow-up* – Be vigilant in ironing out processes until they are as efficient and effective as possible. No detail should be too small to be ignored. Follow up to ensure processes are running well and evidence-based practices are operating with fidelity. This is continuous work.

How much effort you need to devote to an activity or a critical feature of your program is a constant and compelling question. You must delegate. But to whom, when, and to do what? How much can you trust an individual? Trust you must. A good rule of thumb is to judicially decide to delegate, then do it and see how it goes. People rise to the occasion based on trust. Then another unwritten law becomes evident: Your busiest people somehow can do more—up to a point. Then delegation is imperative to avoid burnout. Keep in mind that delegation confers responsibility that plumbs the other person's capability.

Individual programming, usually a prescribed course of therapy and wraparound services delivered during aftercare, ends very quickly. Services are determined by fiat, limited funding, and limited time horizons. Therefore, termination is preplanned at the first visit with a potential program participant.

The message to participants is clear: Make progress in the program or risk expulsion from it. Program staff are realistic about measures of progress. Initially, staff want to see the conditions of probation completed, at least 75 percent of service plan goals met, and a 75 percent accountability rate for program participation, among other benchmarks. Models for Change keeps a real-time dashboard of measures,[121] which suggests data points it's wise to monitor:

- *Risk assessment* – Aftercare should begin with assessment of the prospective client, which will allow you to track progress toward each measure of individual and collective improvement. Again, ensure your measures are along a chain of outcomes mentioned earlier to keep you from getting distracted by measuring nonessentials.

- *Progress* – Monitor how program participants improve their behaviors and post-release skills. Progress may also be measured by rates of return to regular school, and especially graduation rates for former program participants. Zero in on your best charges. Ask to stay in touch and do so. A superstar or two will emerge. Tout the success of a graduate who progresses to post-secondary schooling for a trade or profession. Then sing the praises of the inevitable graduate that has a job, better a career, where he can support a family.

- *Case planning* – Individual case planning is essential to the well running aftercare program. Each client is arguably unique, so the program needs a way to begin, track, adjust, and complete the most appropriate services for every client's unique needs.

- *Focus on high-risk youth* – The best use of your time is to focus on high-risk youth. Their completion of aftercare and return to the community free from crime and substance abuse has the highest return in dollars that won't be spent cycling in and out of the criminal justice system and public supports. Monitor their progress closely.

- *Revocations* – Know how many of your high-risk clients are revoked for technical reasons. This number can be easily reduced by partnering with probation officers. Make them aftercare team members and brokers of appropriate services rather than continually resorting to revocation. Revocation back to the criminal justice system should be a last resort and its limits discussed, defined, and followed. When all understand how revocation can be used, expectations for behavior can be delineated. Everyone, especially the youth, knows both the limits of bad behavior and the real benefits of behaving well. You may also want to know what percentage of your graduates have no new violations within a certain time after program completion, perhaps six months to a year.

The further out you go, the harder it is to track former participants, so set up a mechanism to stay in touch with graduates. Get as much contact information as you can. Ask that they stay in contact, but also take time to call former graduates. You'll find you will lose contact with most of them. However, the few who remain connected will provide valuable information about the long-term effects of their affirming experience. This, in turn, will suggest how to improve your overall program and be a vital indication of how well your aftercare is working.

- *Attendance* – Note attendance and treatment completion rates. Aftercare therapies require constant contact, so spotty attendance doesn't help. Attendance is the first step to being attentive and involved in changing risky or inappropriate behaviors.

- *Meeting needs* – Be aware of the percentage of program graduates who have had their top assessed needs met. For example, how many know what it's like to live with good behavior? Have a (temporary) place to stay, if needed? Have overcome addictions? Another measure may be to note improvements in life skills and program satisfaction. Remember to include family progress and satisfaction.

> Successful program graduates should be able to say, "I don't need you anymore. I'm no longer delinquent—and I intend to stay that way."

The idea is to have a ready snapshot of program performance—pertinent, easy to read, and transferable to targeted, measurable action. These measures are suggestions only. They still need to be linked with post-release services and measures of ultimate success, as overall program success is measured by the strength of the reconnection to the community independent of program and systemic supports. Figuratively and literally, successful program graduates should be able to say, "I don't need you anymore. I'm no longer delinquent—and I intend to stay that way."

Another part of service brokering is to understand barriers that exist for every service offered.

Effective Practice

Map the terrain of service partners to identify barriers to client service access.

Experienced staff also relate that barriers to a client being able to access services represent a significant impediment to stabilizing the entire program. A solution to this conundrum is to map or chart the process of a service's delivery through the systems responsible for its delivery. This is as simple as talking to the people who deliver a service, whether they're in the juvenile justice system, health or human services, a nonprofit or for-profit entity, or the schools, for example. The list of partners is extensive when plumbed. Chart each stop in the services delivery process and indicate anything that's an impediment, such as unreliable transportation to get to the service. While you're charting or mapping, learn about restrictions, policies, and procedures, all of which can be problematic yet suggest a solution. Ask the service providers along the service map what they want and need. Then, based on your vision, mission, and purpose, negotiate a mutually agreeable arrangement, perhaps a formal memo of agreement or understanding, to facilitate the practice or service. Further, you can settle sharing of resources, people, funding, office space. Just asking will turn a page to expected and unexpected possibilities. Mapping service providers is also a method to agree on expectations for who is to do what, when, and where, which facilitates and informs the how.

When you can plan with public agencies, the culture of control may begin to evolve into a hybrid of hierarchy and compassionate collaboration to facilitate the transition of young adults into their communities.

For example, probation officers wanted Rite of Passage to accept juvenile sex offenders. Rite of Passage management denied that request because sex offenders didn't fit their aftercare model. But that discussion opened other alternatives that could serve this population of offenders. By discussing mutual arrangements along the process life cycle of services delivery, all-important relationships are established and ideally continually strengthened. Staff relate that this personal touch of program capacity building really works and is a pleasant, professional, very productive way to project the vision of reformed aftercare. A performance-oriented proven model of public services delivery extends its influence way beyond its bricks and mortar. Best yet, these models have great influence beyond what they know.

The purpose of mapping services and service partners is to find problems and address them before any crises arise. Then they can resolve the problems before they threaten the program. Ideally, purpose ensures as much as possible that anyone in a supervisory, management, or leadership position is committed to course correction and cultural change. This is critical because lack of leadership is a major impairment to this new approach of aftercare programming. People need to be empowered to make prudent leadership decisions.

Rite of Passage executives knew they were making progress when probation officers first began asking how specific program participants were doing in the program. Then they asked how the participants were doing in school rather than simply asking if the conditions of probation were being met or if a revocation was imminent. VQ and Rite of Passage epitomize this evolution from agency short-term control of reentry to collaborating with local strengths-based therapies and services to complete an aftercare program and a successful transition into the community.

When your project is stabilized, mainly indicated by relatively reliable streams of operating income, it also has a history of success and certain experience gained from the trials of existing. The state of capacity building where you can stabilize and expand brings the project full circle, back to understanding processes and improving them. At this stage of project development, staff and key partners should be comfortable with the model, its complexities, and how to safely grow to meet the assessed need without diminishing or threatening the work of aftercare. Your program is institutionalized within your operational systems and your community. Every critical feature of the life cycle is imbedded and getting better with continuous critique, reflection, adjustment, and action. You are ready to assume responsibility for more young adults and perhaps more territory. This is where you *begin* to close the services-to-needs gap.

18. Expand Incrementally and Locally.

The process of expanding is the work of creating movement builders, according to staff at the Annie E. Casey Foundation. Movement builders are aftercare practitioners who believe big change is possible and high-needs youth can achieve purpose, productivity, and satisfaction in the community. It's also about long-range planning in an uncertain environment marked by complex, interdependent, competing agencies and relationships. Even with the struggle to keep an aftercare effort alive, those involved in the aftercare movement know that its survival depends on expansion, while it's a stumbling walk into the unknown based a good bit on faith that they have the *what* and *how* to make it work.

Expansion is a continuation of the flow of planning, operations, and stabilization as the program matures. This maturity, for example, is a board of directors that changes its roles from planning, implementing, and stabilizing this idea to one of an avuncular advisor. It's a natural progression as is the experience of these Movement Models. Movement building is, according to the Choice director of Community Partnerships, a lot of little things done well via attention to detail—no detail too small, continuously developing new and strengthening old relationships, and constantly improving processes. Expansion is not simply a matter of finding more office space; expansion is complicated by the need for cultural change and reform.

Program expansion is an extension of the planning you have been doing all along, hence the organic body and soul, alive nature of planning. Each program has a body, which is its process and its physicality by being rooted in the community. Its soul is the belief in the transformative potential of its clients. Still, expansion is different from original planning, as long-range strategic planning cannot begin unless the organization enjoys reasonable stability.[122]

The planning document at this stage of the project life cycle should be an inspiring statement about what you, the collective of stakeholders, want your organization to look like when the expansion is complete. It's a process of learning about growing so it can be done again almost of its own volition as the process compels the next best thing. This part of the life cycle is where you take a much longer view. That view includes where you are, where you want to go, and how to get there.

Long-range planning is as necessary to good governance[123] as it is nearly mystical. Just how do a few people look into the future and convince others of their view of how things will be? This type of planning has an element of dreaming about possibilities and tends to be a little difficult to fathom for most potential participants, so support may be less than ideal. That's okay. This service is not about perfection. It is, however, about making a difference one life at a time.

Thus, staff need to begin with the intention of making a realistic long-range strategic document for expansion that will engender support and the intention to succeed. Leadership and especially line level supervisors must fully endorse this strategy initially and continuously, especially during implementation, when any plan is the most fragile. Proceed carefully on this first expansion because in many ways it will be the template for further growth. It's helpful to have a single body responsible for the process.

Effective Practice

Designate a single body to guide strategic planning for expansion.

Seeing this process through is better served by the oversight of a dedicated body. Naturally, the composition of it will be dictated by the nature of the project and should be determined by the functions that each member can perform. That is, each member should materially contribute to planning and implementing the expansion. An important function is to be a liaison between the program and the private and public sector stakeholders, as successful expansion depends on finding common ground with the different cultures found in these varied sectors.

Ideally, this single body needs to have a few key people from each level of your program organization. You also need representation from a few well selected external stakeholder groups, such as service providers, court officials, local municipal officials, and the private sector. When the detailed course of action begins to take shape, it must be picked apart to ensure each action item is doable and will lead to a successful expansion. It's easy to go astray as people dream about possibilities. It's best to go small and local as well as one small step at a time, especially if this is a first expansion.

Select a service to pilot the expansion process. Say it's behavior therapy, as you'll have proven modalities, if not the experience of your initial program. Expand first by increasing client load, one individual at a time if need be. Then move the expansion effort to a nearby location. Proximity matters. Once the plan has been agreed to and all are satisfied that it's practical and feasible, implementation can begin. Remember, implementation is often where good public service ideas go to die. Make no mistake; expansion is a version of implementation, so pay attention to the details of each of the critical life cycle features outlined in the above two chapters covering planning and operations.

The best way to keep implementation on track is by evaluating and monitoring processes for efficiency and effectiveness and tracking goal progress and attainment. Do only what can be done very well with reasonable surety.

> **It's best to go small and local as well as one small step at a time, especially if this is a first expansion.**

Don't be afraid to act. Be collectively, reasonably comfy with the next stage. This is not perfect 100 percent confidence, just the feeling that it's time. Problems of implementation and management compound as reach increases, which is why it's important to keep the expansion project near the home, or central, operation at first. Models such as Rite of Passage and Reclaiming Futures with interstate sites took decades to reach that level of expansion. Those in charge of implementation should be close enough to the expansion site for monitors to have daily access. Thus, they can quickly detect even small inefficiencies or lack of fidelity to the model and correct them on the spot if possible. Build communication loops into the process. It's about reasonably resolving the accumulation of little mistakes and oversights that can sink your effort. Even when your new program is realized, planning is well served by being continually updated. Keep focused. Your expansion must succeed for subsequent expansions— your ultimate goal—to succeed. According to Models for Change, your overarching purposes should be to:[124]

- *Enhance capacity* – Programs are not built by proclamation; they depend on effective, efficient processes.

- *Become evidence based* – Goal accomplishment depends on maintaining practice fidelity, which will be one of your most difficult issues. The only way you'll know if your program is making a lasting and positive difference is if the client data show it.

- *Stay on goal* – These programs are founded on good data that tell the story of how a project is working and when it isn't.

- *Constantly get better* – You cannot and must not stagnate. Not evolving risks being overwhelmed by the top-down enforcement/control model of aftercare, which generally finds it difficult to support the learning culture of strengths-based aftercare.

Enhancing capacity is the priority, and it has been so from the first meeting of local change agents and leaders. It's the basis of being data-driven, on goal, and improving with each expansion. Aftercare is a basic concept that reflects the locale in which it's tried. Thus, each expansion site must be customized according to local environments and conditions. VQ is now connected to HomeQuest,[125] sponsored by the Department of Justice Office of Justice Programs. HomeQuest treats delinquent youths or those with mental health issues in their own homes. Choice reflects the partnership with AmeriCorps. Reclaiming Futures is an extension of the courts. They all believe in youth.

Effective Practice
Design a strategic planning process for modest expansion.

When you've done this type of strategic planning well, you will know it in two ways. First, it will lead to a feeling, a comfort level, if a little uneasy, that you're ready to take the leap. None of the many people interviewed saw this work as totally analytical, as if planning a rocket launch. It's a sense of arrival when people somehow discover they can make a commitment to next-step actions. Secondly, the process of capacity building, when diligently done, has certain characteristics that describe the bottom-up nature of this level of planning.

- *It establishes buy-in.* – Key stakeholders, again, must be true partners—believers and doers. They can't wait to do something for the cause. The criterion for inclusion is if each member can add materially to goal accomplishment. It's a mutually agreed upon process. The fewer but necessary people included in this core group the better.

- *It's about the plan, not services programming.* – There's a tendency for discussion and agendas to drift to the more comfortable topic of services to the exclusion of more basic topics such as narrowing scope, lining up resources, and getting staffing right. Be aware of this and avoid it. First things first: Build support systems so your services will evolve and can develop instead of being abandoned for lack of funding or adequate referrals.

  > **Your program must sit juxtaposed with traditional hard services and be as commanding as they are for limited tax dollars.**

- *It's shared.* – Be aware that aftercare is only one concern of the municipality. See that your project fits with the overall municipal plan for general services, all of which compete for political and operational support. Parenthetically, you're competing with basic services on a fixed automatically renewed budget line item such as roads maintenance, recreation, policing, garbage collection, water, and more. Your justification must be as solid as these local tangibles. Thus, your program must sit juxtaposed with traditional hard services and be as commanding as they are for limited tax dollars. Ultimately, it must pay in dollars and cents, not cost.

- *It supports the core project.* – Expansion should strengthen the original program and not allow drift away from core values, original goals, and principal strengths, mainly building services delivery capacity. Biting off more than the project can handle is a particularly risky reality at this stage. Success tends to build over-confidence and an inflated desire to do more to please friends, neighbors, and the town council.

- *It has clear direction.* – Stakeholders down to and including those at the line level should clearly understand how the expansion will be done and their individual key part in it. The strategic plan for expansion should be written in the language of stakeholders, particularly those responsible for local implementation.

- *It emphasizes client independence.* – Never forget this is about preparing youth for success in the community.

- *It's based on the experience of other programs.* – Rely on the many established aftercare experiments throughout the country, especially the Movement Models, for proven ideas, processes, procedures, and abundant encouragement.

- *It relies on data and analysis.* – This is twofold. You can have numbers, low hanging fruit, that mean little. Data is refined by analysis, which proves its worth and determines direction. The expansion plan itself explores various scenarios and how they may impact effectiveness and costs. Obviously, if revenue streams don't support the idea, don't go forward, or wait until they do. Secondly, expansion should remain data driven marked by progress. That progress, as noted, is to begin to close the services-to-needs gap. In itself, this gap is a compelling argument in dollars and cents for support and more.

Realize at this stage your program represents more than your working project. It's an example for the rest of your municipality for designing and providing meaningful, impactful public services. You exemplify governance at its practical finest. *Failure is just not an option.*

Your failure would not be just the tragic demise of *your* program but the nameless, numberless good ideas that die aborning, unknown.

Next, your strategic planners should understand how your program has come to its present situation by conducting a good look at the strengths of the current aftercare program, all the significant things that went wrong as it progressed, and how they were overcome. This helps decision makers avoid painting an unrealistically rosy picture of their accomplishments and the false sense of accomplishment that comes with it. Keep notes on the discussion, because the things that went wrong tend to happen again. This descriptive eclectic model of aftercare relies on process, and strategic planning is no exception. Following is a good take on such a process.[126]

- *Decide on a process.* – People need to know what expansion is all about, especially how it will affect them and who is supposed to do what, when, and how.

- *Do an environmental scan of externalities and internalities.* – Assess externalities, outside the boundaries of your program world, and how your organization fits in the community, whom it serves, and who are your friends, allies, and competitors. Public projects and programs all compete for very limited funding and helpful involvement. Internally, know your staff capabilities, how you are performing, the sophistication of your support systems, and what it takes to succeed.

- *Have a feel for key information.* – Be particularly mindful of how sustainable operational funding will be secured. Have as many funding streams as possible. Be leery of grants. They have strings attached, are terminal, and tend to end at the worst possible time. A grant is good if you can get it, but treat it as tangential to more reliable sources of support.

- *Review the basics.* – Are the original vision, mission, goals, and values still pertinent? Perhaps an expansion is a good time to see that they are current and can guide the path beyond the stresses of doing more. Make sure any fact- and performance-driven revisions are shared with all concerned.

- *Develop goals for the years specified in the plan.* – This is where the lofty statement of vision becomes real, as reaching targets requires an action plan. Each goal needs its own strategy for completion. A statement of beliefs strengthens the vision, staff, and supporters.

- *Write an action plan on a timeline.* – This specifies details about what work the plan will require and deadlines for when actions will reasonably be completed. It will take constant adjusting, but its main purpose is to keep the end goal clearly visible, on track, and challenging.

- *Publish the plan.* – Make it a convincing, practical, working document that stands up to the scrutiny of a public airing. Encourage comments, as that's another way to gain buy-in.

- *Follow up.* – Ensure progress of the process. Collectively, you want staff to have done something meaningfully good at the end of the day.

There are many ways expansion can be hampered or fail outright. It's easy to neglect monitoring during expansion. Do not! Executing a strategic planning process is a complex dynamic with continuous internal and external threats. Be aware when they impinge on the expansion. Anticipate them and head them off. Have a realistic discussion about each threat and anticipate their negative consequences with solutions. Data collection is tough, but persist in developing it with the intention of making it as easy as possible to collect and analyze, interpret, and distribute your data.

Any quantitative justification for your program will be compelling in an environment where long-term effects are nearly impossible to state without supporting numbers, especially for an idea that successfully tackles a vexing problem.

Build an eclectic expansion effort based on established aftercare models. The basic model tends to be strengthened with expansion. There tends to be a hybridization of improvements building on improvements with each iteration as more services are offered to wider populations of wayward youth. Find program champions and put them in charge of expansion efforts. Make sure your plan drills down to daily goal-directed activities. Monitor to find little corrections that collectively will create opportunities for success.

When do you put the plan into effect? Movement practitioners observe that their expansion efforts began when there was a "discontent that there can and needs to be more" and the core group has had

> **It's easy to neglect monitoring during expansion. Do not!**

enough planning. The moment of beginning can come suddenly with the availability of funds or, as in most cases, the group finds itself outfitting facilities and hiring people. The result of planning will be a responsive plan of action that coalesces your disparate partners and focuses their multiplied energies on implementation. Witness collective intelligence and, again, the whole becoming greater than its parts. Then persist with the plan until it blossoms into the envisioned expansion.

The seriousness of expanding was captured by a Choice executive. She said implementing or expanding one of these programs is not merely assuming an evidence-based practice. Replication or expansion is the avenue to changing the way more people think and act about strengths- and community-based aftercare by making room for them to participate. The more the merrier.

Chapter 5

THOUGHTS ON REENTRY AND THE AFTERCARE REFORM MOVEMENT

Chapter 5

THOUGHTS ON REENTRY AND THE AFTERCARE REFORM MOVEMENT

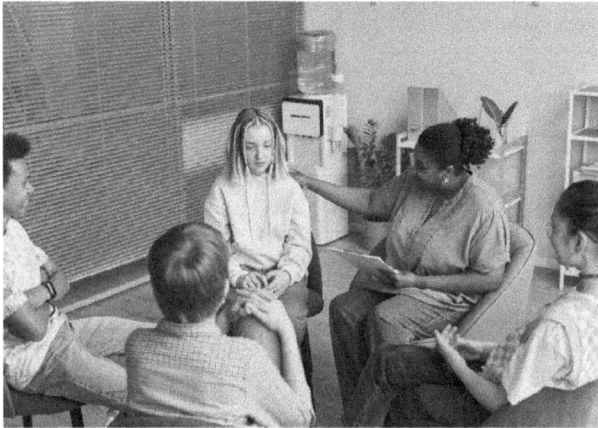

There will come a time when our descendants will be amazed
that we did not know things that are so plain to them ....
– Seneca

The two innovations that mark this new wave aftercare movement are genuine Capacity Building organized by the Life Cycle and the *bottom-up,* not top-down nature of Capacity Building. These features allow local services to be built in a matrix critical to defined program services. This is efficient, effective, targeted governance. The township is where plaguing problems manifest *and* real solutions lie. Thus, local people define *their* problem with *their* answers and *their* resources, and they take responsibility to solve *their* problem. With that ownership and commitment, they have a "can't fail" work ethic and the best of collective, creative intelligence prevails. The whole grows greater and greater. It must prevail because the problem of reentry continues in all its difficult, tragic, and expensive realities. If you can tackle and tame a thorny concern such as reentry, you can do just about anything.

Lastly, the way forward rests on proven action items and Effective Practices. The concept works and tames endemic chaos. Just follow the proven Capacity Building checklist! Your peers in the trenches wrote it!

Another innovation is evidence-based assessment, to be differentiated from an evidence-based process or practice. From the moment a youngster becomes a possible candidate for a community-based aftercare program, you need to lay out a detailed and accurate profile of strengths and risks. With an assessment of risk and resiliency factors, young adults are understood more for who they are, the good and the bad, and not through an adult lens. That adult lens tends to assess bad behavior and, in turn, results in reactions to control that behavior. On the other hand, assessment deals with the causal factors that influence young behaviors. Once these are identified, they can be addressed and corrected.

This precise screening allows for tailoring of individualized plans to help a client toward independence via evidence-based working practices and therapies to change wayward behavior, thinking, and decision making. In other words, a package of services is matched to each youth as accurately as possible and case managed through aftercare. Upon client independence, the practitioners in the model programs highlighted herein then become brokers for juvenile services. This manner of service provision is changing the practical function of criminal justice professionals from controllers to guides and mentors, from just coordinators to collaborators. For example, probation officers shift from supervisor-enforcer to monitor-broker of services, one officer at a time. Still, much needs to be done to realize the promise of juvenile aftercare.

It is not enough to assume a probation officer, for example, will simply get the intention of and assume the additional role of service broker. They must be trained in how to explain Functional Family Therapy, for one, to clients and aftercare stakeholders.

> **Assessment deals with the causal factors that influence young behaviors. Once these are identified, they can be addressed and corrected.**

They must realize that a main job duty is to help build the network of friends, partners, and collaborators. Everyone is a recruiter to your aftercare innovation.

Training of staff in services delivery techniques and stakeholders in the benefits of aftercare and understanding its long-term effects as well as the application of capacity building are some of the issues holding back the expansion of juvenile aftercare.

Next, strengths-based aftercare programs need to be replicated with the ambitious but necessary intention of having at least one in every county nationally. Why not dream? Even with so much evidence and experience that these programs work and are reforming the system, it's still difficult to determine their long-term effectiveness. However, we know it's good and it's important. Program graduates melt into life, which is a good thing, but it's maddening to try to track their life trajectories. It would take years, if it's even possible, to determine if they've made an acceptable transition to independence and are good family members and neighbors.

However, it's encouraging that these Movement Models have remarkably low recidivism rates while clients are in the programs. Anecdotal reports from a few graduates who stay in touch with their program staff affirm that they have indeed made a successful transition.

Established sites still struggle with the work of expanding their idea to different locations and markets even though their accomplishments over the past decades are most impressive. It would be helpful if they had a much better practical understanding of capacity building and leading from the bottom up. Plus, existing and planned aftercare program practitioners need to strengthen services delivery capacity, as it's the key to proliferating this model Reform Movement. Complicating the situation is the fact that our service systems and the families of high-needs youth are still dysfunctional. In addition, according to local practitioners, resources continue to dwindle in the new reality of downward spiraling austerity.

This cultural change of bottom-up local determination is simply not working its way through the court system and local services fast and deep enough. The new model is not secure. The VQ lead executive points out that this cultural change is a threat to established systems. It appears to deflect service provision away from agency providers. This view is a matter of misunderstanding. The aftercare Movement aims for a *collaboration* between a public agency and local private or private nonprofit providers, *not* replacing what an agency offers. The Rite of Passage director of Student Services observes that working with the professionals in the criminal justice system will help clear up this misunderstanding.

Movement aftercare practitioners need to better explain what their programs do and how agencies have a vital part to play. In the opposite but complementary direction, agency professionals need to look for ways to collaborate. Work with the status quo, the Rite of Passage executive suggests. However, make it a blend of conventional criminal justice and agency-based answers to delinquency combined with community- and evidence-based aftercare. This will create opportunities to rationally demonstrate—with data—that conventional control-based programming just does not have the results of capacity-built evidence-based programming.

First, understand that most young adults and juniors need only a strong nudge to stay on the straight and narrow to being a good, productive citizen. However, our public systems focus on asocial and criminal activity. It's easy to post the unacceptable recidivism rates of incarcerated youth. Further, they do not perform well in school, and many youths become more criminalized because of being incarcerated. Considering the above institutional dynamics of adapting to Reform Movement aftercare, who knows how long it will take to significantly improve the "cuff 'em and stuff 'em" mentality.

Thus, a major task is to grow these Movement programs and promote learning, so key court and public safety officials see that good aftercare is a way to accomplish *their* jobs. Why can't we have aftercare schools that focus on vocational training while offering evidence-based practices and therapies? Our major public institutions, such as criminal justice, can be greatly improved by collaborating with Movement model reformers and refocusing from what is to what can be.

Chapter 6

A LOOK OVER THE HORIZON – THE REFORM PUBLIC SERVANT-SCIENTIST

Chapter 6

A LOOK OVER THE HORIZON – THE REFORM PUBLIC SERVANT-SCIENTIST

Putting things off is the biggest waste of life: it snatches away each day as it comes and denies us the present by promising the future. The greatest obstacle to living is expectancy, which hangs upon tomorrow and loses today. … To what goal are you straining? The whole future lies in uncertainty: Live immediately.
– Seneca

While juvenile aftercare is nascent with respect to the (vast) need, it's always productive to ask what comes next. When asked this question, practitioners suggested three areas it would be productive to probe.

Conduct long-term studies. First, there's a significant need to conduct long-term studies of the graduates of aftercare programming. We don't know with any reliability if the youngsters who seem to do well immediately after graduation progress into being productive citizens with prospects for a long-term, adequately paying career and a well-adjusted family life. Common sense suspects many do. Success is not newsworthy. A picture of how they're doing at least five years after they leave a program would more accurately yield recidivism rates and shed light on possible reasons why they recidivate. This then could suggest ways to improve project development and programming. It would also help make the cost-effectiveness/trade-off arguments.

Build true collaboration. Next, our public institutions, systems, and agencies will be well served to collaborate on aftercare services. Success here informs and improves other service ideas. This is not cooperation as it largely has come to be. Cooperation, simply defined, is working to get to the end of the day. It's task oriented and usually done by one person in relative isolation. Now, what is *true* collaboration!

Collaboration is when a team or an organization willingly works overtime to realize a vision. Work becomes fulfilling. It's a can-do attitude. Obstacles are opportunities to learn, strengthen, do, and grow. Collaborators are motivated, even inspired, to do their part because their leader

> It would be extremely helpful if probation officers were equipped with the tools of aftercare and became part of the therapeutic rebuilding of court-involved youth.

leads by example. They see the need to work together as the whole becomes much greater than the parts. When effort makes a real difference in lives, the project lives on. The people smile broadly and say, "We did this."

Our criminal justice system simply cannot do the work of reentry alone. Our health and human services agencies simply cannot provide all the services at-risk or delinquent minors need. Plus, the stark fact is that public funds for services to effectively transition troubled teens away from crime and back into the community are limited and dramatically dwindling. A Models for Change senior executive suggests, for example, that the juvenile correctional system begin developing evidence-based probationary practices to connect to community-based aftercare services. These pages have frequently mentioned the need for probation officers to become brokers of services and not merely people who enforce a court order when the ultimate threat of noncompliance is revocation or parole. It would be extremely helpful if probation officers were equipped with the tools of aftercare and became part of the therapeutic rebuilding of court-involved youth.

Rigorously test, prove, and re-prove Capacity Building. This model of aftercare needs to be tested by being implemented over and over. The best result of this eclectic Movement Model is that it evolves via replication. By the experience gained from every iteration, it reforms our juvenile justice and public health care systems toward collaborating on local networked matrices of services assembled for aftercare.

The hope of this model is that it enables practitioners to capture the unique qualities of troubled youth and draw light and a flame from the ashes of a young life crashing. This requires a different kind of service provider—one compelled to be a servant first. Movement practitioners demonstrate that we need to develop reform leadership capable of forming public and private partnerships, which will multiply the effect of combined resources.

The people who are leading this reform recognize that their insightful system of reentry-aftercare captured herein is complex, if only because of its relative newness. It's a new combination of each sector—public, private, and private nonprofit, neighbor by neighbor—guided by the principle that youngsters, even the wayward, are capable of blossoming as adjusted adults and are masters of their fates. They need understanding and guidance, but with a certain strictness and high expectations.

> **The heart of success in aftercare is focused on the strengths of the youths, but that philosophy extends to anyone involved in the Movement.**

Reform Movement professionals practice the art of harnessing intrinsic motivation. People generally want to be involved in the Movement, whether they find themselves on a foundation board or are the child who has had a first court appearance. Practitioners in these community-based programs are modern shape shifters in their ability and willingness to step into nearly any task while on the job. The heart of success in aftercare is focused on the strengths of the youths, but that philosophy extends to anyone involved in the Movement. People then form unique ad hoc groups brought together by the recognition of *their* problem with *their* solution, not that of an outsider or someone in a distant executive suite. This forms buy-in that becomes commitment approaching zealotry but toned by the gravity of doing something of a lasting nature.

This bottom-up approach to forming problem-solving matrices with one's neighbors has a human capital multiplier effect that's rarely seen in the top-down control model. These Movement Model solutions to the problem of delinquent youth are creative, entrepreneurial, and very practical. Participants take the long view beyond program development to how *systems* can be strengthened and updated for efficiency and effectiveness, for energizing goals, missions, visions, and beliefs. In the process of delivering reentry-aftercare, they are becoming reform public servant-*scientists*.

The *how* of going about this work is becoming clear. It is one step, one youngster at a time, to state the obvious. That is how all these remarkable Reform Movement models tackled obstacles: slowly and incrementally but with inexorable progress.

Following are more suggestions from the trenches:

- *Augment a drug court.* – For example, drug courts can accommodate Reclaiming Futures aftercare services to complement court-ordered substance abuse treatment.

- *Enrich drug court.* – Enrich your drug court by making it part of the matrix of services devoted to completing reentry with aftercare. Further enrich the court by the experiences of other models.

- *Broker aftercare.* – Improve parole by it becoming a brokerage of aftercare therapies and services.

- *Institutionalize continuum services.* – Establish a continuum of standard, evidence-based practices and more importantly, service suggestions you will develop according to your problem definition.

- *Modify drug court to aftercare court.* – This recognizes that solving a teen's drug abuse condition is only part of what needs to be done to set them on a path to productivity.

- *Grow strengths-based residences.* – Let Models for Change provide an example of how to build and run local residential facilities.

- *Energize partners.* – The Choice program teaches how to multiply the energies of volunteers and the resources of sponsors and a host agency.

- *Expand, expand, proliferate with Capacity Building.* – VQ teaches how to penetrate the idea to just about any community.

- *Make a cadre of believers.* – Pick your friends and partners well; relationships must be positive, enduring, and productive.

- *Understand what works and what doesn't.* – Analyze without being paralyzed by all there is to know.

Your greatest threats happen during implementation. The cure for threats is to plan well and then act; nothing goes to the timid. Focus on lasting capacity. In other words, you and your program are seeking to become part of the fabric of the community, if not a leader of it.

Practically, these programs have demonstrated declining recidivism rates and have documented efficiencies, cost-effectiveness, trade-off value, community betterment. Don't forget that success with these Model programs means support and success for other ideas similarly imagined, planned, built, and sustained. Their operational resources are relatively stable, they have built a network of services, and they have political support. Staff are also inspired and trained to be responsible for this new wave of services delivery in and of the community for the long term.

> **You and your program are seeking to become part of the fabric of the community, if not a leader of it.**

When established, your aftercare program will lead the community as a model program for the 21st century—one that defines a local solution to a local problem with largely local resources. One thing is quite certain; you will be successful if you base your reentry-aftercare program on bottom-up Capacity Building.

A sincere Thank You for your efforts!

ABOUT THE AUTHORS

JAMES KLOPOVIC, Major, USAF, retired, holds a Doctor of Public Policy (DPP) from Charles Sturt University, Sydney, Australia, with concentration on service program capacity building at the organizational and community levels.

James is helping cultivate the next generation of leaders via character-based education and development. He promotes the understanding of how to build teams that accomplish more than the sum of the parts and combines this passion with developing better ways to deliver municipal public services with collaborative capacity building.

After retiring from the United States Air Force, James continued providing leadership at federal, state, and local levels for a total of 45 years. He served as a senior staffer for 25 years on the North Carolina Governor's Crime Commission, where his responsibilities encompassed strategic planning, municipal governance, financial development, federal granting, and community and organizational development, implementation, and evaluation. Now he writes, publishes, and consults.

One of the numerous programs he created detailed the processes and procedures for School Resource Officers, which resulted in continuously improving learning environments statewide while making schools safer. Those programs continue today.

As the principal investigator/program director on a series of research programs, he analyzed and proposed model local programs leading to grant proposals for dozens of municipal and state initiatives. He has broad experience in logistics, training, and education. His expertise in program design, implementation, and management includes ensuring program and organizational permanency. His technical support to numerous local government entities created and enhanced service ideas such as delinquency prevention, reentry, and decriminalizing people living with mental illness.

James is cofounder of The Nicole and James Klopovic Family Charitable Foundation, which lends support to local social programs with funding and knowledge of Capacity Building to encourage *Permanent Solutions to Permanent Problems*.

He has authored numerous publications regarding community policing, community development, and effective/efficient delivery of public services as well as books for fun. In descending order of date, they include the following:

The Good Life: My Legacy for You. A memoir. (Morrisville, N.C.: Affinitas Publishing, 2023) Available through Amazon and *http://www.affinitaspublishing.org.*

Volume I, Capacity Building Series: *Building Capacity from the Bottom Up: The Key to Sustaining Local Services.* (Morrisville, N.C.: Affinitas Publishing, 2024) Available through Amazon and *http://www.affinitaspublishing.org.*

Volume II, Capacity Building Series: *Decriminalizing Mental Illness: A Practical Guide for Building Sustainable Crisis Intervention Teams.* (Morrisville, N.C.: Affinitas Publishing, Second Edition 2024) Available through Amazon and *http://www.affinitaspublishing.org.*

Volume III, Capacity Building Series: *Accelerating Juvenile Reentry: A Practical Capacity Building Model for Sustaining Aftercare.* (Morrisville, N.C.: Affinitas Publishing, 2024) Available through Amazon and *http://www.affinitaspublishing.org.*

Volume IV, Capacity Building Series: *Accelerating Adult Reentry: A Practical Capacity Building Model for Sustaining Post-Release Transitional Services.* (Morrisville, N.C.: Affinitas Publishing, 2024) Available through Amazon and *http://www.affinitaspublishing.org.*

Becoming a New Wave Leader: Principles and Practices to Live and Lead Well. (Morrisville, N.C.: Affinitas Publishing, 2021) Available through Amazon and *http://www.affinitaspublishing.org.*

Your Moral Compass: A Practical Guide for New Wave Leaders. (2020) Available through Amazon and *http://www.affinitaspublishing.org.*

Little Stories: A Legacy of Living, Laughing and Loving. (Morrisville, N.C.: Affinitas Publishing, 2019) Available through Amazon and *http://www.affinitaspublishing.org.*

The Honest Backpacker: A Practical Guide for the Rookie Adventurer over 50. (Morrisville, N.C.: Affinitas Publishing, 2017) Available through Amazon and *http://www.affinitaspublishing.org.*

Effective Program Practices for At-Risk Youth: A Continuum of Community Based Programs. (Kingston, N.J.: Civic Research Institute, Inc., 2003). Available through Amazon and *https://civicresearchinstitute.com/index.html.*

Contact: *jklopovic@gmail.com*

NICOLE KLOPOVIC is the daughter of James Klopovic. She holds a Doctor of Medical Science and is a certified Physician Associate (PA-C), practicing in the areas of Emergency Medicine, Urgent Care, Aesthetics, Weight Management, and Primary Care. In addition, she is a captain in the U.S. Air Force Reserve Medical Corps and is pursuing her Air Force career concurrently with her career as a PA-C.

She stays active with dance instructing, weightlifting, hiking, and cycling and enjoys cooking and traveling, striving to embrace the motto *carpe diem* while maintaining her passion to mentor, help, and teach others.

Nicole is cofounder and CEO of The Nicole and James Klopovic Family Charitable Foundation, which lends support to local social programs with funding and knowledge of Capacity Building to encourage Permanent Solutions to Permanent Problems.

APPENDIX

Checklist: A Capacity Building Tool for Juvenile Aftercare

For your convenience and review, the wisdom from all the aftercare practitioners is summarized in Figure 1-B in the same checklist presented in Figure 1-A on pages 7-10. The checklist makes beginning, operating, and stabilizing your idea less daunting. You have a place to start, a path to follow, and an end to anticipate. Since it's based on building the capacity of a proven idea, that of community- and strengths-based services, be assured that you are embarking on a journey of building a permanent aftercare program that truly makes a difference in the community. This life-cycle sequence of juvenile aftercare effective practices is an implementation checklist complete with practitioner recommended action items. Furthermore, you can see your program and how to do it in a few pages.

An added benefit is that you can use it as a readiness tool to begin the discussion of your aftercare programming or rerun it when you're considering an expansion. It can also be used to strengthen an existing program.

The first thing to determine is whether your community wants to proceed. If there's consensus to do so, then your decision-making team ought to begin assessing where weaknesses and strengths lie. Weaknesses require particular attention because of the tendency to avoid them. Especially the weakest link in the chain. The capacity building tool that follows is a good way to confront the unknown with proven ideas to accomplish critical features of project development. So, use the checklist to size up your willingness to proceed, what needs to be strengthened, and how to do it, then begin assigning work with confidence.

Note that this Effective Practices Action Checklist mirrors (albeit with different populations) that of the other three programs in the Capacity Building series. They each address a local reentry strategy to ameliorate the vexing and expensive problem of recidivism. Capacity Building is the business beneath the business of service deliveries with the mantra: *Permanent Solutions to Permanent Problems.*

To review, these guides in sequence include:

Volume I. *Building Capacity from the Bottom Up: The Key to Sustaining Local Services*

Volume II. *Decriminalizing Mental Illness: A Practical Model for Building Sustainable Crisis Intervention Teams*

Volume III. *Accelerating Juvenile Reentry: A Practical Capacity Building Model for Sustaining Aftercare*

Volume IV. *Accelerating Adult Reentry: A Practical Capacity Building Model for Sustaining Post-Release Transitional Services*

Together, these guides outline in detail how to proceed with a very tangled local problem. Each addresses unique clients with its corresponding approach. All are organized around the program Life Cycle, which conveniently details what must be done and when. A new take on capacity building for permanence ties them together.

Each model can be tackled separately or collectively as resources and will dictate. The promise of this model of delivering public services makes solutions to permanent problems practical and thus doable. By thinking big and acting small, reentry is improved significantly, thus greatly reducing recidivism. Just take it one effective practice at a time.

Always remember that this is your checklist. Keep the integrity of the process then modify as experience informs you. Hence you are building the plan for your next idea.

Figure 1-B. Capacity Building Checklist for Juvenile Aftercare – PHASES I-III, with Key Action Items and Effective Practices
Phase I: Plan and Implement
1.   **Structure leadership to build and preserve core values.**
Effective Practice: Publish and distribute a signed state-level joint policy statement that commits agencies to the new vision of aftercare.
Effective Practice: Organize senior core stakeholder groups according to bottom-up, community-based aftercare critical functions.
Effective Practice: Organize your overall operations staff as Task Teams responsible for specific program core values.
Effective Practice: Organize site-level leadership around a strong judge.
Effective Practice: Organize services delivery stakeholders according to their expertise with and influence on building and using evidence throughout your program.
2.   **Assess capacity to deliver services by understanding your client.**
Effective Practice: Assess organizational capacity to deliver services as preparation for implementation.

Effective Practice: Define your transitional services in terms of your target populations.	

3.	**Narrow your scope to include what can be done.**

Effective Practice: State a vision with a purpose that is motivating by its challenge and tempered by scope that considers what can and can't be done.	

Effective Practice: Define the project scope in terms of your target populations' needed competencies for productive independence in the community.	

4.	**Design analysis and evaluation to preserve core programming components.**

Effective Practice: Design a logic model for the chain of outcomes to define project results and means to get there.	

Effective Practice: Operationalize impact analysis and process evaluation according to core components to ensure evidence-based practice fidelity.	

5.	**Plan for stable resources.**

Effective Practice: Conduct annual strategic planning devoted to sustaining resources, which include personnel, equipment and material, and funding streams with multiple goal-oriented purposes.	

6.	**Build evidence-based services on an evidence-based program and processes.**

Effective Practice: Build an evidence-based program and processes to support your evidence-based practices.	

Effective Practice: Build a single plan for individualized, comprehensive treatment that focuses on post-program aftercare.	

Effective Practice: Collect data that support the evidence-based practices adopted.	

7.	**Build key staff to support and deliver strengths-based services.**

Effective Practice: Select staff with a multi-step vetting process.	

Effective Practice: Create an organizational structure that's lean and flat, in which everyone must be qualified and ready to deliver line services.	

Phase II: Operate and Stabilize
8. Operationalize the plan.
Effective Practice: Practice hands-on developmental leadership and train to sustain.
Effective Practice: Continuously engage the citizens.
Effective Practice: Engage collaborative leadership skills, especially with external change agents.
Effective Practice: Understand programming readiness to help determine capacity to deliver defined services.
Effective Practice: Extend capacity assessment into a statement of cost effectiveness.
Effective Practice: Carefully limit project scope to keep from overextending service delivery capacity.
Effective Practice: Become data driven by putting the components of evidence gathering in place.
Effective Practice: Develop a dashboard of results-based accountability.
Effective Practice: Maintain resources by keeping stakeholders informed.
Effective Practice: Have the money follow youth targeted by aftercare.
Effective Practice: Have the aftercare services continuum emphasize capability for independent living.
Effective Practice: Create a workplace to tap intrinsic motivation.
Effective Practice: Tame turnover by managing employee and leadership succession.
Phase III: Sustain and Expand
9. Sustain operations via brokered services and mapped service systems.
Effective Practice: Sustain the brokerage of services.
Effective Practice: Map the terrain of service partners to identify barriers to client service access.

10. Expand incrementally and locally.
Effective Practice: Designate a single body to guide strategic planning for expansion.
Effective Practice: Design a strategic planning process for modest expansion.

GLOSSARY

Capacity building

This infrastructure is a matrix of those resources and services specifically chosen for their long-term commitment and capabilities toward resolving the local problem addressed. These supports are both internal (organizational) and external (private, community, state, and federal). They include a combination of:

- *Political will* – The collective means and determination to see the project through to sustainability.

- *Human capacity* – Staff developed for their wholistic contribution to building the service idea.

- *Leadership* – An executive director and board chosen for the will to succeed by long-term collaboration. They believe in and live bottom-up leadership based on humility and introspection.

- *Dedicated matrices of local services* – A team of local entities chosen for their applicability, dedication to the program, and willingness to collaborate inter-organizationally.

- *Facilities* – Ideally located in the municipality served, including equipment and supplies, with funds for replenishment, operation, and measured expansions.

- *Capability* – Operational capability, such as financial management and training.

- *Funding* – Separate reliable streams/sources of financial support for program development, maintenance, and expansion.

- *Processes* – A measurably effective means of service delivery; the efficient and effective daily work of the project. For the purposes of Capacity Building, a process is continuous versus a project, which is terminal. The former focuses on vision; the latter aims at getting a task done. Processes must be effective (doing the right things) and efficient (doing the right things well).

- *Measured effectiveness and efficiency* – A means of analysis in place to measure the effectiveness of improving the target population and developing the "picture" of success for program justification. The best effectiveness measures easily translate to cost-effectiveness, that is a dollar invested yields a dollar plus in "profit." This is basic to making the trade-off argument to support your idea. Analysis of efficiency is also necessary.

The overall goal of capacity building is to *close the services-to-needs gap.*

Chain of Outcomes

The chain of outcomes illustrates what a project is doing and why. It's a key management tool to help you do what you say you will and justify your program. It includes *immediate inputs,* such as the tools and work of reentry. These work elements connect to *intermediate outcomes,* which can be numbers, such as the number of participants served. Finally, *ultimate outcomes* measure progress toward prosocial behaviors and independence. The chain demonstrates how the work done today connects to community involvement and pro-social strengthening to reach a vision tomorrow and continuously going forward.

- *Inputs* – These are the *activities and tools* of capacity building. They enable productivity and efficiency.
    - Planning – Establishing what to measure to tell the story of progress
    - Building the business of delivering reentry – Putting the activities, tools, and people in place

- *Intermediate Outcomes* – These are largely numbers, which connect to goals. This is about effectiveness (doing the right things).
    - Program enrollment and participation
    - Skill development and education

- *Ultimate Outcomes* – These are changes that translate to successful youth independence and ultimately community betterment.
    - Behavioral change – Making good choices. Completing school. Learning a trade or getting post-secondary education.
    - Community reintegration – Getting and keeping a meaningful job that can support a family
    - Community safety and well-being – Reduction in delinquency and recidivism as a result of your reentry program

The importance of the chain of outcomes for Capacity Building is threefold. First, the chain keeps the program, people, and infrastructure focused on goals, mission, and vision. Secondly, impact can be measured then converted to a Return on Investment (ROI) statement. Simply, doing juvenile reentry does not cost; it makes a profit. Lastly, it's aspirational, as progress can be seen and noted in the chain outcomes that prove the idea is working. Each step in this chain of outcomes builds upon the previous one, illustrating how a comprehensive reentry program can lead to positive changes for juveniles and their communities.

Effective practice

This is an action that's been proven by application and experience of successful practitioners to be practicable and productive, and which leads to measurable good effect.

However, it's *not* a "best" practice, because what's best is uniquely individual to a project, determined by myriad variables, and not easily replicable. What's effective in one locale has relevance to another only when properly implemented via Capacity Building and proven to work in that new locale. Effective practices are the *essential* activities that can be applied in whole or in part to other service development projects.

Evidence-Based Practice (EBP)

An EBP is a practice proven to be efficient and effective by practical application over time. It's the careful use of the best evidence in making decisions or acting. Understanding this concept is fundamental to delivering an idea that makes meaningful and cost-beneficial improvements. In other words, a project must make a good argument for spending public dollars. An EBP contributes significantly to sustainability.

Its research basis determines that, under certain conditions, the practice can have, must have, a measurable, positive result or results—usually a favorable change in the behavior of a target population. More important, the way an EBP is conducted is continually informed by meaningful data. A few performance measures will tell the story of program progress and effect, and they must be quantified in dollars to compute cost effectiveness. The language of money is the best argument to win a little of very limited funding.

Relative to capacity building to deliver local public services, sometimes the term "evidence-based practice" is misconstrued as the label for the entire task of building capacity or the program itself. An EBP is only *part* of, yet essential to, capacity building.

It is a service or procedure within the wider work of building the supporting infrastructure for that service or procedure. EBPs are organized by major action items. Taken together, they form a logical process to build your idea to "bricks and mortar" in the community. If you can't prove an action is first cost effective then makes a difference, the project dwindles and fades away.

Implementation

Implementation for Capacity Building describes the practical sequence of activities that brings a service idea from concept to permanent presence in the community. It does this by planning, operating, sustaining, and expanding a service over time. Learning how to implement an idea with transformative possibilities takes time, experimentation, and determination.

While the Capacity Building process herein provides a promising, proven process for implementation, every idea for local service is unique, and practitioners must learn and adjust as they go.

Leader

The leader of today and especially tomorrow lives and works by continuously practicing virtue, developing character, and promoting well-being in self and community. Thus, they exemplify leadership to their staff. These leaders continuously work on the Ancients' Cardinal Virtues of Justice, Wisdom, Courage, and Temperance while pursuing well-being for self, family, organization, and community. Likewise, they constantly practice character through humility and introspection. They inspire the organizational body to be more than the sum of its parts, with a worthy vision of what can and should be. They are participatory by truly serving staff, bottom up. They see problems and obstacles as opportunities to grow and stretch. Thus, they improve staff, hastening the march to individual self-worth and organizational success.

Leadership

Leadership is much contested and discussed. The Teal Trust refers to modern interpretations from noted scholars: Peter Drucker stresses that a leader simply has followers. John C. Maxwell reduces leadership to the simple ability to influence others. Warren Bennis describes the abilities of a leader such as self-awareness, building trust, and being effective. This author would add the qualities of humility and introspection guided by evolving morals.

Leaders who understand capacity building are essential to the successful implementation and stabilization of public service ideas. Leadership, then, consists of certain qualities in these stakeholders. They must inspire the staff of an organization to achieve defined goals and enable others to be leaders in an atmosphere of calculated risk, learning, and fun. Bottom-up leaders in this reform movement to build the business beneath the business of delivering public services are the guiding lights of social transformation.

Partner vs. Collaborator

A partner is an individual or agency bringing resources—monetary, physical, political, or human—to an endeavor. This distinguishes a partner stakeholder from a collaborator. While the partner brings expertise and/or resources to the project, the collaborator becomes an *integral part* of the effort and idea.

The capacity building effort may require partners who can provide labor or donate in-kind hard goods. The service idea must also have collaborators who may be able to sway political will—an elected body, for example—to support the project under development. They are believers. Put more commonly, partners are pursued for the *things or people* they can provide, whereas collaborators are pursued for their *creativity, ideas, and connections.*

The terms partnership, cooperation, and collaboration are usually used interchangeably. This can lead to confusion, especially when targeting recruiting and development strategies to each category of supporter. Partnerships and collaborations are broader and longer term than those who may simply cooperate with your project in a limited way. People can cooperate on a task to get to the end of the day. This is a vast difference from people who see a vision and work to get there. The best partners are also collaborators who help the project achieve its vision.

A partner's contribution of material support such as a donation, supplies, and perhaps a few volunteer hours is important but terminal. A collaborator makes a permanent contribution to building or sustaining the idea. You may approach a partner such as a local business representative because he upgrades his many computers every few years and donates the old ones. Or, you may approach a corporate lawyer as a partner for his expertise in writing a start-up charter for your board. If that lawyer becomes involved in the long term as a legal representative, he or she would be considered a collaborator. Differentiation is necessary as each group of supporters needs to be courted for what they believe and can do and what they bring to the table, preferably for an extended period.

Partnership

A partnership is an agreement, usually formal, between parties who agree to a common endeavor. When a partnership is successful, it's marked by cooperation, the taking of collective and individual responsibility, and being accountable for attaining stated goals. When a partnership is formed, ideally the partners involved become collaborators.

Relative to the concept of Capacity Building, partnership has several meanings depending on the phase of a project's life cycle.

- *Planning* – During the planning stage, the essential partnership is the constellation of founding members, which includes at least the executive director and grows from there.

- *Operation and Stabilization* – During operations, partnerships greatly expand to include individuals and agencies that bring necessary talent and services to the effort. This goes considerably beyond necessary program staff. These partnerships may include service providers or agencies, consultants, and advisors, plus those connected to resources such as hard goods, volunteers, or funding.

- *Sustained growth* – When a service idea is in the hard-fought and won position to expand, partnerships expand, especially if the expansion is to another locale. A partnership then becomes an assembly of likeminded people of varying talents. They all have a long-term goal of delivering a service to address a social ill that continually improves the target population and thus the community.

Process

The word "process," as used in this study, has characteristics specific to the task of capacity building in the public sector. It's based on the life cycle of the project idea—from concept to reality to perpetuation. The correct process leads to *permanent solutions to permanent problems* in the local public sector.

The process of building business and administrative infrastructure to deliver a service actualizes the resources of networked entities representing a matrix of talent and skills. The multiplier effect of organized, focused networks of people allows the whole to be greater than the sum of its parts. The matrices of people and services are specifically structured by the needs of and solutions to the problem at hand.

The local project development process evolves and grows organically as capacity building directs resources to answer local service needs, resulting in well-being, community betterment, and social transformation.

Public service project

Many local public sector ideas are for one-time purchases of supplies, equipment, or training, for example. Other projects are part of a much larger whole. An example is an effort to enhance the academic success of elementary school children. Only one part of that project is a school readiness program that offers parenting classes and health screening for infants and preschool children. Capacity Building attacks the tangled root causes of social dysfunction, such as having a single parent, female head of a household of several children.

In this study and its reform movement models, a service project is a local idea to deliver a service, over time, with the purpose of effecting positive behaviors in a target population. In turn, the project gradually, measurably, collectively, leads to improvements in social conditions and thus in community betterment.

Recidivism

"Recidivism," according to the Bureau of Justice Statistics, "is measured by criminal acts that result in the re-arrest, reconviction, or return to prison with or without a new sentence during a three-year period following the prisoner's release."[127]

A problem with this definition is that recidivism is usually only measured while an inmate is still under court supervision or in a reentry program when measurement is easier to manipulate. What about, for example, measuring revocation back to a cell? It's that much more remarkable that aftercare reduces recidivism at far greater rates than criminal justice system-sponsored reentry programs.

Recidivism, therefore, doesn't reflect the true performance of the aftercare programming necessary to complete the inmate's transition to home and community. Still, the recidivism rate is used as a primary measure of institutional or agency program reentry "success." The term, thus the measure, can mean many things. Is it a return to injurious behavior, for example, a relapse to substance abuse? Is it a re-arrest or a reconviction? Or is it simply a return to criminal activity? It is all these, so clarity is needed.

Recidivism should be measured in yearly increments after all programming is completed, but this is quite expensive and difficult to do. A simple definition elucidates what the result of a criminal justice-oriented project versus a local aftercare service project should realistically be. A return to criminal behavior signifies a return to social dysfunction and unproductivity, a probable return to dependency on expensive social and private support networks, more victimization, and the loss of a potentially productive citizen.

The term recidivism needs to be reconsidered because, as it's now used, it only measures reincarceration for the short term. It doesn't reflect the reality that the work of reentry is only done to prepare for the long-term work of successful post-release aftercare. It's aftercare that completes the individual's transition to the community and away from bad behaviors and crime to productivity. To accurately reflect the effect of reentry/aftercare programming, recidivism must have a long-term reference. It should refer to a return to criminal behavior, usually several years after a sanction or rehabilitation program, whether there's a re-arrest, a reconviction, or a return to incarceration. Recidivism defined this way is better suited to measure the effect of a good aftercare program, part of an overall local re-entry strategy.

Social capital

Social capital is the collective quality and strength of a social organization. It's human capital that springs from individual qualities and strengths.[128] Social capital is understood in the context of how a community facilitates bringing people together to problem solve when motivated by a common cause. It springs from a program of human capital development that focuses on wellness, well-being, and character education and development.

Social capital in this present study refers to the collective capability of networks of services and people established by Capacity Building to support and develop local social services projects.

Socially transformative

A service project is socially transformative when it fosters measurable improvements in individuals that ultimately contribute to community well-being. A post-release aftercare services program, for example, improves the employability of a former inmate, which results in long-term self- or family-supporting employment. Another example is a program for school readiness, which helps children stay in school and thus out of eventual trouble with school failure, risky behavior, drugs, or the law. This can translate to being a productive adult with skills for a self-sustaining career. As the individual becomes a productive citizen, so the community is transformed—one person at a time.

Success

A primary focus in studying the reform models highlighted herein is on the formal measurement of impact and results, or success in achieving stated goals. Analyzing the impact or result of a program is difficult. It takes years to establish a project and more years to reach a target population. Then it takes yet more years to begin to measurably change the behavior of that group. Thereafter, it can take a few additional years to conduct a sound, rigorous analysis of results, or degree of program success. Thus, few long-term studies are done that test program impact at least one year after program completion, let alone longer term.

Since project stakeholders cannot begin to assess meaningful impact until the project is self-renewing and permanent, let's use a simple funds-based criterion of success. A successful project is one that's still accomplishing originally stated goals, with permanent operational resources in place, at least one year after any start-up soft funding has evaporated.

Stability

Project stability means operational processes have become routine and are supported with staff and reliable resources. It does not necessarily mean the project has worked out the details of efficiency and effectiveness nor achieved success in making a positive difference in the local community.

Stability as used in the Capacity Building Life Cycle refers to Phase II: Operations, in which the project reaches its first level of daily function facilitating service delivery. It's the state of project development that focuses mainly on processes leading to permanency.

One difficulty with service project development is that it's difficult to link a program to ultimate measures of community improvement. Therefore, successful programs must focus on interim measures that link to community well-being. A school program, for example, may track graduation rates and placement in post-secondary education. This is an interim measure, as post-secondary education is only a step. There's no guarantee it will result in an individual's long-term employment in a career that will sustain a family. This distinction is relevant because many projects focus on stability as a primary end goal, whereas it's an *initial* goal and, at best, an *interim* goal of Capacity Building.

Stability, then, is a state of routine operations with the focus on improving processes and conducting initial analysis to determine downstream measurable impact to justify sustainability.

Sustainability

An enterprise that has reached sustainability has a reliable business infrastructure, operational capacity, and especially permanent resources to persevere. The project ultimately has the *potential,* usually after years of successful operation, to become transformational in the community. Moreover, a service programming idea made permanent proves the model for other ideas to solve a social need.

Sustainability for any service project means that the project is generating adequate administrative, material, human, and financial resources to function productively for the long term.

Project sustainability is also determined by its contribution to general community well-being as evidenced by a thriving or at least measurably improving target population. Note, however, that this state of project development precedes a project becoming fully transformational.

Transformational

A *transformational* public service, in terms of Capacity Building, refers to a municipal public service that produces significant, long-term, positive behavioral changes within its community. Its goal is to build *permanent solutions to permanent problems.* When this eventually happens, the service is *fully transformational* for both the target population and the community.

Well-Being versus Wellness (of a community)

A distinction between community well-*being* and well*ness* will elucidate how the terms apply to Capacity Building.

Wellness herein refers to public or project infrastructure devoted largely to health. For simplicity's sake, it's the purview of the medical professions and helping arts. While health is certainly critical for thriving, wellness is only a few pixels in the whole picture of well-being.

Well-being connotes quality of life, which encompasses but expands beyond physical health. A community's well-being is determined by having positive activities and services available to support thriving and the conditions of happiness for the individual to discover. The community has little well-being if dysfunction—e.g., crime, drugs, poverty, food insecurity, mental illness, unemployment, inadequate schooling—is at toxic levels.

When discussing the ultimate result of community services, it's helpful to under-stand it in terms of community betterment and eventual well-being. This keeps the project focused on what it should be doing day-to-day to positively affect the community. Well-being reflects a community's strengths and attributes as a favorable place in which to live, work, recreate, and especially, raise a family. A community that displays well-being is a thriving community.

Most programs wrongly focus on immediate results, which are usually the numbers of people going through a program, for example. This may or may not lead to a better community or effects such as higher primary school graduation rates and lower recidivism rates during court supervision. *What matters is how the behavior of service recipients changes and how that change ultimately improves the individual and consequently the community.*

Understanding well-being and how a project effects it is vital to gathering the right data, support, and decision-making, and having a successful project well beyond implementation and stabilization.

The goal is to help citizens become free of public support by being self-sufficient and thriving. Living independently is a responsibility and its own reward; it's called pride.

REFERENCES

Altschuler, D., Armstrong, T., "Intensive Aftercare for High-Risk Juveniles: A Community Care Model," Office of Juvenile Justice and Delinquency Prevention, 1994. *https://www.ncjrs.gov/pdffiles/juvcc.pdf.* Viewed March 3, 2024.

Altschuler, D., Armstrong, T., *Intensive Juvenile Aftercare Reference Guide,* the Juvenile Reintegration and Aftercare Center, Sacramento, CA, 2004. *http://www.csus.edu/ssis/cdcps/intensiveaftercarereferenceguide.pdf.* Viewed April 1, 2013.

Annie E. Casey Foundation, "Equal Voice," 2012. *http://www.aecf.org.* Viewed March 21, 2024.

Annie E. Casey Foundation, "A Road Map for Juvenile Justice Reform," 2013a. *A Road Map for Juvenile Justice Reform - The Annie E. Casey Foundation (aecf.org).* Viewed March 25, 2024.

Annie E. Casey Foundation, "Juvenile Detention Alternative Initiative, Core Values," 2013b. *http://www.aecf.org/MajorInitiatives/JuvenileDetentionAlternativesInitiative/CoreStrategies.aspx.* Viewed April 10, 2013.

Armstrong, T., Altschuler, D., "Intensive Aftercare Program," 2000. *http://www.csus.edu/ssis/cdcps/iap.htm.* Viewed April 1, 2013.

Bamburger, M., Hewitt, E., "Monitoring and Evaluation: What Can They Do for Me?" *Monitoring and Evaluating Urban Development Programs, A Handbook for Program Managers and Researchers,* World Bank Technical Paper no. 53, Washington, D. C., 1986.

Bilchik, S., "Five Emerging Practices in Juvenile Reentry," Center for Juvenile Justice Reform, Georgetown University Public Policy Institute and The National Reentry Resource Center, 2014. *https://csgjusticecenter.org/2014/03/24/five-emerging-practices-in-juvenile-reentry/.* Viewed March 25, 2024.

Blase, K., Fixsen, D., "Core Intervention Components: Identifying and Operationalizing What Makes Programs Work," U.S. Department of Health and Human Services, 2013. *https://aspe.hhs.gov/reports/core-intervention-components-*

identifying-and-operationalizing-what-makes-programs-work-0.
Viewed March 25, 2024.

Bliss, M., Emshoff, J., "Workbook for Designing a Process Evaluation," 2002. Viewed May 2, 2013.

Bolmant, L., Deal, T., *Reframing Organizations: Artistry and Choice and Leadership,* 4th ed. San Francisco: Jossey-Bass, 2008.

Butts, J., Roman, J., "Changing Systems: Outcomes from the RWJF Reclaiming Futures Initiative on Juvenile Justice and Substance Abuse," A Reclaiming Futures National Evaluation Report, Portland, Ore.: Reclaiming Futures National Program Office, Portland State University, 2007.

Dubin, J., "Metamorphosis: How Missouri Rehabilitates Juvenile Offenders," American Educator, Summer, 2012.

Evans, J., "The Most Important Part of Strategic Planning: Operationalizing Strategy, Method Frameworks," A Division of Forte Solutions Group, 2012. *http://www.methodframeworks.com/blog/2012/most-important-part-strategic-planning-%E2%80%9Coperationalizing%E2%80%9D-strategy/index.html.* Viewed May 29, 2013.

Fulmer, R., "Choose Tomorrow's Leaders Today: Succession Planning Grooms Firms for Success," Grazaidio Business Review, v. 5, iss. 1, 2002. Graziadio School of Business and Management, Pepperdine University, Malibu, Calif.

Carey, M., "EBP Step-By-Step Planning Guide: Summary Page." *http://www.thecareygroupinc.com/documents/EBP%20Step%20by%20Step%20Planning%20Guide.pdf.* Viewed May 30, 2013.

Cary Group, "Checklist: Building and Sustaining an EBP Organization," 2011. *http://www.thecareygroupinc.com.* Viewed April 25, 2013.

Collins, J., *Good to Great . . . in 30 Minutes: A 30-Minute Expert Summary.* Berkeley, Calif: Garamond Press, 2012.

Council of State Governments 2005, "Report of the Re-Entry Policy Council: Charting the Safe and Successful Return of Prisoners to the Community," Council of State Governments, Reentry Policy Council, New York: Council of State Governments, January 2005. *http://reentrypolicy.org/Report.* Viewed March 25, 2024.

Covey, S., Merrill, A. R., and Merrill, R. R., *First Things First*. New York: Free Press, 1996.

Crane, T., *Using Transformational Coaching to Create a High-Performance Coaching Culture,* 3rd ed. San Diego: FTA Press, 2009.

Dubin, J., "Metamorphosis: How Missouri Rehabilitates Juvenile Offenders," *American Educator,* Summer 2012.

Greenwood, P., *Changing Lives: Delinquency Prevention as Crime Control.* Chicago: University of Chicago Press, 2006.

Griffin, P., Steele, R., & Franklin, K., "Aftercare Reality and Reform," *Pennsylvania Progress,* Pittsburg: National Center for Juvenile Justice, 2007.

Henderson, M. & Hanley, D., "Planning for Quality: A Strategy for Reentry Initiatives," *Western Criminology Review,* 2006, vol. 7(2), pp. 62-78. Accessed March 31, 2024.

Jaszczolt, K., Potkanski, T., Alwasiak, S., "Internal Project M & E System and Development of Evaluation Capacity," 2013.*http://webcache.googleusercontent.com/ search?q=cache:VYmfGZzUuZ4J:ec.europa.eu/regional_policy/sources/docconf/ budapeval/work/jaszczolt.doc+&cd=1&hl=en&ct=clnk&gl=us.* Viewed June 30, 2013.

"Joint Policy Statement on Aftercare: Commonwealth of Pennsylvania," 2004. *http://www.modelsforchange.net/publications/153/.* Viewed March 2, 2024.

Kaye, B., Jordan-Evans, S., *Love 'Em or Lose 'Em: Getting Good People to Stay.* Oakland, Calif.: Berrett Koehler Publishers, 1999.

Klopovic, J., Vasu, M., Yearwood, D., *Effective Program Practices for At-Risk Youth.* New York: Civic Research Institute, 2003.

Lipsey, M., Howell, J., Kelly, M., Chapman, G., Carver, D., "Improving the Effectiveness of Juvenile Justice Programs: A New Perspective on Evidence-Based Practice," Georgetown, Washington, D.C.: Center for Juvenile Justice Reform, 2010.

Marguerite Casey Foundation, "Organizational Capacity Assessment Tool," 2012. *http://caseygrants.org/resources/org-capacity-assessment.* Viewed April 22, 2013.

Search Marguerite Casey Foundation Organizational Capacity Assessment Tool for updated link.

Mendel, R., "The Missouri Model: Reinventing the Practice of Rehabilitating Youthful Offenders," 2010. Baltimore: The Annie E. Case Foundation. *https://njjn.org/uploads/digital-library/model.pdf.* Viewed March 25, 2024.

Models for Change, *Pennsylvania's Juvenile Justice System Enhancement Strategy: Achieving our Balanced and Restorative Justice Mission Through Evidence-Based Policy and Practice,* 2012. *http://www.modelsforchange.net/publications/342/.* Viewed March 25, 2024.

National Institute of Corrections, "Implementing Evidence-Based Practice in Community Corrections: The Principles of Effective Intervention," 2004. *http://nicic.gov/Library/019342.* Viewed March 25, 2024.

North Carolina Department of Juvenile Justice Division of Juvenile Justice, *Service Plan Protocols,* n.d. OJJDP Model Programs Guide, n.d., Office of Justice programs. *http://www.ojjdp.gov/ojp.gov/model-programs-guide/home.* Viewed March 25, 2024.

Pennsylvania Commission on Crime and Delinquency, "Pennsylvania's Juvenile Justice System Enhancement Strategy: A Monograph," 2012. *http://www.modelsforchange.net/publications/342/.* Viewed March 25, 2024.

Pressman, J. & Wildavsky, A., *Implementation: How Great Expectations in Washington are Dashed in Oakland.* Berkeley: University of California Press, 3rd ed., 1984.

SAMHSA, Substance Abuse and Mental Health Services Administration, *Access to Recovery Implementation Toolkit,* 2010. HHS Publication No. (SMA) 10-4596. Rockville, MD: Center for Substance Abuse Treatment, Division of Services Improvement, Substance Abuse and Mental Health Services Administration. *https://www.yumpu.com/en/document/view/44361711/access-to-recovery-implementation-toolkit-samhsa-store-.* Viewed March 25, 2024.

Shilling, D., n.d., "Retention Strategies for Key Employees in B-to-B Companies." *http://www.americanbusinessmedia.com/images/abm/pdfs/resources/Retention_Strategies.pdf.* Viewed July 7, 2013.

Taylor-Powell, E., Steele, S. "Collecting Evaluation Data: An Overview of Sources and Methods," Program Development and Evaluation, University of Wisconsin Cooperative Extension, Madison, WI, 1996.

UNESCO 2011, "Results-Based Programming, Management and Monitoring (RBM) Approach as Applied at UNESCO - Guiding Principles," *https://www.coe.int/t/budgetcommittee/ Source/RBBSEMINAR/UNESCO_RBMguide_en.pdf*. Viewed March 25, 2024.

Vincent, G., Guy, L., Grisso, T. "Risk Assessment in Juvenile Justice: A Guidebook for Implementation," 2012. The John D. and Catherine T. MacArthur Foundation. *http://modelsforchange.net/publications/346*. Viewed March 25, 2024.

Virginia Department of Juvenile Justice "Virginia Department of Juvenile Justice Re-Entry Initiative: Four-Year Strategic Plan Executive Summary," 2010. *http://www.djj.virginia.gov/initiatives/pdf/ReentryExecutiveSummary_12142010.pdf*. Viewed April 10, 2013.

Wiebush, R., McNulty, B. & Le, T. "Implementation of the Intensive Community-Based Aftercare Program," *Juvenile Justice Bulletin*, 2000, Office of Juvenile Justice and Delinquency Prevention.

World Bank 2012, "Decentralization and Subnational Regional Economics – Service Delivery," *http://www.worldbank.org*. Viewed May 16, 2013.

Zastava, D., "Measuring Actual Project–Benefits - How to Maintain Your Project Profile and Funding," 2000. *http://gisdevelopment.net/proceedings/gita/2000/people/ peoi056pf.htm*. Viewed June 20, 2013.

Links to Practical Advice

https://s3.amazonaws.com/static.nicic.gov/Library/021041.pdf (Viewed May 25, 2024.)

Implementing Effective Correctional Management of Offenders in the Community Outcome and Process Measures. This report presents the outcome and process measures used to gauge the effectiveness of the Integrated Model in reducing offender recidivism. Each component found within a measure has information regarding its definition, tool/data source, description, frequency, and individual who collects the data. Components are organized into the following measures: recidivism; risk; proxy risk; supervision length; dosage; revocation and violation; program effectiveness; assessment; case plan; workload; violations; organizational climate; and collaboration.

http://nicic.gov/Library/019342 (Viewed May 25, 2024.)

Implementing Evidence-Based Practice in Community Corrections: The Principles of Effective Intervention. Topics discussed include: evidence-based practice (EBP); term clarification; and eight principles for effective interventions. The authors consider the following matters: assess actuarial risk/needs, enhance intrinsic motivation, target interventions, skill train with directed practice, increase positive reinforcement, engage ongoing support in natural communities, measure relevant processes/practices, and provide measurement feedback; components of correctional interventions; implementing EBP principles; applying the principles at the case, agency, and system levels; seven recommended strategies for implementing effective interventions; and levels of research evidence.

https://www.yumpu.com/en/document/view/44361711/access-to-recovery-implementation-toolkit-samhsa-store- (Viewed May 25, 2024.)

Access to Recovery Implementation Toolkit. The Access to Recovery (ATR) Implementation Toolkit consists of three workbooks prepared by the Substance Abuse and Mental Health Services Administration (SAMHSA) ATR program. The workbooks were developed as planning, implementation, and operational tools to assist the Single State Authority and tribal program officials and their project management teams. SAMHSA hopes the information contained in the workbooks is also useful to others interested in learning about ATR's provision of services using vouchers and the integration of diverse services within a single collaborative system. The workbooks include many lessons the grantees learned in the first two ATR cohorts from 2004 to 2007 and from 2007 to 2010. Many practical tools are available in these documents, especially the step-by-step workbooks and ATR Tips.

http://www.raguide.org (Viewed May 25, 2024.)
The *Results-Based Accountability Implementation Guide: A Comprehensive Resource for the RBA/OBA Community* is a helpful sequence of penetrating questions about building a results/outcomes-based service program. This guide is intended for those who are implementing some form of Results-Based Accountability™ in their community, city, school district, county, state, or nation. Implementation is no small matter. The leap from theory to practice requires courage, time, discipline, and some knowledge about HOW to do the work, to which this guide is devoted. It's an attempt to summarize as much of what we know about implementation as possible. The guide is organized by questions—the hardest ones you might ask—and then followed by the most effective practical answer possible.

https://nicic.gov/resources/nic-library/all-library-items/tools-trade-guide-incorporating-science-practice (Viewed May 25, 2024.)
Tools of the Trade: A Guide to Incorporating Science into Practice. This guide explains the application of evidence-based research findings to the practice of offender supervision. Sections of this manual include: supervision as a behavioral management process to reduce recidivism; behavior and change; assessment and planning; communication tools; information tools; incentives to shape offender behavior; service tools; offender types; and guiding principles.

http://www.modelsforchange.net/publications/342/ (Viewed May 25, 2024.)
Pennsylvania's Juvenile Justice System Enhancement Strategy. The goals of Pennsylvania's Juvenile Justice System Enhancement Strategy (JJSES) align with those of Balanced and Restorative Justice (BARJ). JJSES seeks to reduce harm by applying the best-known research to the principles and goals of BARJ. A few ways that JJSES supports a BARJ mission of reduced harm include: using actuarial assessment tools, cognitive behavioral interventions, and performance measures to make incremental improvements, and addressing not just the youthful offender but the entire family. This monograph provides juvenile justice system stakeholders with practical information on how daily practices can be improved to achieve better juvenile justice outcomes. The

monograph divides and groups the implementation activities of JJSES into four stages and identifies support resources for each stage.

https://www.aecf.org/resources/juvenile-detention-alternatives-initiative (Viewed May 25, 2024.)
The Annie E. Casey Foundation helped pave the way for the Missouri Model. The Juvenile Detention Alternatives Initiative (JDAI) was designed to support the Casey Foundation's vision that all youth involved in the juvenile justice system have opportunities to develop into healthy, productive adults. After more than 15 years of innovation and replication, JDAI is one of the nation's most effective, influential, and widespread juvenile justice system reform initiatives.

JDAI focuses on the juvenile detention component of the juvenile justice system because youth are often unnecessarily or inappropriately detained at great expense, with long-lasting negative consequences for both public safety and youth development. JDAI promotes changes to policies, practices, and programs to:

- reduce reliance on secure confinement;
- improve public safety; reduce racial disparities and bias;
- save taxpayers' dollars; and
- stimulate overall juvenile justice reforms.

Since its inception in 1992, JDAI has repeatedly demonstrated that jurisdictions can safely reduce reliance on secure detention.

http://modelsforchange.net/publications/36 (Viewed May 25, 2024.)
Risk Assessment in Juvenile Justice: A Guidebook for Implementation. This guide provides a structure for jurisdictions, juvenile probation, or centralized statewide agencies striving to implement risk assessment or to improve their current risk assessment practices. Risk assessment in this guide refers to the practice of using a structured tool that combines information about youth to classify them as low, moderate, or high risk for reoffending or continued delinquent activity, as well as identify factors that might reduce that risk on an individual basis. The purpose of such risk assessment tools is to help make decisions about youths' placement and supervision and create intervention plans that will reduce their level of risk. The guide is practical and can be used as part of overall aftercare program planning and implementation.

http://www.ncjj.org/About/History.aspx (Viewed May 25, 2024.)

The *National Center for Juvenile Justice* (NCJJ), located in Pittsburgh, Pennsylvania, is the research division of the National Council of Juvenile and Family Court Judges. It's the oldest juvenile justice research group in the United States, having conducted national and subnational studies on crime and delinquency since 1973. NCJJ is a private, nonprofit organization dedicated to effective justice for children and families through research and technical assistance. For four decades, NCJJ has conducted research and provided objective, factual information that professionals and decision makers in the juvenile and family justice system use to increase effectiveness.

http://www.elc-pa.org (Viewed May 25, 2024.)

The *Education Law Center* is a nonprofit legal advocacy and educational organization dedicated to ensuring that all of Pennsylvania's children have access to a quality public education.

Funding

One of the biggest challenges faced by reentry programs is how to establish funding. Depending on the services offered by your organization, various funding sources could be available. The trick is finding them. The following are a few resources on how to discover the latest information about available funding for criminal justice initiatives, courtesy of The Urban Institute:

The National Reentry Resource Center collects and presents information about funding opportunities for reentry. The mission of the Center is to advance the reentry field through knowledge transfer and dissemination and to promote evidence-based best practices. The Center is a project of the Council of State Governments Justice Center, with these key project partners: the Urban Institute, Association of State Correctional Administrators, and the American Probation and Parole Association. The Center is also guided by Advisory Committees, which help coordinate support and services for Second Chance Act grantees and the reentry field. Their objectives are to:

- Provide a one-stop, interactive source of current, user-friendly *reentry information.*

- Identify, document, and promote *evidence-based practices.*

- Deliver individualized, targeted *technical assistance* to the Second Chance Act grantees.

- Advance the reentry field through *training, distance learning, and knowledge development.*

www.nationalreentryresourcecenter.org/ (Viewed May 25, 2024.)

The Report of the Reentry Policy Council is a good source for tips on funding strategies for reentry efforts. The report includes a chapter on securing funding streams for reentry initiatives with comprehensive information and suggestions. The Reentry Policy Council (RPC) was established in 2001 to assist state government officials grappling with the increasing number of people leaving prisons and jails to return to the communities they left behind. The RPC was formed with two specific goals in mind:

- To develop bipartisan *policies and principles* for elected officials and other policymakers to consider as they evaluate reentry issues in their jurisdictions.

- To facilitate *coordination and information-sharing* among organizations implementing reentry initiatives, researching trends, communicating about related issues, or funding projects.

https://csgjusticecenter.org/publications/ (Viewed 25 May 2024.)

Candid, formerly The Foundation Center, offers a directory of U.S. private foundations. (Information was current at the time of this writing.) It's supported by close to 550 foundations and is the leading source of information about philanthropy worldwide. Through data, analysis, and training, it connects people who want to change the world to the resources they need to succeed. Candid maintains the most comprehensive database on U.S. and, increasingly, global grant-makers and their grants—a robust, accessible knowledge bank for the sector. It also operates research, education, and training programs designed to advance knowledge of philanthropy at every level. Thousands of people visit Candid's website each day and are served in its five regional library/learning centers and its network of 450 funding information centers located in public libraries, community foundations, and educational institutions nationwide and beyond.

https://candid.org/?fcref=lr (Viewed 25 May 2024.)

Grants.gov provides public access to comprehensive information on new federal funding opportunities. This site allows users to register for daily email updates. Grants.gov is your source to find and apply for federal grants.

www.grants.gov (Viewed 25 May 2024.)

Contact Links for the Model Programs

http://www.modelsforchange.net/index.html (Viewed 25 May 2024.)
Models for Change supports a network of government and court officials, legal advocates, educators, community leaders, and families working together to ensure that kids who make mistakes are held accountable and treated fairly throughout the juvenile justice process.

http://www.aecf.org/~/media/Pubs/Initiatives/Juvenile%20Detention%20 Alternatives%20Initiative/MOModel/MO_Fullreport_webfinal.pdf (Viewed 25 May 2024.)
The Missouri Model's approach offers a promising alternative to current top-down agency-centered juvenile justice.

vq.com (Viewed 25 May 2024.)
The VQ program provides extraordinary experiences and relationships that allow youth, staff, and families to redefine and reach their highest potential.

https://choice.umbc.edu/ (Viewed 25 May 2024.)
The Choice Program is a community-based, family-centered case management approach to delinquency prevention and youth development.

https://www.reclaimingfutures.org/ (Viewed 25 May 2024.)
Reclaiming Futures is a model for improving juvenile justice through community integration.

riteofpassage.com (Viewed 25 May 2024.)
Rite of Passage is a leading national provider of programs and opportunities for troubled and at-risk youth from social services, welfare agencies, and juvenile courts.

https://www.aspireyouthandfamily.com (Viewed 25 May 2024.)
The mission at Aspire Youth & Family Inc. is to assist young people in overcoming behavioral, emotional, or substance abuse obstacles, so they may realize their full potential.

ENDNOTES

1   D. Altschuler & T. Armstrong, "Intensive Juvenile Aftercare Reference Guide," the Juvenile Reintegration and Aftercare Center, Sacramento, CA, 2004. *http://www.csus.edu/ssis/cdcps/intensiveaftercarereferenceguide.pdf.* Viewed April 1, 2013.

2   Annie E. Casey Foundation, "A Road Map for Juvenile Justice Reform." *http://www.aecf.org/.* Accessed February 4, 2024.

3   Ibid., p. 1.

4   Ibid., p. 6.

5   Ibid., p. 8.

6   Ibid., p. 10.

7   Ibid.

8   Ibid., p. 12.

9   Ibid., p. 15.

10   Annie E. Casey Foundation, "A Road Map for Juvenile Justice Reform," 2013a. *A Road Map for Juvenile Justice Reform - The Annie E. Casey Foundation (aecf.org).* Viewed March 25, 2024.

11   Ibid.

12   Pennsylvania Commission on Crime and Delinquency, "Pennsylvania's Juvenile Justice System Enhancement Strategy: A Monograph," 2012. *http://www.modelsforchange.net/publications/342/.* Viewed March 25, 2024.

13   Annie E. Casey Foundation, "Juvenile Detention Alternative Initiative, Core Values," 2013b. *http://www.aecf.org/MajorInitiatives/JuvenileDetentionAlternativesInitiative/CoreStrategies.aspx.* Viewed April 10, 2013.

14   Op. Cit., Pennsylvania Commission, 2012.

15   Virginia Department of Juvenile Justice, "Virginia Department of Juvenile Justice Re-Entry Initiative: Four-Year Strategic Plan Executive Summary," 2010. *http://www.djj.virginia.gov/initiatives/pdf/ ReentryExecutiveSummary_12142010.pdf.* Viewed April 10, 2013.

16   There is a significant difference between wellness and well-being, especially for the purposes of Capacity Building. Wellness is largely the responsibility of health professionals who deliver medical services, whereas well-being encompasses the totality of an idea—body, mind, and spirit if you will—and the people making it work. It helps define ultimate goals and results to build communities in which people can thrive to their innate potential and define the conditions for happiness to occur.

17   Adapted from http://www.choiceprograms.net. Accessed February 5, 2024.

18   Adapted from The Missouri Model: Reinventing the Practice of Rehabilitating Youthful Offenders. For a full report on the Missouri Model, refer to the Annie E. Casey Foundation, *www.aecf.org.*

19   Ibid.

20   For more details, refer to *http://www.modelsforchange.net/index.html.* Accessed February 5, 2024.

21   *www.reclaimingfutures.org.* Accessed February 5, 2024.

22   Adapted from the VQ website: http://www.vq.com. Accessed February 5, 2024.

23   Adapted from www.reclaimingfutures.org. Accessed February 6, 2024.

24   Adapted from and for further reference see the Aspire home page: *http://www.aspireyouthandfamily.com.* Accessed February 6, 2024.

25 Adapted from *http://www.riteofpassage.com*. Accessed February 6, 2024.

26 T. Armstrong & D. Altschuler, "Intensive Aftercare Program," 2000. *http://www.csus.edu/ssis/cdcps/iap.htm*. Viewed April 1, 2013.

27 The Models for Change bottom-up movement to do community-based aftercare is also changing the way philanthropy is done. Philanthropies such as the MacArthur and Annie E. Casey Foundations recognize they can do the most to effect change by reforming service delivery systems. They do this not by imposing a policy direction but by collaborations that recognize the essential need for grant recipients to chart their own course. The commonality is research. These foundations chart the general goals for a project, present dramatic research to justify it, and work hand in glove, daily in some cases, to see the project to a successful conclusion. Every dollar must produce results.

28 R. Mendel, "The Missouri Model: Reinventing the Practice of Rehabilitating Youthful Offenders," 2010, p. 51. Baltimore: The Annie E. Case Foundation. *https://njjn.org/uploads/digital-library/model.pdf*. Viewed March 25, 2024.

29 With the kind permission of the Marguerite Casey Foundation: *https://www.501commons.org/resources/tools-and-best-practices/assessment/CaseyTool.xls/view*. Accessed February 13, 2024.

30 Ibid.

31 Ibid.

32 Ibid.

33 Adapted from Pennsylvania Commission on Crime and Delinquency, "Pennsylvania's Juvenile Justice System Enhancement Strategy: A Monograph," 2012, p. 14. *http://www.modelsforchange.net/publications/342/*. Viewed March 25, 2024.

34 Vincent, Guy, & Grisso, *Risk Assessment in Juvenile Justice: A Guidebook for Implementation.* MacArthur Foundation, 2012.

35 Ibid.

36 The Cary Group, 2011. *https://www.thecareygroup.com/reports-guides*. Accessed February 12, 2024.

37 The Cary Group, *Building and Sustaining an EBP Organization.* (Adapted from p. 9 of this Checklist & Worksheet.) A free resource to help organizations identify what to do to make further progress on building and sustaining their evidence-based framework. *https://www.thecareygroup.com/reports-guides*. Accessed February 12, 2024.

38 Op. Cit., Vincent, Guy, & Grisso, 2012.

39 Op. Cit., Pennsylvania Commission on Crime and Delinquency, 2012.

40 VQ: *https://www.vq.com/about-us#Scroll*. Viewed June 12, 2024.

41 Ibid.

42 Adapted from *http://caseygrants.org/*. Viewed February 14, 2024.

43 Council of State Governments 2005, "Report of the Re-Entry Policy Council: Charting the Safe and Successful Return of Prisoners to the Community," Council of State Governments, Reentry Policy Council, New York: Council of State Governments, January 2005. *http://reentrypolicy.org/Report*. Viewed March 25, 2024.

44 Op. Cit., Pennsylvania Commission, 2012.

45 K. Blasé & D. Fixsen, "Core Intervention Components: Identifying and Operationalizing What Makes Programs Work," U.S. Department of Health and Human Services, 2013, p. 3. *https://aspe.hhs.gov/reports/core-intervention-components-identifying-and-operationalizing-what-makes-programs-work-0*. Viewed March 25, 2024.

46 Ibid. Adapted from pp. 7-8.

47 M. Bliss & J. Emshoff, "Workbook for Designing a Process Evaluation," 2002. Viewed May 2, 2013.

48 SAMHSA, Substance Abuse and Mental Health Services Administration, Access to Recovery Implementation Toolkit, 2010. HHS Publication No. (SMA) 10-4596. Rockville, MD: Center for Substance Abuse Treatment, Division of Services Improvement, Substance Abuse and Mental Health Services Administration. *https://www.yumpu.com/en/document/view/ 44361711/ access-to-recovery-implementation-toolkit-samhsa-store-.* Viewed March 25, 2024. *https://www.samhsa.gov/grants.* Viewed February 18, 2024.

49 J. Butts & J. Roman, "Changing Systems: Outcomes from the RWJF Reclaiming Futures Initiative on Juvenile Justice and Substance Abuse," A Reclaiming Futures National Evaluation Report, Portland, Ore.: Reclaiming Futures National Program Office, Portland State University, 2007, p. 26.

50 Op. Cit., SAMHSA.

51 National Institute of Corrections, "Implementing Evidence-Based Practice in Community Corrections: The Principles of Effective Intervention," 2004, p. 2. *http://nicic.gov/Library/019342.* Viewed March 25, 2024.

52 World Bank 2012, "Decentralization and Subnational Regional Economics – Service Delivery," *http://www.worldbank.org.* Viewed May 16, 2013.

53 Ibid.

54 Ibid.

55 Op. Cit., National Institute of Corrections.

56 Ibid.

57 Op. Cit., Adapted from Models for Change, *Pennsylvania's Juvenile Justice System Enhancement Strategy: Achieving our Balanced and Restorative Justice Mission Through Evidence-Based Policy and Practice,* 2012, section 1.9, p. 9. *http://www.modelsforchange.net/publications/342/.* Viewed March 25, 2024. Adapted also from (Op. Cit.) National Institute of Corrections, 2004, pp. 3-8.

58 Op. Cit., SAMHSA.

59 Motivational interviewing is a collaborative, person-centered form of guiding to elicit and strengthen motivation for change. It's an empathic, supportive counseling style that supports the conditions for change. Practitioners are careful to avoid arguments and confrontation, which tend to increase a person's defensiveness and resistance. *http://www.samhsa.gov/ co-occurring/topics/training/motivational.aspx.* Accessed February 19, 2024.

60 Op. Cit., National Institute of Corrections.

61 Adapted from P. Griffin, R. Steele, & K. Franklin, "Aftercare Reality and Reform," *Pennsylvania Progress,* Pittsburg: National Center for Juvenile Justice, 2007, p. 5.

62 Models for Change, *Pennsylvania's Juvenile Justice System Enhancement Strategy: Achieving our Balanced and Restorative Justice Mission Through Evidence-Based Policy and Practice,* 2012. *http://www.modelsforchange.net/publications/342/.* Viewed March 25, 2024.

63 Op. Cit., National Institute of Corrections, p. 16.

64 J. Dubin, "Metamorphosis: How Missouri Rehabilitates Juvenile Offenders," American Educator, Summer 2012.

65 Jim Collins, *Good to Great: Why Some Companies Make the Leap and Others Don't.* New York: HarperBusiness, First Ed., 2001, pp. 5-6.

66 This description of the Choice Program's organizational structure was accurate at the time of this writing.

67 Anonymous from the Pennsylvania Commission on Crime and Delinquency, 2012, p. 16.

68 J. Evans, "The Most Important Part of Strategic Planning: Operationalizing Strategy, Method Frameworks," A Division of Forte Solutions Group, 2012. *http://www.methodframe works.com/blog/2012/most-important-part-strategic-planning-%E2%80%9Coperationaliz- ing% E2%80%9D-strategy/index.html.* Viewed May 29, 2013.

69 R. Wiebush, B. McNulty, & T. Le, "Implementation of the Intensive Community-Based Aftercare Program," *Juvenile Justice Bulletin,* 2000, Office of Juvenile Justice and Delinquency Prevention.

70 M. Henderson & D. Hanley, "Planning for Quality: A Strategy for Reentry Initiatives," *Western Criminology Review,* 2006, vol. 7(2), p. 75.

71 Op. Cit., Wiebush, McNulty & Le, 2000.

72 Op. Cit., Altschuler & Armstrong, 2004.

73 Op. Cit., adapted from Altschuler & Armstrong, 2004, pp. 4-3 – 4-5.

74 The Implementation Index can be obtained from the national offices for Reclaiming Futures housed in the Regional Research Institute of the School of Social Work at Portland State University. *https://www.reclaimingfutures.org/our-model.* Accessed March 2, 2024. Viewed June 25, 2024.

75 *https://modelsforchange.net/publications/346/.* Accessed June 25, 2024.

76 Op. Cit., Adapted from Vincent, Guy, & Grisso, 2012, pp. 8-9.

77 P. Griffin, R. Steele, & K. Franklin, "Aftercare Reality and Reform," *Pennsylvania Progress,* Pittsburg: National Center for Juvenile Justice, 2007.

78 Extracted from the Reclaiming Futures Implementation Index (2014), in use at the time of this writing.

79 Reclaiming Futures 6-Step Model. *https://www.reclaimingfutures.org/our-model.*

80 J. Klopovic, M. Vasu, & D. Yearwood, *Effective Program Practices for At-Risk Youth.* New York: Civic Research Institute, 2003.

81 Op. Cit., Models for Change, 2012.

82 P. Greenwood, *Changing Lives: Delinquency Prevention as Crime-Control.* Chicago: University of Chicago Press, 2006.

83 Op. Cit., Pennsylvania Juvenile Justice System Enhancement Strategy, p. 13.

84 Op. Cit., Models for Change, 2012.

85 Ibid.

86 Ibid, p. 14.

87 L. Bolmant and T. Deal, *Reframing Organizations: Artistry and Choice and Leadership,* 4th ed. San Francisco: Jossey-Bass, 2008.

88 Op. Cit., Klopovic, Vasu, & Yearwood, 2003.

89 S. Covey, A. R. Merrill, R. R. Merrill, *First Things First.* New York: Free Press, 1996.

90 Ibid.

91 Ibid.

92 Ibid.

93 E. Taylor-Powell, S. Steele, "Collecting Evaluation Data: An Overview of Sources and Methods," Program Development and Evaluation, University of Wisconsin Cooperative Extension, Madison, WI, 1996.

94 M. Bamburger & E. Hewitt, "Monitoring and Evaluation: What Can They Do for Me?" *Monitoring and Evaluating Urban Development Programs, A Handbook for Program Managers and Researchers,* World Bank Technical Paper no. 53, Washington, D.C., 1986.

95 Output is starkly different from outcome, yet they are symbiotic. Outputs are measurable, tangible results, measured as work quantity. Outcome tells the story of impact—results or consequences derived from the work. It can assess the program's success or lack of it. They fit, as output numbers can be translated to percentages for comparisons over time, for example. Both output and outcome are served well by being laid on a chain of outcomes to make sure work is connected to overall goals.

96 D. Zastava, "Measuring Actual Project–Benefits - How to Maintain Your Project Profile and Funding," 2000. *http://gisdevelopment.net/proceedings/gita/2000/people/peoi056pf.htm.* Viewed 20 June 20, 2013.

97 D. Altschuler and T. Armstrong, "Intensive Aftercare for High-Risk Juveniles: A Community Care Model," Office of Juvenile Justice and Delinquency Prevention, 1994. *https://www.ncjrs.gov/pdffiles/juvcc.pdf.* Viewed March 3, 2024. S. Bilchik, "Five Emerging Practices in Juvenile Reentry," Center for Juvenile Justice Reform, Georgetown University Public Policy Institute and The National Reentry Resource Center, 2014. *https://csgjusticecenter.org/2014/03/24/five-emerging-practices-in-juvenile-reentry/.* Viewed April 1, 2024.

98 Ibid., Bilchik.

99 M. Lipsey, J. Howell, M. Kelly, et al, "Improving the Effectiveness of Juvenile Justice Programs: A New Perspective on Evidence-Based Practice," Center for Juvenile Justice Reform, Georgetown, Wash. D.C., 2010.

100 Ibid.

101 Ibid.

102 Ibid., p. 37.

103 Ibid., Lipsey et al, 2010.

104 Op. Cit., Altschuler & Armstrong, 2004.

105 North Carolina Department of Juvenile Justice Division of Juvenile Justice, *Service Plan Protocols,* n.d.

106 Op. Cit., Altschuler & Armstrong, 2004

107 Op. Cit., Altschuler & Armstrong, 2004, p. 6-2.

108 Cit., Altschuler & Armstrong, 2004.

109 Op. Cit., Vincent, Guy & Grisso, 2012.

110 Ibid.

111 D. Shilling, "Retention Strategies for Key Employees in B-to-B Companies," n.d. *http://www.americanbusinessmedia.com/images/abm/pdfs/resources/Retention_Strategies.pdf.* Viewed July 7, 2013.

112 Ibid.

113 B. Kaye and S. Jordan-Evans, *Love 'Em or Lose 'Em: Getting Good People to Stay.* Oakland, Calif.: Berrett Koehler Publishers, 1999. Ibid., Shilling, n.d.

114 T. Crane, *Using Transformational Coaching to Create a High-Performance Coaching Culture,* 3rd ed. San Diego: FTA Press, 2009.

115 Fulmer, R., "Choose Tomorrow's Leaders Today: Succession Planning Grooms Firms for Success," *Grazaidio Business Review,* v. 5, iss. 1, 2002. Graziadio School of Business and Management, Pepperdine University, Malibu, Calif.

116 Ibid.

117 Op. Cit., Dubin, 2012. *https://eric.ed.gov/?id=EJ973192.* Viewed March 31, 2024.

118 Op. Cit., Evans, 2012.

119 D. P. Mears & J. Travis, "Youth Development and Reentry," Sage Journals, 2004. *https://journals.sagepub.com/doi/10.1177/1541204003260044.* Viewed March 31, 1014.

120 Op. Cit., Models for Change, 2012.

121 Ibid.

122 J. McKay and P. Marshall, "The Dual Imperatives of Action Research," ResearchGate, 2001. *https://www.researchgate.net/publication/220437083_The_dual_imperatives_of_action_research.* Viewed March 31, 2024.

123 Ibid.

124 Op. Cit., Models for Change, 2012.

125 "The HomeQuest program treats delinquent youths and youths with mental health problems while they remain living in their own homes. HomeQuest is part of VisionQuest (VQ), which uses a milieu treatment approach and a multidisciplinary staff to give severely troubled adolescents the chance to achieve success through positive experiences and to avoid institutionalization." *https://www.ojp.gov/ncjrs/virtual-library/abstracts/homequest-program*. Viewed March 16, 2024.

126 Op. Cit., McKay, 2001.

127 Bureau of Justice Statistics. *http://bjs.ojp.usdoj.gov/index.cfm?ty=tp&tid=17*. Viewed April 1, 2024.

128 S. Burt, "The Contingent Value of Social Capital," *Administrative Science Quarterly*, Vol. 42, No. 2, 1997, pp. 339-365. *https://www. jstor.org/stable/2393923*. Viewed April 1, 2024.

www.ingramcontent.com/pod-product-compliance
Lightning Source LLC
Chambersburg PA
CBHW051317020426

42333CB00031B/3390